To Hillary,
Run Fast!

-Nick

Life Outside the Oval Office:

THE TRACK LESS TRAVELED

Nick Symmonds

Published by
Cool Titles
439 N. Canon Dr., Suite 200
Beverly Hills, CA 90210
www.cooltitles.com

The Library of Congress Cataloging-in-Publication Data Applied For

Nick Symmonds—
Life Outside the Oval Office: The Track Less Traveled

p.   cm
ISBN 978-1-935270-32-4
1. Autobiography 2. Sports 3. Running I. Title
2014

Printed in the United States of America

1 3 5 7 9 10 8 6 4 2

Book editing and design by White Horse Enterprises, Inc.

For interviews or information regarding special discounts for bulk purchases,
please contact cindy@cooltitles.com

Distribution to the Trade: Pathway Book Service,
www.pathwaybook.com, pbs@pathwaybook.com, 1-800-345-6665

"I shall be telling this with a sigh, Somewhere ages and ages hence: Two roads diverged in a wood, and I, I took the one less traveled by, And that has made all the difference."

—Robert Frost

Dedication

This book is dedicated to Coach Sam Lapray. Without his never-ending love and support very little of this would have been possible.

Foreword

The first time Nick Symmonds came onto my radar was in Indi-
anapolis, Indiana. Nick had just graduated from Willamette University and
was at the USA Outdoor Championships. He gave a fabulous performance
for a Division III kid in the men's 800 meter. I was very impressed, and
arranged to have someone introduce me to him. I knew I was leaving my
current coaching position with the Nike Farm Team in Palo Alto and helping start Nike's Oregon Track Club in Eugene, Oregon, near where Nick
had gone to school, so I asked if Nick wanted to train with me.

While I had been impressed with his running, I didn't know then
about Nick's tremendous heart to be a winner. Nick Symmonds is a very
hard worker. From weights, to flexibility, to distance running, to speed
training, Nick always gives more than 100 percent. He also has enough
sense to know when he needs a break and then he goes fishing. That balance makes him a better runner, and the first time I saw that was at the
Prefontaine Classic in Eugene in May of 2007.

I met Nick in June of 2006 and he was training with me by September of that year. The Prefontaine was Nick's first really big race and it is
held every year at historic Hayward Field. I'll let Nick tell you more about
the field. On this particular day there was a gigantic crowd and Nick was
running against a really great field, including Russian Olympic gold medalist Yuriy Borzakovskiy.

At that time, Nick had a problem of hanging too far back in his races before his big kick across the finish line. "You can't do that in this race," I said. "These runners are the fastest you've ever met. You have to be close." So the race goes off and there's Nick, with 200 meters to go in an 800 meter race, not last, but close to it. With 150 to go I see he's gotten himself boxed in and that's usually the end of it for a runner, there is no way to get out of the box to pass other runners. But somehow, Nick found a way out and kicked down the stretch and won the field.

Nick took his victory lap and did his press interviews. All the time I'm standing on the warm-up track waiting for him. After thirty or forty minutes he comes running up. "Wasn't that great?" he asked. "Wasn't that a great race?" I looked at Nick for a split second before I grabbed him by his shirt. "You didn't listen to me, Nick. You still hung back."

The look on Nick's young face said it all. He learned a big lesson that day. Even though he got out of the box and went on to win, he could just as easily have remained trapped between runners and finished toward the back.

It is no secret that Nick has a brilliant mind. Anyone who has ever met him knows how intelligent he is. He has also surrounded himself with some really good people and has a supportive family. Nick's one weakness, though, might be Mortimer. Mortimer is Nick's pet rabbit. You'll find out in the book how Nick came to get this rabbit, but I don't think when Nick first got Mortimer that he knew he'd actually like the rabbit. But he did. Nick used to bring Mortimer to a lot of our team events, such as photo day. Half the time when Nick was driving around town running errands there Mortimer was in the truck riding right alongside Nick.

The men's 800 meter race is one of the most competitive, and this is true around the world. Over the years, Nick Symmonds has been very, very consistent at the top of this race. He has been a national champion and so far has twice gone to the Olympics. Looking into the future, I believe that when it is time for Nick to hang up his track shoes, as impressive as his career has been (and still is), Nick will be remembered as someone who was never afraid to speak when he believed in something. So many people are afraid to say something, but Nick is definitely not one of those people. I know you'll enjoy reading about several ways Nick has broken industry barriers, just by speaking up and out.

I also know you'll appreciate reading about Nick. I think he is a wonderful man and I am honored to have been asked to be part of his book.

Coach Frank Gagliano
July 2014

Introduction

It's a warm summer evening in 2008, and I stare down at the familiar rubbery surface of a running track. I am twenty-four years old and have spent thousands of hours on tracks just like this one. This particular track is a beautiful shade of red. It looks like most others: flat, rounded at the ends, with eight equally wide lanes.

I keep my gaze down, and am fixated on the soft, red surface, afraid to look up. I know if I do, what I see will cause my adrenal gland to dump a large amount of adrenaline into my system and send my heart racing. I want to save this adrenaline for the fight I am about to take part in—a fight for which I have been preparing for a decade.

As I stand nervously and shift my weight back and forth, I decide to look up to the sky, another familiar sight. The sun has descended past the horizon, but a brilliant sunset helps light the stadium. Large floodlights add to the quickly fading sunlight and set the mood.

I close my eyes and take a few deep breaths to calm my nerves and I feel my heart slow down inside my chest. My body begins to feel entirely at peace, when suddenly I am shocked back into the moment by a loud voice booming through stadium speakers. The voice is calling my name. I can no longer ignore my surroundings, so I open my eyes and look.

Around me are twenty-three thousand screaming spectators. Many are friends, some are family, and there are those who would very much like to see me fail tonight. The roar of the crowd is deafening and reminds me that the following two minutes will be two of the most important of my life.

I am at the 2008 Olympic Trials for track at Hayward Field in Eugene, Oregon. I have spent ten years preparing for this race—a race that will decide which men and women will represent our country at the Beijing Olympic Games.

Though my shaggy hair and nervous fidgeting suggest I am nothing but a young boy who is in over his head, the bulging, sinewy muscles of my legs suggest otherwise. Furthermore, what cannot be seen is the blood running through my body, being fed oxygen by my large lungs and pumped by my powerful heart.

In both a literal and metaphorical way, this heart of mine has carried me from obscurity all the way to this championship starting line. Though many people have told me a short, stocky, white kid from Idaho will never make an Olympic team, my heart has always said otherwise.

Now it is time to find out who is right.

1

In one of my very first memories I am five years old, watching my little sister run for the first time. My sister's name is Lauren and she is exactly twenty-seven months younger than I am. I watch as Lauren stumbles from the security of our mother's arms down the hallway to the door that leads to my parents' bedroom and back. I didn't realize it at the time, but it is very prophetic that this should be my earliest memory: my mom crouching next to me, and my sister doing laps around the house in her diaper. These are two of the people most close to me and it makes sense that this scene would cement itself in my mind.

The only person missing is my dad, Jeffrey, who I am equally close to. No doubt Dad was at the hospital where he has practiced vascular surgery for the past three decades. Every day, Lauren and I waited patiently, playing games with our mom until Dad came home in the evening. Our favorite game was to attach ourselves to his ankles as he came through the door, using his size twelve shoes as our seats. As my dad's long, bowed legs walked toward the kitchen where Mom prepared dinner, Lauren and I flew through the air, giggling.

As I grew older I thought my family was a bit of a cliché: two parents together and in-love, two kids (one boy and one girl) and a few pets. We sat around the dinner table most nights enjoying a home cooked meal and sharing the events of our day. Now that I am grown up and have moved out of that wonderful home, I can appreciate how rare and special it was. I was surrounded by never-ending love and support as I strived to impress the people I loved most—my family.

Since then, as I have traveled the world, I realize that I was born into a truly fortunate family. We were not overwhelmingly rich, but we were far from poor and my parents made sure that my sister and I never wanted for anything. Though I often took this for granted as a child, I now understand the sacrifices Mom and Dad made to ensure that I had everything I needed to be successful in life.

My mom, Andrea, was born in southern California, the youngest of four children. She spent her youth, as many California kids do, playing on the beach and life guarding at the local pool. She is a classic California beauty with blonde hair and brilliant green eyes. Though she only stands five foot three she seems much larger (and scarier) when she is mad. This seldom happens, though, as the majority of the time Mom has a huge smile on her face and enjoys everything life has to offer.

After high school Mom attended the University of California-Irvine where she majored in theater. Though she went on to pursue a career in teaching, Mom has always viewed the entire world as a stage. Whether at dinner with family and friends or at her job as an English teacher at the high school I attended, my mother has an incredible ability to make people feel welcome and engaged, both in conversation and thought.

On the other hand, Dad, who is quiet by nature, can sometimes seem intimidating. The son of a doctor and the youngest of three children, he grew up in Rochester, Minnesota. At six feet even, his dark coloring and sharp features reflect the Cherokee blood found on his side of the family. He has tan skin stretched taut over long muscles, and is so lean that you might assume he is an endurance athlete of some kind. In fact, Dad rarely works out—aside from climbing the hospital stairs dozens of times a day to visit patients, or puttering around the twelve-acre farm in Boise, Idaho where my sister and I grew up. Dad also has a deep voice that he uses to speak with knowledge and eloquence. My quiet, introverted dad could rival the most gifted orators.

Dad attended Colorado College as an undergrad and went on to earn his MD from Duke University. When I listen to Dad dictate medical charts, the words and terminology he uses sound as though he is speaking a foreign language. He is the epitome of Midwestern stoic, so it can, at first, be hard to know what Dad is thinking, though he loosens up considerably after a couple of beers.

My parents have been married thirty-three years and are still very much in love. People say that opposites attract, and my parents are a good example of this. Though they are very different in their personalities and interests, they balance each other well. Where Mom is tender and full of emotion, Dad is more even tempered. My mother is a lover of the arts and claims that math gives her a headache, while my dad still remembers his calculus and could probably list all of the known elements in order. They both, however, are encouraging and positive, and have supported my sister and me in nearly all of our endeavors.

Though neither parent was a professional athlete, both are athletic. Dad was a great hockey player growing up and in college, while Mom has been an avid swimmer and jogger all her life. When asked where I get my athletic abilities from, she laughs and swears it must have something to do with the fact that while pregnant with me she jogged until the day she gave birth.

My parents met in San Francisco in the late 1970s and many times I have heard, and been enraptured by, the telling of their meeting by my mother. "I still remember the first time I saw him," my mother always begins. "He was tall, dark, and handsome, and he walked on these incredibly long bowed legs around San Francisco State Hospital where I worked as a ward clerk. The first time I ever laid eyes on him he had just stepped off the elevator onto my floor and I knew right then and there that he was the man I was going to marry."

Dad usually allows mom to tell the story, but always backs her up with a smile.

My parents dated in the Bay Area for four years before getting married on May 14, 1980. Shortly after, my dad completed his medical residency and my parents moved from the hip streets of San Francisco to rural Blytheville, Arkansas. My father owed the US military several years of service for putting him through medical school, and the air force base in Blytheville was where he was needed. On their placement application form my parents listed Manila, Philippines as their top choice. There was a Manila, Arkansas not far from Blytheville, so I suppose the military thought it was close enough.

Needless to say, it came as quite a surprise when Mom and Dad found they were going to be stationed in the American South. While they found the other military families and the people of Blytheville extremely welcoming, they had just uprooted their lives from a major metropolitan city and felt the culture shock. Mom and Dad had weekly bowling nights and potluck dinners, but Mom felt something was missing. Apparently I was that something, and at six A.M. on December 30, 1983, she had an extremely cranky baby boy to keep her happy and busy.

The three of us finished our time in Blytheville and moved to Rochester, Minnesota shortly after my first birthday. My dad was to finish his residency at the Mayo Clinic—where his father had practiced medicine for thirty years. It was at this hospital that my sister was born.

Though we share DNA and were raised in the same home, my sister Lauren and I are very different. Where I have blonde hair and blue eyes, she has the dark features of my dad. I can be somewhat cynical toward the world and my sister, a social worker, takes it upon herself to change the world one child at a time. Her altruistic nature inspires me every day. One thing we do share, however, is athletic talent. My coaches like to joke that my sister, a multiple state champion in soccer and track, still has several years of collegiate eligibility that she never used. I have many fond memories of Lauren and me practicing soccer skills together, or racing our bikes. We were competitive in nearly everything we did and I often wonder if my athletic talents would have developed the way they did without my little sister there to push me from an early age.

Not long after Lauren was born, my family relocated again, this time to Boise, Idaho where my dad joined a medical practice called Boise Surgical Group. I believe this move was important for my future athletic career, as Boise was the perfect city for a young athlete to grow up in. Its moderate altitude and never-ending possibilities for outdoor recreation had me active all the time. There was never a season where Lauren and I weren't outside playing sports or enjoying the outdoors. The house we grew up in backs up to the Boise foothills, and during my high school days, I covered hundreds of miles on the hilly, single-track trails that criss-cross them.

When it came time for Lauren and me to go to school, my parents had a dilemma. Mom was raised Catholic and Dad Methodist. Though neither practiced their religion, they felt my sister and I should be brought up with some exposure to it. At the urging of my maternal grandparents we were both baptized into the Catholic Church. As Catholics ran most of the private schools in Boise, it made sense that Lauren and I both attend one of them. Early on, though, this presented a bit of a problem.

I began at St. Mark's Elementary at the age of six and enjoyed school very much. Report cards typically read: NICK IS A BRIGHT AND ATTENTIVE STUDENT WITH A PASSION FOR LEARNING. ONE AREA HE COULD WORK ON IS CLASSROOM BEHAVIOR. NICK CAN SOMETIMES BE A DISTRACTION TO HIS CLASSMATES. Sounds about right.

I enjoyed most subjects, however our daily theology classes and weekly mass bored me to tears. I often told my parents this and they encouraged me to use it as meditation time. This worked well until fourth grade, when we were introduced to the catechism of the Catholic Church. This mind-numbing piece of literature spells out the tenets of the church and is pounded into young impressionable minds all over the world.

One day at school I remember listening intently as my teacher and the priest, a man I'll call Father McBride, tried to explain to a room full of nine year olds how the Holy Trinity worked. "Well, God is God, but

God is also Jesus," the priest droned. "But God is also the Holy Spirit, and Jesus is the Holy Spirit, too."

My young mind struggled around this three-in-one idea. Really, none of it made any sense to me. At home, whenever I was confused about something my parents encouraged me to ask questions. I found that doing so usually alleviated my confusion and I approached the Holy Trinity this same way. In class I raised my hand and said, "This doesn't make any sense. There is no way for one thing to be three separate things or three things to be one thing."

With a furrow of his brow Father replied, "You must have faith that it can be so."

I raised my hand again. "But how can I have faith that any of these three things exist if I've never seen them, much less that they all exist together and are separate at the same time?" I'm sure my argument wasn't quite that well put together at the age of nine, but you get the idea.

Father's response was simply, "Have faith, my son."

It seemed that any time I had a question about anything in the Catholic Church, that was the default response. Have faith. I continued over the next days and weeks to ask questions during religion class as I tried to make sense out of what I was being taught, but never got anywhere.

Eventually my teacher stopped calling on me, but I still talked to my parents about what I learned in class when we sat around the dinner table. Lauren was two years behind me in school and listened intently to our discussions. "I like stories about Jesus," I said one night. "He seemed really nice, but it doesn't make sense to me that he was the Son of God, and at the same time God, too. And then also, at the same time, the Holy Spirit." My parents always encouraged Lauren and me to come to our own conclusions, and to that end gave a brief history of Christianity and what it meant to be a Christian.

One day not too long after this, Father McBride visited my sister's class and began to give the same lecture that he had given my class. When he got to the Holy Trinity part my sister raised her hand and said, "My brother doesn't believe in the Holy Trinity."

The priest looked my seven-year-old sister in the eyes and said, "Then pray for his soul, because he will not be going to heaven."

You can imagine how Lauren took the news that her big brother would not be joining her in the "eternal kingdom." She began to cry and no amount of consoling comforted her. Eventually school staff called Mom and she came to school, probably right from her own teaching job, to get Lauren to stop crying. With her arms wrapped around Mom, Lauren cried, "Nick will never go to heaven!" and explained what had happened.

Infuriated, Mom stormed into Father McBride's office. "How dare you? Telling my daughter that her brother isn't going to heaven!"

"Your son does not believe in the Holy Trinity and therefore is not Catholic," he said. "Not only will he not be going to heaven, he is no longer welcome at my communion rail."

Father's holier-than-thou attitude was absolutely the wrong way to talk to Ma Symmonds. In a tone that could raise the hair on your neck my mother leaned over the priest's desk and said, "My son is a baptized Catholic and if he wants to receive communion you will give it to him. We both know you do not have the power to excommunicate him. You can count on me being at mass this Friday with my son." With that, she stormed out of his office.

It is no secret that I have always had some trouble with authority. Though I sometimes wonder *when* my disdain for rule makers and enforcers began, I never wonder *where* it came from. My mother is an extremely confident woman who calls it like she sees it, and is quick to speak out against any injustice. She raised me to do the same and has always had my back when I speak up for what I believe in.

Lauren and I remained in the Catholic school system, but our relationship with the church was never the same. A church that told a seven-year-old girl her brother was going to hell, a church that could not take time to answer a confused question from a nine-year-old, was a church we wanted no part of. Years later, as they took a hard line on women's rights, gay marriage, and covered up dozens of child molestation cases, we were pretty pleased with our decision to distance ourselves from the Catholic Church.

2

Although my initial exposure to religion had been rough, my expo-sure to sports had been life changing. My parents encouraged me to try many sports and were quick to sign me up for any team I showed interest in. I tried many, and found my first real love to be soccer. Like so many kids in the United States, I grew up running around in a recreational league wearing one of those mustard/ketchup reversible jerseys.

I was fast and had decent ball handling skills, and at the age of eleven was picked up by a traveling team called the Boise Capitals. For several years I was competitive in this league, usually playing forward. I loved to score goals and lived for the breakaway. This exciting play pits a sole at-tacker against the goalkeeper in a one-on-one, and I loved every second of it.

Often, I parked myself at half-field and patiently waited for one of our defenders to kick the ball over everyone's head. Then, evenly posi-tioned with the other team's larger, slower defenders, I'd break off in a sprint to beat them to the ball. Early on there were very few people I couldn't beat in a footrace.

However, toward the end of middle school, that started to change. All the kids I used to be able to beat were suddenly beating me. Though I had always been small for my age, I was suddenly tiny in comparison with the kids around me. They were clearly going through puberty, and I clearly was not. I found myself getting less and less playing time in soccer games, and instead, frequently rode the bench. It infuriated me that I was working as hard or harder than my teammates and not getting equal playing time. Though I didn't know it then, it was partly for my own safety that my four-foot-ten, ninety pound self wasn't often allowed on the playing field.

One hot August day, just before I began my eighth grade year, I voiced my soccer frustrations to two friends as we sat by our local pool. My friends had just signed up for the cross-country team and suggested I do the same. Normally I would have laughed at the idea of "running for fun," but these weren't just any two friends. Rather, I was lounging poolside with the two prettiest girls in my class. I had a huge crush on one of them and would have gone out for the dance team if she had asked me to. Hormones had recently kicked in and I found the opposite sex fascinating.

As soon as I got home I told my parents that I wanted to run cross-country that fall. As always, my parents were supportive. Just as they had done with my interests in golf, hockey, and skiing, they made sure I had all the gear I needed. In hindsight, they were probably relieved to find that all I needed for cross-country was a new pair of running shoes.

From the first day of practice I could tell two things about my new sport. One, co-ed practices were awesome, and two, distance running sucked. I quickly got to know many people on the team and liked most of them, but the idea that we were going to run, for an extended period of time with no real purpose, seemed absurd to me.

We often practiced with the high school team and one afternoon, before our scheduled workout, a senior girl asked if I wanted to buy one of the T-shirts they were having made. She showed me a mock up of the shirt. On the front it read BISHOP KELLY XC (which was the name of our high school) and on the back, OUR SPORT IS YOUR SPORT'S PUNISHMENT.

Are you serious? I thought. *That's exactly what this is: punishment. Why in the world are we doing this?* I was just about to say this to her when, as if on cue, the girl I had joined the team for said, "I want one." Immediately, I echoed, "Oh, yeah, me too!"

I showed up at cross-country practice every day after school excited about the social aspect of being on the team, but dreading the athletic part. My teammates kept telling me how much fun the meets were, but I secretly dreaded them. I got nervous before soccer games, but calmed my fears with the knowledge that a bad performance reflected on the entire team, not just me. On the other hand, if I ran poorly, there was no one to blame but myself. I imagined people laughing at me and asking how I could be so good at the mile in P.E. class, but so bad at cross-country running.

As the first meet neared I began to think of ways I could get out of it. *Surely if I throw up during class they won't make me run. If I twist my ankle during the warm up I bet Coach will let me out of racing.*

I expressed my concerns to my mom and she told me not to worry, to just have fun with the race. "Win, lose, or draw, just make sure you are the one to shake everyone's hand and congratulate them after the race," she said.

Her words did little to ease my nerves, and my concerns ran through my head all the way until the moment I toed the start line. With a bang the gun went off and several hundred middle school kids took off in a sprint. Once I was running, my mind calmed and I simply ran. I keyed off the other kids and every so often did a check to see how my heart, lungs, and legs were feeling. With only a half-mile to go I found myself nearing the lead. Though my legs and lungs ached, I took off in a sprint. To my surprise, the pain didn't increase. Instead, my legs simply went numb. This numbness quickly took over my entire body and I rigged hard in the final stretches of the race. I was passed just meters away from the finish line, but managed to hold on for second place.

Apparently, the boy who beat me had built up a pretty big name for himself as a distance runner in the southern part of the state and people were surprised to see me, a newcomer, this close to him. When I crossed the line people ran over to congratulate me. "Who is this kid?" people asked. Boys shook my hand and girls came up to talk to me.

Several years of riding the bench in soccer and struggling to figure out how to connect with the opposite sex had left my self-esteem in tatters. I felt my peers had left me behind socially and I wondered how I would ever catch up. That day, as I looked around and saw the respect and admiration I so desperately craved, I began to wonder if running could ultimately help me get all that I wanted in life.

To put this idea to the test, I knew I needed to continue with competitive running. As hard as it was for me to do so, this led me to skip tryouts for the high school soccer team my freshman year so I could run cross-country instead. Many of my friends, however, weren't sure that was a good idea.

"Distance running is lame!" they said.

"You are a good soccer player and will have way more fun playing soccer," my soccer teammates said.

"Soccer players are the most popular kids in school. Can't say that for the cross-country runners," some girls laughed.

Still, there was something about the unity of the cross-country team, the fact that everyone got equal playing time, and that all my hard work would pay *me* dividends. I liked that. I stuck with my gut and showed up for the first day of cross-country practice. As expected, I had a love-hate relationship with high school cross-country from day one. Of course, I still loved the coed practices and cherished being part of a team.

I also really liked our coach, Tom Shanahan. Tom was a young, energetic Irishman who had run distance for Boise State University. He was tough at times, but he loved us and never pushed us beyond our limits. I really didn't like practice and he could tell. More often than not I sat in the back of the group as he explained the workout while I looked at the ducks or geese walking by. If I did manage to keep my attention toward practice it was only to check out the girls in their Spandex. Of course, this always led to me having no idea what the workout for the day actually was, and I invariably messed it up.

On one very memorable occasion, I recall Coach saying something about hill repeats, but tuned out how many or for how long. I started on the first repeat and ran until I was tired and then turned around and walked back down. At the bottom, waiting for me, was Coach Shanahan and his wild Irish accent.

"Ye were 'sposta run ta da green three!'"

"Huh?" I replied, trying to catch my breath.

"Da green three! Da green three!" he shouted pointing at a nice looking green tree on the side of the road about 300 meters away.

"Ahhh, you mean the green *tree*. Yeah, I'll run to the *tree* next time, Coach." I responded as irreverently as possible.

Though I had grown to love Coach Shanahan in just a few short weeks, my disdain for authority ran deep. I knew he was working hard to help me accomplish goals I had set for myself. However, anytime someone told me to do something it set me off inside. Needless to say, I would not have done well in the military.

Thankfully, Coach Shanahan has always been a very patient man. He often allowed me to be a part of the decision making process when it came to my races so that I felt I wasn't being controlled or bossed around. On that particular day near the hill and the green tree, Coach Shanahan just laughed, rolled his eyes, and said, "Git yer arse movin'."

Coach worked hard to prepare us and we worked hard to avoid running. Often, on our easy days, we left the track at Bishop Kelly High School and ran to the nearby shopping mall to get free food samples. Other days we ran to nearby Borah High School where we jumped the fence to swim in their beautiful outdoor pool. Occasionally, if we were running along the Boise River, we stopped at a rope swing to play around for a few minutes before getting back to our run. In those days, training never seemed as important as having a good time.

The camaraderie I felt on the cross-country team kept me coming back each day. I still had not gained an appreciation for distance running, but goofing around at practice with everyone made it tolerable.

I played club soccer in the spring of my freshman year of high school, but in the middle of every practice, every game, I wondered what kind of times I could be running on the track. Coach Shanahan wondered the same thing and urged me to join the track team my sophomore year. I struggled with the decision to give up soccer completely, but after my first track season all of my reservations about switching sports disappeared. In cross-country I was good, but on the track I was great.

In cross-country everyone competes at the same distance. In high school that distance is typically 5,000 meters, just over three miles, and is run over grass, dirt, and asphalt. Though I was a decent distance runner, my soccer background had developed a certain amount of explosive speed in my legs. This kind of power is better suited for hard surfaces and shorter distances. On the track, events were contested from lengths of 100 meters up to two miles—and everything in between. I quickly found several distances I was built for.

That first year, as a sophomore, I finished second at the Idaho State Championships at 800 meters. I did not it know at the time, but I would not lose another 800 meter final for seven years. That same year I finished very well in the mile and the two-mile. By the time I completed high school I had racked up nine state championships in events ranging from the 4x400 meter relay all the way up to 5,000 meter cross-country.

With this success came the attention and recognition I had always wanted. Though I was small for most of my high school career, five-foot-flat at the outset, guys now treated me with respect. And, while many of the girls were much taller, they flirted with me during and after school. I was too incompetent to do much with their attention, but I appreciated their efforts nonetheless.

Like many teenage boys, I had sex on the brain most of the time. My mind constantly wandered to girls who were in my class and at practice. I recall being absolutely tortured about finding out what breasts felt like. It was terrible to want something so badly, and to have no idea how to obtain it.

As a late bloomer, it was apparent to me that most guys in my class were more advanced than I was when it came to the opposite sex. When

I did hang out with a girl, it was almost always with one who was much younger. I felt more comfortable around younger girls, because I hoped they were as inexperienced as I was. Usually we spent our time together holding hands and watching movies. Occasionally, I worked up the nerve to kiss one goodnight. For the most part, that was the extent of my high school love life.

Fortunately, I had sports. I threw all of my teenage angst and frustration into whatever sport was in season, and usually played at least two simultaneously. In the fall I ran cross-country and hunted upland game birds with my dad. In the winter I was on both the ice hockey and ski teams. In the spring I ran track and biked. Summers were devoted to all things outdoors, as Boise is the perfect place for hiking, boating, and fishing. I was also very active in scouting and, shortly before my eighteenth birthday, had the honor of becoming an Eagle Scout.

My family has given me many things, but of all their gifts the one I will always be most grateful for is the passion they instilled in me for the outdoors. From as early as I can remember, each weekend we went out to explore the mountains and rivers of the Northwest. We hiked, biked, rafted, fished, and climbed almost every surface in southern Idaho. When I was young I appreciated all the time that I got to spend with my family and the fact that my need for adventure was satiated each weekend. However, as I got older, I began to realize that the outdoors had become much more than a playground to me. It had become my church.

Today I feel most grounded and most connected to something larger than myself when I am climbing a tall mountain or chasing a big fish. These moments remind me of my grandfather teaching me how to cast my first fly rod, and of canoe trips down the windy Snake River with my little sister giggling behind me. In times of both joy and frustration, I turn to the wilderness to calm me, and remind me of my place in this world.

Aside from providing me with the spiritual side that formal religion never could, my passion for the outdoors kept me out of trouble, helped me make friends, and gave me a sense of identity. Though distance running was intrinsically linked to the outdoors, it still ranked right at the bottom of my list of favorite things to do. However, I knew deep down that it was the sport I was best at. I didn't love it, yet, but I was curious to see where it could take me.

Initially I thought running could take me to college. Going into my senior year of high school I was the defending state champion in the 800, 1600, and 3200 meter races. I was the anchor on our state-winning 4x400 meter relay team, and in the fall of my senior year won the 4A state championship cross-country title, the second largest division for schools in Idaho. However, despite all these accolades, I did not receive a single Division I college scholarship offer. Division I is the highest level of intercollegiate athletics sanctioned by the National Collegiate Athletic Association (NCAA), and I wanted to be at one of those schools.

There were very few kids in my state that I couldn't beat at any distance, and I shook my head wondering where the scholarship offers were. Envelopes from schools all over the country poured into my family's mailbox and calls came to our home phone. Though many coaches expressed an interest in working with me, none offered me a scholarship. I was confused and upset.

To be fair, I did not aggressively pursue an athletic scholarship. When I speak to high school kids today, I tell them to be proactive about their careers, to write letters and make calls to college coaches expressing their desire to work hard for them and be part of something great. I did not write a single letter, nor did I make any calls.

The few coaches I did speak with were even less interested in me when I told them I planned to study pre-medicine. They often laughed and said that was not an option if I ran for them. At least, that is what I was told from the (then) head coach of the University of Oregon. Not only did he say that it was next to impossible to balance the rigorous course load of a pre-med major with the athletic work load, I was told I was not talented enough to merit an athletic scholarship. At best, as a walk on, I could become a member of the track team without receiving any form of athletic scholarship.

This was devastating news. Like most high school runners, early on I had learned of several legendary distance runners who had attended the University of Oregon. One was Steve Prefontaine, who broke many

American records. His coach, Bill Bowerman, with the help of some of his athletes, created what became Nike, Inc. The history ran deep, and I wanted to be a part of it.

Discouraged, I began to look at other options in the Pacific Northwest. I liked the idea of being relatively close to the University of Oregon. Even if I was unable to be a part of the Ducks, Oregon's track and field team, I liked the idea of racing at the University of Oregon's historic Hayward Field regularly. Some of the most memorable races ever had taken place on this track and I wanted to be able to add to that history.

One school that piqued my interested was a small liberal arts university in Oregon's capitol city, Salem, just an hour north of Eugene. As an NCAA Division III school, Willamette University (pronounced Wil-AM-et), was unable to offer athletic scholarships. Athletic scholarships were only available at Division I, II and National Association of Intercollegiate Athletics (NAIA) schools. However, as a spoiled middle class kid, my parents offered to foot the bill for my tuition, no matter what school I chose. This incredible gift allowed me to continue my college search with the intent of choosing the program that was truly right for me.

I spoke with the Willamette University head coach Kelly Sullivan over the phone. "At Willamette," he said, "you will be a student-athlete, not the other way around." He went on to say that at Willamette I could major in whatever I wanted, and that they would work practices around my academic schedule. He even went so far as to say I could continue to play hockey in the winter, if I so desired.

The fall of my senior year I applied to three schools: Northern Arizona University, Dartmouth College, and Willamette University. Though only one of these is located in the Pacific Northwest, I wanted to apply to a diverse set of schools and the coaches at these other programs had been particularly supportive. The seven thousand feet of altitude at Northern Arizona University intimidated me, and I was wait listed at Dartmouth. Thus, my decision to go to Willamette University was made quite easily.

I made one visit to Willamette and absolutely loved it. The tiny campus of red brick buildings and beautiful, lush green lawns was exactly how I imagined a university to be. I trusted Coach Sullivan who, in 2001 had been an assistant coach for Team USA at the Track and Field World Championships. His assistant, Matt McGuirk, was the head men's distance coach and seemed like he really cared about his athletes. They both told me that they very much wanted me on the team.

Matt was the best recruiter I had talked to during the entire college recruiting process and he even flew to Boise to meet with my parents and me. During my visit on campus I had gotten along great with the guys on the Willamette cross-county team and thought Oregon was a beautiful state. At the time, I felt very confident that Willamette was the right choice for me.

Looking back on the way I handled selecting a college, I can say I took a lazy approach. I was not proactive in my search and did not make a single recruiting visit to a Division I or Division II school. At the time I felt overwhelmed by the whole process, and was much more interested in trying to win my first state cross-country title or get a girlfriend.

My parents also liked Willamette University best and I figured at WU I would have the freedom to pursue all of my interests without someone telling me what to do, just because I was on an athletic scholarship. The fact that Willamette University offered me a partial academic scholarship made me feel that they really wanted me, and made the pricey tuition slightly more affordable.

Aside from my parents, who were ecstatic about my choice, Willamette University was a rather unpopular one. Most people in the Idaho running community were disappointed that I chose a Division III school. It is not often that runners from Idaho are able to run for a Division I program and I certainly had the ability to walk on to most school's track teams.

Those at my high school were disappointed as well, as it is not often BKHS places an athlete into a Division I program. Teachers, coaches, and students alike all looked at me quizzically when I told them I had committed to Willamette University. Even members of my own extended family expressed doubt about my choice. One of my uncles went so far as to ask me, "Is it because you're not fast enough? Will no Division I school take you?"

Comments like these were a huge kick to my ego, but in my heart I knew that I was fast enough to run at any school. There were many times I had to look at myself in the mirror and remind myself of this fact. Even so, sometimes I wondered if I was making the right choice.

When I imagined life at college I saw myself next to a bunch of test tubes eagerly learning, and hanging out at sporting events with my friends. I also saw myself walking across a grassy quad on a warm spring day, holding hands with a girl. Very seldom did I imagine myself running. The fact that competitive running was only my third or fourth priority reinforced my belief that a Division III school was right for me. My gut told me I was making the correct choice, so, against all of the unsolicited advice, I went with my instinct and committed to Willamette.

3

On a warm morning late in the summer of 2002, my dad and I finished packing up my bright red Toyota 4Runner with most of my worldly possessions. Mom and Lauren stood crying by the front door of the house I had grown up in. I wanted to cry too, but I held back the tears knowing they would only make it harder to say goodbye. I gave them both a hug and got behind the steering wheel, while Dad sat in the passenger seat.

The drive from our house in Boise to Willamette University is almost exactly five hundred miles and is one that I have done many times now. None of the trips, however, have been as exciting as that first trip with my dad. I loved growing up in Boise, but as a new high school grad I was desperate for a change of scenery and ready to experience new things.

We worked our way west on I-84, and passed some of our favorite hunting spots. When we crossed the Snake River and entered Oregon, I had a rush of adrenaline. This state was going to become my new home. But for how long? What kind of opportunities waited for me here?

Eight hours later we parked the 4Runner in a lot next to the university library. There were parents and kids headed in all directions carrying books, boxes, and furniture. I walked to a line of tables that had been set up near the quad and gave them my name, where I was issued a few items and assigned to an "Opening Days" group.

One of the items I had been given was a map of campus. Dad and I looked at the map to find Baxter Hall, the substance-free dorm I had been placed in. I had requested to live there because it was where most of the cross-country team was housed. As a young athlete who had never touched, much less seen, an illegal drug, this seemed like a great spot for me. Though I had tasted some of my dad's drinks over the years, and been drunk on a couple of occasions, I had never been into alcohol or parties. The large red brick building of Baxter Hall seemed like a great place for me to call home, despite its ironical positioning adjacent to campus fraternities.

I met many people that first day, including my freshman year roommate who was also on the cross-country team. His name was Erik and he had just arrived from Minnesota. He was a bit taller than me, and much skinner with a mop of curly blonde hair. He came off as a guy with a goofy sense of humor, but he was also quite friendly. I had a feeling we would get along well. Erik and I shared a tiny room that faced south, a typical dorm room with two beds, two desks, and two closets. Erik had staked out the west side of the room so I began setting up on the east.

Dad helped me unload my car and we somehow managed to fit the truckload of stuff I had brought with me into my half of the small room. With the heavy lifting complete we got some dinner. While we ate, Dad and I talked about what he remembered of college, and then about what I was most looking forward to in my four years at university. I admitted to him that I was a bit afraid of all the change. The drive and the moving had exhausted me, and the thought of finding my way around a new city for the first time was stressful.

"But that's what's so fun about living in a new place," Dad said. "Every time you leave campus is a new adventure. A chance to eat in new restaurants, see new things, and meet new people."

He knew how deep my need for adventure ran and this was the perfect advice to send me on my way.

After dinner I drove my dad to the Salem airport. I assisted him with his bag and thanked him for all his help. Then I shook his hand and gave him a hug good bye. As soon as I had done so, tears welled up in my eyes and I rushed back to the SUV, because I didn't want him to see me cry. The second I hit the road, tears began streaming down my face and I cried the entire way back to the dorm. As excited as I was to start this new adventure, I knew how much I was going to miss my family. With my dad now gone, I was on my own for the first time.

That first week was a lonely one for me, but fortunately there were so many new and interesting things going on, that I didn't have much time to feel it. I explored the campus and the city of Salem, and made new friends every day. Each night Erik and I would talk about our days and, of course, discuss the cute girls we had crossed paths with on campus.

I absolutely loved my freshman year of college. Every day I met new and interesting people and learned cool new things in my classes. I made some good friends on the cross-country team and quickly established myself as the best incoming freshman runner. I was almost always a scoring man on our team, and the guys treated me with a lot of respect. I recognized that I probably would not have been one of the top incoming freshmen at many Division I schools. This kept me grounded and hungry to become better. Although I was beating many upper classman, I did my best to do so with humility.

The classes I was taking were relatively easy for me, and the course load was light compared to what I had studied the year before. Bishop Kelly High School had prepared me well for college.

That first semester I got along with the coaching staff quite well. Coach Kelly Sullivan was clearly an intelligent and thoughtful man who had worked with amazing talent over the years. Coach Matt McGuirk had run the steeplechase (a race just shy of two miles that takes competitors over barriers and through a water pit) for the University of Oregon, and competed at the Olympic Trials himself. Both very clearly cared a great deal for their athletes.

These two coaches had similar philosophies regarding training, but were very different in the way they communicated with athletes. Coach

Sullivan was the kind of guy who put his arm around you and asked how you were feeling about school, life, and family. Coach McGuirk was more reserved and had a single-minded focus for running. They balanced each other well, and I found it worked well for me because I could get the attention I needed for whatever the situation called for.

Early on, however, I was bothered by one aspect of the cross-country and track programs. At the beginning of each season we were given a pair of shorts and a singlet, which we were expected to hand back at the end of the season. As for warm ups, we were told that we needed to buy these ourselves. The day after this was announced at one of the first cross-country practices I made an appointment to speak with the coaches.

"I know this is not a Division I program," I began at the appointed day and time, "but the least you can do is buy us some freakin' warm-ups." Sounding like the spoiled kid I was, I went on. "You want us to race Division I athletes every weekend and they are getting thousands of dollars worth of free gear each season!" Then I sat back in my chair to hear what they had to say for themselves. Coach Matt looked at Coach Kelly and raised his eyebrows as if to say, "You're the head coach, why don't you take this one."

If I mention only one thing that exemplifies how great a coach Kelly Sullivan is, it is how he responded to me that day. In a calm, soothing voice he said, "Nick, yes. You will need to buy your own warm-ups. Or, better yet, keep wearing those beat-up sweatpants and that hole-ridden sweatshirt you have been wearing to practice for the past few days. Own those sweats. When you roll up to University of Oregon this spring and compete at historic Hayward Field against the Oregon Ducks decked out in all of their brand new Nike gear, think how embarrassed each one will be when the kid in the trashy sweats from little Willamette University kicks their ass."

As he talked, I could feel goose bumps spread down my arms and legs. I wanted to find my beat up sweatshirt and go for a ten-mile run in it. In less then twenty seconds Coach Sullivan had not only saved his budget several thousand dollars, but had also set for me an attitude that would carry me through my entire collegiate career. From that point on I looked at those sweats with more pride than almost anything else I owned.

As for school, I was getting near perfect grades on all my exams. I had expressed my interest in studying pre-medicine to several of my professors and they suggested I look into Willamette's biochemistry program. Apparently, this course of study had the highest percentage of students accepted into medical schools. I looked over the required course work for the program and while it would be rigorous, I felt I could handle it and declared myself a chemistry major with an emphasis in biochemistry.

It wasn't that I loved science or the idea of being a doctor as much as I had no idea what I wanted to do with my life. Nothing jumped out at me as fascinating, but I did enjoy general chemistry and biology classes. Furthermore, I came from a long line of doctors and it seemed a wise enough choice.

As a student-athlete I found I was constantly trying to balance three things: academics, athletics, and a social life. My friends warned me a student could only do two of the three really well. I clearly chose the first two during my freshman year at Willamette, and my social life was left to revolve almost entirely around the cross-country team.

Fortunately, I liked most of the guys I ran with, and as in high school, the practices were co-ed. There were also a few girls on the ladies cross-country team that I flirted with often. I spent most of my free time with the Bearcat Pack, as we were called, due to the fact that we were often seen packed together in races, and also for Willamette's unusual mascot, the bearcat.

During my first week at Willamette University I met an incoming freshman from Spokane, Washington. His name was Cooper, and though he had come with the intention of running on the cross-country team, it became clear early on that he was going to put his social life above all else. Cooper was a tall, muscular guy and had always done well with the opposite sex. He was emotional and moody, but more often than not came off as happy, charismatic, and full of life. I was drawn to his high-energy mannerisms and we quickly became friends, despite the fact that he dropped the cross-country team just two weeks into the season.

I liked having a friend who wasn't on the team. When I was burnt out on running or tired of team drama I went to Cooper's dorm room to hang out. I also liked having a friend who pushed me outside my comfort zone. I think it is important for everyone to have such a friend, and for much of the past decade that person, for me, has been Cooper.

I wouldn't say Cooper and I were best friends our freshman year. He was constantly getting high on marijuana, drinking, or spending his nights with one girl or another, and I was pretty much always running or studying. Most Saturday nights I was at his dorm room playing video games or watching a movie. Occasionally, we cracked some beers. After a long hard week of work, hanging with Cooper was a good way to let off steam and press the reset button.

One night after a few beers while sitting in Cooper's dorm room, he asked how old I was when I lost my virginity. "I'm still a virgin," I replied with much embarrassment. He could not hide his shock, but was not insensitive about it either. Cooper went on to tell me that he had lost his virginity at the age of thirteen and had been sleeping with women at a ravenous pace ever since.

Cooper was the life of the party. He always paid for the beer, and as soon as I finished one he was at the fridge getting me another. Cooper preferred weed but accepted that I was focused on running well and never asked me to smoke with him, even though I occasionally hung out with him, and a few other people he had met while they were smoking.

I was curious about marijuana, and found it interesting to see them talk nonsense together with their blood-shot eyes. One night during finals week of my first semester, I went to Cooper's dorm to hang out. When I got there he said he was supposed to meet some guys to get "baked," but said I was welcome to hang out.

As I watched them take several hits, I sat back and complained about how hard my chemistry final was going to be. With a somewhat glazed look in his eye, Cooper said what I really needed to do was take a hit, that it would calm me down and help me study. I laughed and thanked him for the offer, but declined.

"Symmonds," he said with a confident and slightly disappointed tone, "you are almost done with your first semester of college, in Oregon mind you, and you have yet to try weed."

I was curious about the skunky smelling stuff and thought it would be quite an adventure to try it, but I had reservations. I looked down at my shoes and said, "I know. It's just that I heard you can't get high your first time and I'm focused on running and school and stuff."

I wasn't the most self-confident person at the time, but I knew how to say no to peer pressure. Cooper watched me and seemed to be listening, but the look on his face said he felt disappointment for me. He knew I was good at saying no to peer pressure, and my lame response conveyed that I was not trying very hard to pass up his offer.

"Well, I guess cross-country season *is* over," I said. With that, Cooper's face lit up.

The THC, the active chemical in marijuana, didn't affect me right away, but when it did, it hit me like a train. I went from totally sober to higher than a kite in a matter of seconds. I don't remember all of that evening, but what I do remember is that I fatigued my abdominals by laughing so hard, and was so sore that I couldn't do a sit up for a week. I also remember eating an entire pizza, and once it was finished I ate vanilla ice cream out of a plastic gallon container by the handful. At some point I passed out.

The next day I woke up and felt like a dried out dog turd. I didn't feel hung over, at least not the way I did after the few times I'd had too much. I looked down at my body and wondered how much harm had been done. Chemicals aside, how many calories had I consumed? I felt sick thinking about it and decided that what I needed was to burn the calories off and sweat out the toxins. I put my running shoes on and headed out the door.

The funny thing about THC is that it is stored in your fat cells. When I went for my run my body began to metabolize these fat cells, and in the process released the THC back into my bloodstream. I made it about four miles along the Willamette River when I suddenly realized I was high again. I looked around and admired the beautiful park, the green grass, the blue sky, and slowly walked back to campus.

My first experience with marijuana taught me that the drug wasn't for me. I had experienced what weed did to me and what it had done to many people around me. It made me feel lazy and dirty, and I knew that feeling lazy and dirty would not allow me to accomplish the goals I had set for myself.

I was able to get through my finals and, while at home for Christmas break, received notification that I had earned straight A's. Convinced that my first semester of college had been a success on all accounts, I returned to Willamette University determined to have an equally successful second semester.

4

My list of priorities at that time in my life was as follows: family, school, running, social life. I kept this list in my mind always, and made sure to allocate time and energy to the highest priorities first. I continued to do well in school so I set my sights on running at the NCAA Division III National Championships for Track and Field. This meet, which takes place at the end of the academic calendar, was the largest and most important competition that I would participate in my freshman year.

My build up for this meet had gone incredibly well and all that stood between racing for my first two national titles was finals week. As was par for the course, Cooper came to me and asked how things were going.

"Pretty well," I replied. We were sitting in our philosophy classroom after class. As we packed our books into our backpacks he asked if I had hooked up with anyone recently. "No, just really focused on classes and nationals right now," I replied.

"Ah, come on Symmonds, don't give me that," he said nudging me with his arm. "You're almost done with your first year of college and you're going back to Boise a virgin?"

I had heard this line of argument from Cooper before and he knew it was a successful way to manipulate me. Looking back, I knew I was being manipulated, but allowed it to happen—and I appreciated it.

Cooper always pushed me out of my comfort zone at a time when I both wanted and needed to be pushed. Growing up without older friends or a big brother I was still very much behind my peers and was often awkward socially. Like many young men, I desperately wanted to lose my virginity, but didn't know where to begin.

"You just gotta find a girl you are attracted to, then ask her out," were Cooper's words of wisdom. He made it all sound quite simple. "Who are you attracted to?" he asked.

There were several girls, I admitted, that I had admired from afar. As chance would have it, one of them happened to be exiting our philosophy class with us. I pointed at the petite brunette who hid her beautiful, brown, almond shaped eyes behind a pair of librarian style glasses.

"Kathy?" he laughed.

"Yeah, I think she's really pretty," I responded.

"Dude, she's way cute. But she's a senior." He paused and then went on. "You're the man, though. You should ask her out."

We watched in unison as Kathy slung her backpack over her shoulder and walked out of the room. "Okay, I will," I said, making no actual effort to do so.

"*Now*," Cooper said, gently pushing me forward.

I didn't want to disappointed Cooper, but I also didn't want to talk to Kathy. Well, I did, but I didn't want to feel that sudden, paralyzing nervousness that overcame me whenever I approached a girl. The feeling was similar to standing on the start line of a race, only once the gun went off at the race the feeling disappeared. In talking to a girl my nervous anxiety just got worse and worse as the conversation went on.

Kathy was three years older, graceful, and beautiful. I was a freshman, awkward, and poorly dressed. Despite this, I chased after her across the quad and caught her near the Mill Stream, the creek that runs through campus. "Kathy!" I called. She turned, and I was tempted to run in the other direction. Somehow, I stood my ground and introduced myself.

Runners eat a lot of carbohydrates before a race to maximize muscle energy, and I recall saying some stupid line about how I had a big race coming up and needed to carb load. Then I asked if she would possibly like to join me for a pasta dinner. Kathy said she was a runner herself, though she didn't run competitively, and that yes, she would like to accompany me. She wrote her number on a sheet of paper in her binder, tore it off, and handed it to me. Then she smiled and walked off while I stood there holding the precious slip of paper, dumbfounded, as the rare Oregon sun shone down on me. *It worked.* It was an early lesson that with great risk comes the potential for great reward.

I remember being a very smooth gentleman on our first date, but Kathy would probably tell you I was a nervous disaster. When I asked her why she agreed to go out with me she said, "You seemed so nervous when you asked me, and also very sweet, so I didn't have the heart to say no." *Whatever works,* I thought as I stared across the table at her. Later, I drove Kathy back to her house and gave her an innocent hug on her doorstep. When I climbed back into my 4Runner I figured that would be the last I'd hear from her.

The big race I was carb loading for was to take place the next day at the University of Oregon, and I wanted to rest up for it. The race was the famous Bill McChesney Mile, named after one of the great University of Oregon distance runners who died from injuries sustained in a car accident in 1992. There was much pride and prestige associated with this invitational event, and many great runners had been invited to race it. Somehow the WU coaching staff had talked the meet director into letting me in. My 1600 meter personal best of 4:20 from high school was not going to get me very far in the race. However, my training had been going really well and I knew I was due for a big improvement.

The race ended up being a cat and mouse game between a high school phenom named Michael McGrath, and me. He had a big lead going into the final lap, but ultimately I was able to hunt him down and win the race with a time of 4:03. I had shaved more than seventeen seconds off my best time! That kind of jump is almost unheard of in the sport of track and field, and I stared in disbelief at my time on the scoreboard. As

I had done often in high school, I looked down at my legs and audibly thanked them for all that they had given me.

I returned to school that night ecstatic with what I had accomplished, but sad that I had not heard from Kathy. I had really enjoyed our first date and wanted to see her again. Saturday came and went, and still nothing from her. Finally, late Sunday night as I was studying in the library, my phone began to vibrate.

It was a text from Kathy! I HEARD YOU DID WELL IN YOUR RACE! CONGRATS! SEE YOU IN PHILOSOPHY ;)

I read the text several more times. *I got a winky face!* I wanted to yell this as loud as I could, but fortunately for the many other kids who were also studying, I refrained. My heart leapt and I smiled a sheepish grin. Not only was I now a 4:03 miler, but I was also conversing with a beautiful woman, three years my senior, who was sending me flirtatious texts.

The next day in philosophy class Kathy and I sat next to each other and made plans to hang out again that night. Kathy and I soon began meeting almost every day after school, and some nights I stayed at her place off campus. One night while we were watching TV I turned to her and said, "Kathy, I'm a virgin." She smiled and said, "I figured." I suppose the fact that we had been hanging out for a while and I had never made a move beyond kissing kind of gave it away. I told her I wanted her to be my first and she smiled, stood up from the couch, and grabbed my hand. Kathy then led me from the living room into her bedroom.

I had waited more than nineteen years for this to happen and at times had cursed my inexperience. However, after that night I was glad I had waited. Kathy was fun and patient and made it an incredible experience. I was, and am, also quite glad that I did not wait until marriage. I learned from that first relationship that sex is an extremely important part of a relationship. In my experiences since, I have also learned that not all people are sexually compatible. While I certainly respect those who choose to wait until marriage, I made the right choice for me.

When I was young my mom taught me about the birds and the bees. In her colorful speech she said, "When two people really love each other they can express their love with sex. Sex is one of life's great joys, as long

as both people involved feel good about it and are engaging in it safely."
I'm pretty sure I had no idea what she was talking about at the time, but
it seemed important so I remembered it. To this day it is the best advice
on the subject I have ever been given.

As for me, I thought sex was incredible and I wanted to make up for
lost time! I actually thought more about sex now than when I had been a
virgin. But, I did my best to remember my list of priorities. I still saw
Kathy each night, but reminded myself regularly that training and running
well at the NCAA's was the higher priority.

A week later I flew to Canton, New York to compete at the NCAA
Division III National Track and Field Championships. I went in ranked
in the top ten for both the 800 and 1500 meter races. Though it had taken
some work, I managed to convince Coach Sullivan and Coach McGuirk
to let me run both. They were nervous that the series of rounds would be
too much for me, and that I would risk my chance at winning one or the
other. I assured them that I was used to running many events at the Idaho
State meet, and that doing so had prepared me for the rounds I'd face at
this championship event.

That weekend I faced very tough competition in each event. In the
800 I was attempting to dethrone two-time defending national champion
Matt Groose of Wisconsin-Oshkosh. In the 1500 I hoped to upset one
of the best distance runners to ever come from a Division III school, Ryan
Bak of Trinity College in Hartford, Connecticut.

The day of the finals was cold and rainy, despite it taking place in
June. Although I was seriously outmatched on paper, I looked at the down-
pour as a gift that would help me overcome the odds. My edge was that I
had spent most of the spring training in exactly these conditions in Oregon. With rain flying off our spikes as we fought for the titles, both men
gave me a great race. But, I was beyond thrilled to leave Canton that weekend as a two-time NCAA Division III national champion.

As I headed to the airport, I remembered how nervous I had been
one short year ago about choosing Willamette University. Having now
upset two of the most decorated athletes to come through Division III, I
felt an enormous sense of pride, both in the hard work I had put in, and

also in sticking with my gut and choosing the program that was completely right for me.

I flew back to Oregon with my two first place trophies tucked into my backpack, and as soon as we landed I went to see Kathy. We celebrated by taking a trip to Lincoln City, a beautiful little town on the Oregon Coast just an hour west of Salem. I remember working on a six pack of cheap lager as we walked along the beach, and being unbelievably happy. Unfortunately, that weekend was the last that I would spend with Kathy. The next week she graduated from Willamette University and shortly after that she moved back to the Bay Area, where she had grown up.

I returned to Boise to begin a summer job around our farm, and though we talked on the phone occasionally, Kathy and I grew apart. Every once in a while, after a big race, Kathy still sends me a congratulatory message. My heart still races a bit when I read them.

That summer, back home in Boise, I wondered what my sophomore year would be like. I felt that my freshman year had been amazingly successful. I had earned good grades, lost my virginity, and won two national titles.

I did receive some news that summer that worried me, though. Coach Kelly Sullivan had been offered the head women's coaching job at Oregon State University—and was going to accept. Coach Sullivan was the one I always went to for advice. With Coach leaving and another coach taking control of the program, the perfect balance that had existed would be gone. I was nervous to see how the team would now be run.

On a call with Coach Sullivan he told me that he felt very comfortable leaving the program in new hands. He told me that I could call him at his OSU office or on his cell anytime, day or night. Coach then went on to say how much potential he saw in me and that if I trained hard, the sky was the limit for my running career. I trusted him and, listening to his advice, trained as hard as I ever had that summer with the goal of being the number one man on the cross-country team in the fall. I returned to Salem in fantastic shape and felt extremely motivated. But, just days before the first meet was set to take place, something terrible happened.

5

On a relatively easy run, I took a step off a curb and felt something pinch in my knee. I had felt this happen before, but this instance was especially painful. I tried to run back to school, but could feel my knee swelling with each step. I slowed to a walk and limped back to campus with tears in my eyes.

My first reaction to an injury is to panic, and this time was no different. I had been relatively healthy during most of my running career, but had suffered a stress fracture and Achilles tendinitis in high school. Those injuries had tested me both mentally and emotionally, and had threatened to end my running career before it got started. Now, as I hobbled back to campus, I began to fear the worst. *How long will it take for the swelling to go down? What exactly is wrong with my knee? Will I ever run again?*

I went to Coach McGuirk's office and told him what had happened. He nodded and told me to take a few days off. I took three days of rest with no improvement. I then took a week off, and then a month. As the injury lingered, I began to accept that I was not going to be able to compete that cross-country season. Even more troubling, I began to realize that almost all of my friends were runners. It pained me to be around them as they talked about the workout they had just completed, or their upcoming races. I began to spend more time with Cooper and less time with the team. I also began spending more time with a couple of guys I knew at one of the campus fraternities, Sigma Chi. This boisterous, glorified dorm building was always full of cold beer and cute girls, and no one there ever talked about running.

I saw a few doctors, but they thought I was suffering from tendinitis and suggested I take more time off. To keep myself from going totally insane, I worked out with the guys from the fraternity most afternoons. Their idea of a workout was quite different from what I had been doing on the cross-country team, and mostly consisted of zero cardio and a whole lot of bench press. After our workouts we would re-hydrate back at the frat house with unhealthy amounts of cheap beer. My weight shot up from a lean 150 pounds, to a muscular, slightly soft 180. As we sat around the house playing drinking games, the guys suggested that I join the fraternity. I gave their offer some serious thought.

Eventually I returned to my dorm room and lay in bed wondering if my running career was over. *How did it come to this?* Just a few months before I had been a two time national champion, preparing to take on the best in the nation at a distance of 800 meters. Now, here I was, an overweight, out of shape, meathead. I stared at the ceiling as tears streamed down my face. Finally, at the suggestion of Coach McGuirk, I agreed to see one last doctor.

I drove the sixty miles of I-5 that links Salem to Eugene to meet with legendary orthopedic surgeon, Stan James. Dr. James had practiced medicine in the Emerald Valley for decades, and had treated many famous runners. Two minutes into my visit he knew exactly what my injury was. "You have some of the most pronounced plica I have ever felt," he said, working his fingers around my kneecap. "You'll need to have it removed arthroscopically." I had no idea what he was talking about, and said so.

Dr. James explained that plica are an extension of the protective synovial capsule of the knee. Occasionally, a little of the plica tissue can become irritated, enlarged, or inflamed causing something called synovial plica syndrome. The plica themselves are remnants of the fetal stage of development and exist in adults as sleeves of tissue called synovial folds. Very few people ever develop plica syndrome, but those who do are often distance runners.

The surgery to remove the inflamed tissue was a relatively simple one and required three tiny incisions. The operating surgeon then inserts a scope and some cutting pinchers through these incisions to extract the tissue. Doctor James told me that if I rested long enough the inflammation would eventually go down, but that I would always be prone to synovial plica syndrome, unless I had the surgery.

I knew the surgery had to be done or I would face this same injury again and again for the rest of my life. The best time to have the procedure done, though, would be over winter break and back in Boise where I could recover at home. Also, I recognized that I am a high maintenance sick or injured person and was counting on my mom to take good care of me.

The surgery was simple, and recovery would have been easy had I not let my body atrophy so badly the past fall. A physical therapist gave me drills to do to that would help me regain the strength and fitness I had lost. But, with the wisdom of youth and immaturity, I tossed the drills aside in exchange for the TV remote.

With my legs bandaged and propped up on pillows, the only thing that kept me from going totally insane was having my little sister with me. Lauren was now a senior at Bishop Kelly High School. Though we had fought often when I was living at home, usually over resources like the dial-up Internet or the phone, we had grown very close since I had moved out. I missed her, and was grateful to have her by my side, watching trashy movies with me as I recovered from the surgery.

Following winter break, I returned to Willamette University. While the surgery had me hopeful that I would one day run again, I still was not ready to spend a great deal of time with my former teammates. Instead, I continued to hang out at the Sigma Chi house where I found diversion and companionship.

With the spring semester underway, the fraternities and sororities were getting ready for rush. This annual tradition where the various Greek houses recruited new members had everyone at the house excited and busy. My friends in the house continued to urge me to rush, but I still had reservations. I liked being able to come over, hang out, and drink beer, but I also liked being able to go back to my room away from the house when I wanted to. As had been the case with running, it was ultimately at the urging of a girl I had a crush on that finally pushed me to join Sigma Chi.

Rumors of my behavior, my new weight, and my joining of the fraternity eventually traveled to my coaching staff and I was sent an email asking me to meet with one of the coaches, a man I'll call Coach Kendrick. At the meeting he sat across from me with his arms folded and bluntly asked me what the hell I was doing. I told him that I was pretty sure my running career was over. I also said that since I wasn't on an athletic scholarship what I did in my free time was none of his business. He didn't directly say so, but I got the feeling that he wanted me to drop my pledge to the house. I held my ground.

Needless to say, the meeting did not end well. I understand now that Coach Kendrick cared about me and didn't want to see me waste my potential. At the time I had trouble seeing that. He and I always had poor communication with each other, and I felt his concern came across as a mandate, rather than as a guy who genuinely cared about me. This failure to communicate would become a defining characteristic of our relationship.

Well into the second semester of my sophomore year I still had not resumed training. Several weeks after my surgery I had attempted to jog a few easy miles, but my knees still hurt. Even more troubling was that my Achilles tendons were starting to hurt as well. My body was clearly rejecting running of any kind, and I was too lazy to do the rehab drills I had been prescribed.

By this point in time, running had completely fallen off my list of priorities. This allowed me to put all my time and energy into school and a social life. I continued to get good grades and was having a great time in the Greek system. I had made more new friends in my first month with Sigma Chi than I had in the three prior semesters I had been at Willamette.

My love life was at an all time high as well, now that three sororities were inviting me to all kinds of events.

One afternoon, as I sat in the Sigma Chi house shooting pool, there was a knock on the fraternity door. One of my Sigma Chi brothers came back to tell me there was "some guy named Sam," here to see me. I set my pool cue down and walked to the front of the house.

On the steps was a young coach I knew from around the track. His name was Sam Lapray and he was a volunteer assistant for the Willamette Track Team. Sam was a tall, good-looking guy who had run track for Willamette University in the early 1990s. He was now in his mid-thirties and still looked pretty fit. I liked seeing Coach Sam around the track because he always brought a lot of energy to practice. Sam and I had chatted a few times in my first three semesters at Willamette University, but we weren't especially close.

The rumor going around the team was that Coach Sam owned millions of dollars in real estate all over Oregon. The guys on the team looked up to him because he was wildly successful and had a beautiful wife. I also liked Coach Sam because he seemed kind, and because he occasionally brought his three young children with him to our practices. They were great kids and Sam seemed like a really good dad. I recognized that this guy was successful in everything he did, and I wanted to know what his secret was.

That day, as we stood on the front doorstep of Sigma Chi, I am sure I looked the complete opposite of successful.

"So, what have you been up to?" he asked.

"Not much," I replied with a shrug. "Mostly just trying to have some fun."

Sam took a seat on the steps and asked me to do the same. He looked me in the eyes and said he recognized a talent in me that was special. He said he had known several world-class athletes before, and that he saw in me what he had seen in them, a passion and drive that would ultimately overcome any obstacle that stood in the way of my goals. He then went on to say that he truly felt I had the potential to make an Olympic team one day and, furthermore, he would help me get there—if that was what

I wanted. I flushed red at the compliment, and then laughed it off. I told Coach Sam that I was pretty sure my running career was over.

"If I find someone to help you with your rehab will you do it?" he asked.

I told him I would think about it and wished him a good evening. Then I went back to finish my game of pool and drink another beer.

That night Coach Sam did some research and found a company in Beaverton, Oregon, a suburb eight or nine miles southwest of Portland, called Function Dynamics. They specialized in helping athletes recognize structural weakness in their bodies. Once these issues were identified, the team at Function Dynamics created a personalized menu of drills that corrected the underlying problem and allowed the athlete to move more efficiently.

On a rainy, February day, Sam picked me up in his truck and drove me to the Function Dynamics headquarters. He also sat with me through an initial consultation where they took pictures and video of me standing and walking.

The Function Dynamics team told me that the human body was designed to handle an incredible amount of stress. If, I learned, all the pieces are in alignment, the body should be able to withstand hundreds of miles of running each week without injury. However, every person has a few weaknesses and it is these imperfections that lead to overuse injuries. Members of their team then showed me the images they had captured, and identified my own personal weaknesses.

I could see right away what they were talking about. My hips were clearly not parallel to the ground, and my right hipbone was an inch higher than the left. From the side I could also see that my weight was not being evenly distributed through my legs, and my now large torso was swaying well over my toes. The team at Function Dynamics said these issues were the underlying cause of my lower leg problems.

I was concerned with the issues and wanted to address them. However, what concerned me most was the way I looked in the pictures. I had never been the type of distance runner who had a long, lean build, but I now did not resemble any kind of runner at all. I stared at the pictures in disbelief, wondering how I had let myself get so big. I missed being in shape.

The Function Dynamics team printed out my menu of drills and then led me through each one, ensuring that I did it correctly. The entire program took about twenty minutes to complete. On our way out, Sam laid his credit card down and said that he would pay for today's visit.

As we climbed back into Coach Sam's pickup I told him I would pay him back. He shook his head and said, "I don't want you to repay me with money. You can repay my by doing those drills every single day, without fail." I told him I would, then he asked me for one more thing. "I want to see you at track practice every day." I started to protest, but he cut me off and continued, "You don't have to do the workouts with the team. Just do your drills, run a lap or two, and then come say hi to me before you go home. Deal?"

I nodded my agreement. Coach Sam's selfless love and support was exactly what I needed at that time. We rode back to Salem listening to music and talking about things unrelated to running. On that drive home I recall being as happy as I had been in months. Though I still wasn't sure I would ever run competitively again, I knew that I had just made a very good friend, one that would last a lifetime. I was wise enough at the time to recognize the importance of this, and smiled at my good fortune.

True to my word, the next day I showed up at track practice decked out in my old, heavy sweats. I completed my drills, and ran a very slow, painful lap. Then I walked to the weight room where Coach Sam was taking a few of his sprinters through a workout.

"Did you do your drills?" he asked.

"Yep. And ran one lap," I replied.

"Well, that's a great start!" he said and put his hand up to give me a high five. I slapped his hand and then gave him a hug. I thanked him and said, "See you tomorrow Coach," as I walked out of the weight room.

Over the next few weeks I was able to add more laps to my daily jog. The drills seemed to be helping and the pain in my lower legs subsided. By mid April I was running close to thirty miles a week and, despite now having to deal with the worst shin splints I had ever known, was almost starting to feel like my old self again. I remained active in the fraternity, but made plans to run track that spring.

My first race back was scheduled to be at Hayward Field. I was still very overweight and seriously under-prepared, but Coach Sam thought it would be good for me to get some competitive juices flowing again. I entered an 800 meter heat and, to my surprise, won with a time not far off my personal best.

Doing so did not feel easy or smooth. As my bulky muscles burned through the little oxygen that my heart and lungs were able to provide them, lactic acid built up in my body. The lactate that formed from metabolic processes taking place in my body during the race had a paralyzing effect on my muscles, and to win, I had to push myself through a level of pain I had never known before. I crossed the line and deliriously stumbled off the track, through the main gates, and onto Agate Street. Coach Sam was soon beside me, along with a few of my teammates. They were all excited that I was "back." But I didn't feel back at all. In fact, I felt like I was going to die and to prove my point, I collapsed on the grass. I then raised myself up onto my hands and knees and began projectile vomiting. Coach Sam laughed and said, "See that guys? That's how you know you went to the well!"

I had always felt that I was a good runner, and made the most of a little bit of natural talent. Given that my body type did not fit the stereotypical mold of a world-class middle distance runner, I assumed that it was my work ethic that had gotten me this far. That day, as I heaved my lunch onto the grass, I had a revelation: I was built to run, and run fast. There is simply no other way to explain how I was able to win that day without having trained most of the previous six months. *What if running is what I was born to do?*

I now know that injuries test every great athlete in every sport. To become one of the best, an athlete must constantly straddle the razor thin line between training hard and over training. Though I didn't feel it at the time, I can now look back on that knee injury with a certain amount of gratitude. In fighting through that injury I learned a lot about myself. I learned that I was born to run, that I had the mental resolve to overcome obstacles and become one of the best, and that to get to the top I needed a lot of help from people like Sam Lapray.

I had a feeling that Coach Kendrick was not going to be part of the support team that took me to the next level, but he was still my coach and we sat down the following week to form a race schedule for the spring. We talked about going back to the NCAA Championships and what it would take to get there. We both knew that I did not have the strength to defend my dual titles. I opted for the shorter of the two and we made a plan to defend my 800 title.

With workouts coming from Coaches McGuirk and Kendrick, and emotional support coming from Coach Sam I clawed my way back to fighting form. In June we flew to Decatur, Illinois to compete at the NCAA Division III National Track and Field Championships hosted by Millikin University. Suffering though a hot, humid climate unlike anything I had ever run in before, I managed to defend my 800 meter national title. As I crossed the line I felt both joy and disappointment. I was running and winning on a national level again. But I had failed to top, or even match, my accomplishments from the year before.

I flew back to Oregon and added my new first place trophy to the two I had earned as a freshman. Then I spent a few days at Coach Sam's house, getting to know Coach and his family better before I drove back to Boise for the summer.

As my 4Runner rolled along I-84 though the Columbia River gorge I replayed the events of that year in my mind. In some ways my sophomore year had been less successful than my freshman year. There had been many more obstacles and low points. There had indeed been many disappointments, but I felt they had tested me and I had learned a lot about myself and about life in working through them.

I turned the music up and rolled the window down to let the hot, Oregon air pass through the car. I smiled, knowing that I was once again healthy and had the entire summer back in Boise to regain the strength I had lost during the winter.

My incredibly tough sophomore year had given me much, but it had also done some permanent harm. My relationship with Coach Kendrick was not the same after the meeting where we discussed my decision to join the fraternity. I think he may have seen my decision as direct disobedience of his authority. We certainly had personalities that clashed. Furthermore, I think it hurt his feelings that it had been Coach Sam who finally got me back running, and not him.

That summer I worked at the hospital as an assistant to an eye doctor. I also trained hard and looked ahead to my final two years at Willamette University, I tried to be optimistic that Coach Kendrick and I would be able to repair our wounded relationship. However, upon my return to campus, my optimism quickly faded.

6

When I returned to Willamette to begin my junior year, Coach Kendrick and I began to seriously butt heads. I had spent much of the summer running in the rolling hills of Idaho, and had regained most of my leg strength. I thought the workouts he gave me that fall were too easy, and I didn't feel challenged. I mentioned this to him, often, and he responded the same way each time. "Oh, so you're the coach now. Why am I even here?"

"No," I'd say, "you are the coach, but I know my body and I can handle more work."

Despite our discussions, Coach Kendrick continued to write workouts that I felt did not challenge me. This, coupled with the manner in which he addressed my concerns did little to reassure me that he was the right person to be coaching me. Though Coach Sam had a continued presence around the track, his job was to train the sprinters and jumpers. I could continue to rely on him for emotional support, but ultimately, I needed someone to help facilitate communication between Coach Kendrick and me on a daily basis.

Fortunately, Willamette University had just hired a young, new assistant coach by the name of Jimmy Bean. Jimmy had just finished graduate school and was eager to be coaching full time. He was only a few years older than me, but I looked up to him. He and I got along very well from day one and I often expressed my concerns to him. With Coach Jimmy facilitating most of the communication that occurred between Coach Kendrick and me, we were able to find something that worked.

Despite having Coach Sam and Coach Jimmy, I was still frustrated with my running career. I was not being challenged enough, both in practice and in competition. I had taken Coach Sullivan and Coach Sam's vote of confidence to heart and began to believe that I might actually have the talent necessary to make an Olympic team.

As I began to dream about making this a reality, I became frustrated with school. Though I loved my general chemistry and biology classes, I loathed my advanced classes. What had been mind-blowing lessons on how lasers worked or why the sky was blue, was now mind numbing lists and charts that had to be memorized. I soon came to resent all the work that had to be done to get good grades. School was still at the top of my list of priorities, but keeping it there was getting in the way of running.

One day, after receiving a particularly disappointing grade on a chemistry test, I jumped in my SUV and started driving as tears streamed down my face. I drove south for an hour, until I finally pulled to the side of the road and called my mom. Sobbing into the phone I told her that if I continued to get grades like the one I had just received, no medical school would ever accept me.

She asked why I wanted to be a doctor. I thought about that for a minute, then said, "People look at doctors with respect, and they make a lot of money and get to wear pajamas to work." Hearing myself say that I added, "Oh, and I guess doctors get to help people too."

Mom laughed, and then patiently explained that there were a lot of jobs that had those kinds of benefits. She went on to say that, although wanting to help people was a good reason to become a doctor, wearing pajamas to work was probably not worth the amount of time and money it would take to earn my MD.

Deep down I knew this, but I desperately wanted to be successful at something and medicine seemed a logical choice. In the back of my mind I wondered if I could ever be really successful at running. Certainly I'd had some success, but it was small compared to what my Division I colleagues were accomplishing. More to the point, my career had stagnated. At the end of my junior year my personal bests were still very similar to the times I had run my freshman year.

I was bored at school and unhappy with the lack of progression in my running. I also felt I had met everyone there was to meet at tiny Willamette University and was bored in Salem. In addition, I often sat through class staring out the window wondering what life would be like as a professional runner. *Where would I travel and what kind of people would I meet? What sort of crazy adventures would I have?* I imagined myself crossing the finish line at the Prefontaine Classic, the most prestigious professional track and field meet in the United States, as thousands of people cheered me on. I wondered how I would celebrate when I crossed the line, and how I would answer reporters' questions. Invariably, I was brought back to reality when a professor called on me to answer a question about tiny bits of matter that I finally understood would never matter to me.

Every day, when classes were finally over, I ran back to the fraternity, packed my gym bag, and headed to practice where Coach Kendrick and I argued about what I should do for the day's workout. I needed a change.

I began to make calls to ask about transferring to a different school. Although every coach I spoke with was interested in having me run for them, all wanted me to redshirt, or suspend, my first year with them so as to extend my collegiate eligibility. I, however, wanted to be done with school and be out in the real world, so this was not an option for me.

My only choice, it seemed, was to drop out of school altogether. Toward the end of my junior year I called my parents to break the news that I was going to leave Willamette University and focus on running full time. Needless to say, Mom and Dad were not thrilled with this plan. I told them I could be really good if I put all my energy into running, but that school prevented me from doing so. I added that I could always come back and finish my degree at a later time.

"Could you put all your energy into running and still get passing grades?" they asked.

I figured if all I did was show up to class I could eek out C's. Knowing that it was either C's or nothing, my ever-supportive parents told me they would back a plan that involved less than stellar grades, but strongly urged me to finish my degree.

I went to the list of priorities tacked up in my mind and pulled it down. It had been: family, school, running, social life. I mentally ripped it up and wrote a new one: family, running, social life . . . school. As soon as this change had been made I felt a giant weight lift off my shoulders. Sure, I was going to get shitty grades, but I could always go back and retake classes if I decided to go to grad school.

This new plan would also allow me to put my youth to better use, and I made a promise to myself to find out just how far I could take my running. The first step was to log some serious miles in the summer before my senior year. Aaron Hollingshead (a teammate of mine and one of my best friends) and I took to the Internet to find a remote location at high altitude where we could train like Kenyan marathoners. Given that neither of us had ever been able to study abroad, due to the fact that we had athletic commitments in both the spring and the fall, we also wanted this location to be outside of the United States.

Our search led us to a town not far from Mexico City called Toluca. Neither Aaron nor I spoke much Spanish so we asked a teammate of ours who was fluent in Spanish if he wanted to join us. His name was Carlos Ruiz and once he was in, we purchased tickets and set about making plans.

I was thrilled to head to my first real training camp, and to live, eat, and sleep running. There was only one thing that separated me from this Spartan existence; the NCAA Division III National Championships. This time it was being held in Wartburg, Iowa, and I was again trying to pull off the 800/1500 double I had managed my freshman year. Without too much struggle, I did.

You might think that these wins would make me happy; I was running well and had just won my fourth and fifth NCAA Division III National titles. But, my triumphs actually made me less happy and more frustrated. I clearly was not racing tough enough competition. Where was the challenge?

Fortunately, I found the challenge of a lifetime when we arrived in Toluca. Situated at 8,750 feet in the mountains of central Mexico, I struggled to walk in the dry, thin air. Aaron, Carlos, and I ran almost every morning and evening of our ten-week stay. When we weren't running we were studying Spanish, eating tacos, or stumbling around aimlessly having consumed a few too many shots of tequila.

My fitness and my Spanish came along quickly during that trip. Both were largely due to the fact that I had begun dating a girl named Betty. She had a dark complexion and curves that conveyed her Mexican heritage. She spoke little English and laughed at my terrible Spanish. However, she was patient and allowed me to butcher her language as I stared into her beautiful brown eyes.

At this point, aside from the time I had taken off for my knee injury, I had been running nearly every day since I first showed up at cross-country practice in middle school. My love-hate relationship with distance running had come a long way since those days, but the hate side generally still won out. In Mexico, however, everything changed. For the first time in my running career I learned to enjoy the pain and sacrifice that comes with running ten miles a day. In Mexico I no longer had to try to cram my workouts between school, a job, or other daily commitments. Finally, I had the time to appreciate both the hard work that goes into creating a great runner and the rest that must accompany it. As I clicked off miles along dirt trails through the high Mexican dessert, I truly began to fall in love with the sport.

After ten incredible weeks, I was forced to say goodbye to Betty when I returned to Willamette University to finish my degree and collegiate eligibility. I was in the best shape of my life, and with a new list of priorities posted in my brain it felt like this year would be very different from the previous three.

As expected, my grades reflected my new order of priorities. Where A's had always been the standard I held myself to, C's seemed just fine now. *C's get degrees*, I told myself as I shoved another barely passing test or paper into my backpack. My professors had begun to worry and asked what was up. I explained to them that running was now my primary objective. They listened and nodded, but were clearly concerned.

I thought my renewed focus in the sport of running might help mend my relationship with Coach Kendrick, but unfortunately, it seemed to do just the opposite. Previously, when he and I had disagreed on something, I had seen it as an annoyance. Now when we disagreed, I saw him as a giant, stubborn obstacle in my way to running greatness.

He continued to give me workouts that I felt were far too easy. I listened as he read out the day's workout to the team, then shook my head. I ran his workouts though, usually in lane two or three to add distance onto each rep, thereby making it tougher. Each day, when I had destroyed the workout and barely broke a sweat, I asked Coach Kendrick for more.

Rather than embrace my eagerness, he'd throw his hands up in the air and say, "Nick, why am I even here? Since you seem to know everything why don't you just coach yourself?"

That was the first thing Coach Kendrick had said in a while that made sense to me! So I did.

On many occasions during my senior year I ran my coach's workouts and then jogged a mile to nearby South Salem High School where I ran a second workout that I had written for myself. Though I would not recommend that most young athlete do this, out of desperation, I felt I had to. It was risky, but it also taught me to be self-sufficient and to take control of my training. It taught me to listen to my body, for this was the only way I could get through both workouts.

Soon, I began to see all the hard work paying off. During my last cross-country season I set a new personal best for 8,000 meters of 24:49, an average of just less than five minutes per mile for 4.97 miles. That season I also won the cross-country conference title, taking down some very talented endurance runners. I had never been a really great cross-country runner, so I knew that I must have gained some serious strength.

Over the Christmas break I allowed myself to take two weeks of down time. I spent the first week with my family in Boise, Idaho. I think they could see that I was now learning to love the sport of running and could clearly see that it was translating to great returns in competition. They continued to support me emotionally, and encouraged me to follow my dream.

After Christmas, I flew to Portland, Oregon to meet up with one of my fraternity brothers and fellow 800 meter runner, Everett Thomas. He was headed to Costa Rica to see his family for a few weeks and had invited Cooper and me. Everett, Cooper and I had all become very close and were actually living together in a house off campus. When Everett invited us along on the trip, we couldn't say no. In the warm, humid climate on the Pacific side of Costa Rica, I ate fried rice, drank coconut milk, surfed, and played with monkeys. This time off was exactly what I needed after the long summer and fall.

When I returned to Oregon, my legs felt fresh and renewed. I transitioned from preparing for 8,000 meter cross-country races, to mid-distance track races, slowly feeding my legs shorter, faster intervals, and more weight in the gym. The strength I had accumulated over the summer and fall, combined with the fresh legs I had after the vacation, had me feeling invincible. I was even surprising myself in workouts and crushing my competitors in every race I entered.

I begged Coach Kendrick to get me into more challenging races, but he asked me to sit back and trust him. That was the last thing I wanted to do. We finally agreed that I should fly down to Mt. San Antonio College in Southern California to compete in a national class men's 800 meter race. I had won the B section of this race the previous year and was certain that the meet director would put me in the A race this year.

Coach Jimmy and I boarded a flight from Portland to Los Angeles. I was very excited to race some of the best athletes in the United States for the first time. However, when we went to get our race packet, I found that I had, once again, been placed in the B race. I was furious, but had already flown all the way to southern California, so I raced anyway. I won, easily. After the race I told Coach Jimmy I would be a while on my cool down. I threw on my trainers and headed out on a five-mile run, grinding the last few miles as hard as I could. I was so angry and frustrated, and tried to let it all flow out through my shoes.

After all the sacrifices I had made, to fly that far and to then be denied a chance to race against the best made me extremely upset. I had earned the right to be in that elite field. In fact, I had never lost an 800 meter final in my entire collegiate career! It just didn't make sense. Over dinner that night I expressed my frustration to Coach Jimmy, and he promised he would get to the bottom of it.

True to his word, Jimmy found out what had happened. As we flew back to Oregon he told me that I wasn't going to like what he had to say. Apparently, the meet director also felt I belonged in the A race with the nation's best half-milers. However, earlier that week he received a call from Coach Kendrick. During that conversation he asked the meet director to put me in the B race. Astounded, Jimmy called Coach Kendrick to find out why he would do such a thing. According to Jimmy, his exact words were, "Because f*** Nick, that's why."

As Jimmy told me this I sat in my seat staring straight ahead, my body shaking. At the end of the trip I gave Coach Jimmy a big hug and thanked him for his help and for being honest with me. I tried to sleep that night, but the anger I felt deep inside wouldn't allow me to do so.

The next day I barged into Coach Kendrick's office. "You *pulled* me from the A race? Why would you do such a thing?" I shouted before I could even shut the door. Coach sat back in his chair, crossed his arms, and said "I heard you were partying last weekend so I didn't think you deserved to be in a race with the nation's best." I looked at him in disbelief before I stormed out of his office.

Looking back, to Coach Kendrick I must have seemed an unruly, arrogant jerk. What he failed to realize was, that to me, he was no longer my coach. He was now simply a guy with a title who stood in the way of where I wanted to go.

Specifically, I wanted to go to the USA National Championships to race the best America had to offer. This annual meet put on by our sport's national governing body, USA Track and Field (USATF), pits professionals and amateurs against each other to decide the nation's greatest athlete in each event. I knew that this competition would be my chance to test myself against the best. However, I needed a qualifying mark to be invited.

Every athlete must have run a time under the qualifying time standard, and within the qualifying window of calendar time. Both the time and the window are set by USATF. For the men's 800, the qualifying time of 1:47.3 was almost a full second faster than I had ever run. I knew I needed to get in a fast race if I was to have any chance of running the time. I scoured the Internet, looking all over the country for an invitational meet, but couldn't find any. At last I found a tiny meet in Nashville, Tennessee, the Music City Distance Carnival, held at Vanderbilt University. It fit into my season well and happened to have a men's 800 meter race.

I emailed the meet director, a great guy by the name of Dave Milner, and explained my situation. I told him I was the three-time defending Division III national champion at 800 meters and had not lost a race at that distance in almost seven years. Dave wrote back that he could guarantee me a spot on the starting line, but had no money to fly me out or put me up in a hotel.

Even though I had a part time job delivering flowers for a local florist, the thousand-dollar price tag of a trip to Tennessee was well beyond my means. I swallowed my pride and went back to Coach Kendrick's office to ask him to pay for it out of the track team's budget. I explained that I had found a high quality meet on a fast track, in a city known to have great weather at that time of year. But once again, this coach dashed my dreams, this time when he said he wasn't going to waste money on a trip like that, and that I should be able to run fast in Oregon.

I stared at him in disbelief. Either he was punishing me, or the guy just didn't get it. I did not believe for a second that the team did not have the money. Besides, I had raced in Oregon dozens of times and never run faster than 1:48. I needed warmer weather and better competition, and the tracks in the Division III Pacific Northwest Conference simply did not offer me those things. I looked him in the eye and said, "Fine. I can't force you to sign off on this trip, but I'm going to Nashville either way."

"If you go to that meet," he said, "you can consider yourself off the team."

I walked out of his office and decided to call his bluff. As I walked the mile back to the house I shared with Everett and Cooper, I stewed in anger and tried to calm down before I phoned my parents. When they answered, I explained. Both Mom and Dad agreed this was an opportunity that I couldn't miss. Mom's main concern was that the race was scheduled the night before my college graduation ceremony. She was worried that I wouldn't be able to make it back in time to walk with my classmates to receive my diploma. I assured her that because Nashville was two hours ahead of Oregon time, if I left early enough the next morning I could make it back.

Reassured, they booked a flight for me to Nashville, along with a two-night stay at a hotel near the track. Several days later I flew to Music City.

When I stepped off the plane I felt the warm, humid weather settle into my muscles. This wasn't the cold, rainy weather I had been trying to run through all spring, this was sprinting weather. I received my race packet and looked over the names on the start list. I didn't recognize all of them, but I did know one man's name: Jebreh Harris. Jebreh was a talented half-miler who had graduated a few years earlier from the University of Tennessee. He was currently ranked number six in the United States and had a personal best of 1:45.9. I knew if I could stay close to him, he would help tow me to a fast time.

When the gun went off late in the afternoon, Jebreh tucked in right behind the rabbit. In distance running, a rabbit is someone who is hired to run the first part of a race to set the pace for the competitors. Rabbits are not used frequently in collegiate meets, but are common in professional races. The rabbit led the field through the fast first lap before stepping off the track. Knowing the pace was honest, I remained patient, tucking in behind Jebreh, just inches away from his long back kick.

With only 100 meters to go I was still just inches from Jebreh. My legs felt good and strong and my mind was no longer thinking about running a fast time. Rather, I was focused on beating the sixth fastest man in the US to the finish line. I swung wide as we entered the home stretch and pulled even with him. Jebreh responded to my move and we ran shoulder-to-shoulder all the way to the finish line. I lunged for it at the last second and just barely out-leaned my worthy competitor. I had won the race and, in doing so, had set a new NCAA Division III national record. My time of 1:47.3 also just barely qualified me for the USATF National Championships.

When I saw the time, I collapsed to the track. I had done it. I had risked everything for this, but the risk had paid off. Jebreh came over and picked me up off the ground. He congratulated me and I thanked him for doing so much of the work in the race. After I told him he helped me shave almost a second off my personal best he asked if I would like to join him for a cool down run. "Yes," I said. "But first I need to call my parents."

I gave them a quick replay of the race and then told them the time that I had run. I heard Mom and Dad rejoicing on the other end of the line, and it made me happy to share this moment with them. I couldn't have done this without their love and support and told them so. As I cooled down with Jebreh, I asked what the USATF Championships were like and what I should expect. He gave me a few good pointers before he wished me good luck.

Tired, but thrilled, I went to a corner of the track where my backpack lay. I put on my old sweats and packed the rest of my gear. Before I got up to return to my hotel I took a minute to look around. It was still very warm and I could smell the fresh-cut grass of the infield. The sun was just starting to set and the sky was a brilliant shade of pink and orange. I ran my hand along the rough, rubbery track and thought *I want* this *to be my office.*

7

That night, after the race in Nashville, I went out for burgers and beers with a few of the other runners. But each time I got up to purchase a beer someone stepped in to buy it for me. "Not every night you get to buy a national record holder a beer," one guy said as he handed me a cold one. As badly as I wanted to stay out and experience the nightlife of Nashville, I knew I had to get up early to fly back to Oregon. So I thanked everyone and called it an early night.

The next morning I woke before sunrise and got on a plane bound for Portland. When I landed, my parents and my sister, who had also just touched down, greeted me. We quickly loaded up a rental car and shared stories as my dad rushed us down I-5 toward Salem. I had my cap and gown packed and threw them on as he pulled into the Willamette University parking lot. As I got out of the car I saw that my classmates were already filling into the quad where the ceremony was to be held, and I sprinted over to find my place among them.

Later that evening, sitting around a table with my family at a very nice restaurant, I replayed the events of the weekend for them. So much had taken place over the previous four years to bring me to this point in my life. I was now an unemployed college graduate with zero job offers, but I had booked my ticket to the USA National Championships where one good race could change my life forever. It seemed that the timing could not have been better. Just as one chapter of my life was coming to an end, the next path that I was to choose seemed to be presenting itself.

As had happened when I chose cross-country over soccer and a Division III school over a Division I program, some people questioned my decision to choose running over a more stable, predictable career. It began during one of my last classes with my fellow chemistry majors. Many of the professors in our department had gathered us together to share what we would be doing the following year. As my classmates rattled off the names of the PhD or MD programs they had been accepted into I felt my heart begin to race. *What am I going to say?* When it came my turn I smiled and said, "I'm going to train for the 2008 Olympic Trials."

Everyone smiled and nodded, but I could tell they all thought I was crazy. One girl who had been on the cross-country team leaned in and whispered, "You're not fast enough to run professionally, are you?" Despite the overwhelming negativity I felt in that room, my gut told me I was choosing the right path. Thankfully, one of my favorite professors came up to me as I walked out and said, "I believe in you," as she squeezed my shoulder.

I have found that when you are on the road less traveled people often doubt your chosen path. Their negativity creeps in and makes you question your own gut decisions. Those few words of encouragement from my professor reminded me that I was on *my* right path, and I clung to her words.

Aside from my family and one lone professor, I knew another place where I could find people who believed in me. The first Monday after graduation I went to the track to knock out a run and some strides. When I walked into the locker room my teammates greeted me with great enthusiasm. Many had sent congratulatory messages after the race in Nashville, but now, nearly everyone came up to personally shake my hand or give me a hug.

Willamette University will never be known for its incredible track and field team the way the University of Oregon is, but the men and women of the Bearcat Pack made my time there special and memorable. All of them—except one particularly stubborn man.

When I walked onto the track I saw Coach Kendrick standing at the fifty-yard line, smack in the middle of the field. As I approached, he asked what I was doing at his practice, and reminded me that after what I pulled in Tennessee I was no longer part of his team.

I had expected this, and told him I would be happy to talk to a school administrator to find out more official thoughts on the matter. I went on to say that I was pretty sure the administrator would want me to represent the university and defend the five national titles I had already earned for Willamette. At this, Coach Kendrick stepped toward me, just inches from my face. Though he was considerably larger, I was prepared to kick his ass if he so much as touched me. Instead, he said I would be allowed to defend my titles, but that he would no longer coach me.

I think he saw his pronouncement as some kind of punishment, but it was music to my ears. Not only would I get to finish my collegiate career and defend my titles, I was going to get to do so my way. I had already been supplementing his workouts with my own, and now I had the freedom to write the entire program myself! I had just over four weeks until the USATF Championships and saw this as an enormous opportunity to prepare.

After I walked off the field, I started my first warm-up as a liberated athlete. At the time, my anger and frustration with Coach Kendrick prevented me from putting myself in his shoes. Had I done so, I would have seen that he just wanted me to be successful. At least, he had in the beginning. At some point our failure to communicate prevented us from forming a solid coach-athlete relationship.

I have had many coaches in my history as an athlete and have gotten along with most. The ones I have had the best relationship with view a coach-athlete relationship as a partnership. They never talked down to an athlete and always included them in the decision making process. Coach Kendrick, on the other hand, wanted to run his program like a Division I dictatorship. What he failed to realize was that he was coaching a Division III program, and therefore did not have any of his athletes under scholarship. This limited the amount of leverage he had when he tried to force an athlete to do something.

When Matt McGuirk had visited my home in Boise when I was being recruited by Willamette University he asked my mother one question: how do I get Nick to buy into the program? She laughed and replied that I was stubborn and opinionated, but that I was also very logical. She told him that if he took the time to explain his plan and walked me through why he had me do each workout, I would eventually buy into his program.

While most of my coaches followed this plan, Coach Kendrick did not. I like to think that he was just young, and was cutting his teeth on me. I hope that he has since learned that being a dictator typically does not work with amateur athletes who are not under scholarship, or with elite athletes who want to have some say in their training and race schedule. I hope for his current athletes' sake that he has learned to communicate better. I don't know if he has or not, as he and I stopped talking, for the most part, after that day at the fifty-yard line.

I was clearly stubborn and arrogant at this time in my life, but at least I had the good sense to make a phone call before throwing myself into training for the USATF Championships. The call I made was to Coach Shanahan, my former high school coach who was still whipping Bishop Kelly High's youth into shape back in Boise. Coach Shanahan had been one of those coaches who always took time to listen. He also took time to explain the method to his madness. I was glad that we had stayed close since my graduation from high school.

Coach Shanahan offered to help write my workouts and said he would serve as a sounding board for me if I needed help in my preparations. I gratefully accepted his offer. To sweeten the deal, Coach Jimmy Bean agreed to continue to implement the workouts that Coach Shanahan and I wrote together. Between Coach Shanahan's experience and Jimmy's loyal support I had the perfect set up to get me where I needed to go. And, as always, Coach Sam was by my side. I grinned when he told me he had already booked his ticket to Indianapolis where the championships were being held.

During this transition period, the end of my amateur career looked a lot like the beginning of my pro career. I had my support team in place and was living the life of a pro, with one exception: I could not yet accept money. I first had to finish my NCAA eligibility by competing at my last NCAA Division III National Championship.

I flew with the Willamette track team to Lisle, Illinois to defend my titles. Needless to say, there were some awkward moments with Coach Kendrick. With Coach Sam and Coach Jimmy keeping us as far apart as possible, I was able to remain focused. As I had in every NCAA Division III Track and Field national title race, I crossed the finish line in first place, twice.

When I had accomplished this the year before I had felt a sense of anger and frustration. Now I only felt joy and completion. This was the perfect way to end my collegiate career. Where I felt like I was lacking a challenge during my junior year, I now looked at my NCAA races as the perfect way to get my body ready for the USATF Championships.

After the meet I cooled down with a friend, Will Leer. We had only met a few weeks prior to these championships. Though he was a year younger than I was, he ran with the strength and maturity of someone much older. Added to this was the fact that he wore a thick, glorious mustache. I liked him immediately. I liked him even more when he suggested we go to the nearest convenience store and grab a case of beer. We spent the rest of that sunny afternoon lying on a grassy berm, watching the other races while we took pulls from our brown-bagged, ice-cold lagers.

When I returned to Oregon my first order of business was to pack up my things. The lease that Everett, Cooper, and I had signed was up and the house had to be vacated. This left me in a tough position, as the USATF Championships were still several weeks away. I asked for a meeting with an administrator at Willamette University.

The administrator began our meeting by congratulating me on all the titles I had won for the school. I said thank you, and then asked what kind of assistance Willamette University could offer me through the end of the current track season.

At most universities it is not uncommon for a school to support their spring athletes until the end of their seasons, especially if the athlete is going to represent the university at a major sporting event, such as the USATF National Championships. I proposed that in exchange for temporary housing in a dorm and a plane tickets to Indianapolis, I would continue to wear my Willamette University singlet and, in doing so, provide the school with some incredible national exposure.

Unfortunately, the administrator must not have seen the value in this. I was wished luck in my future athletic endeavors, but told that WU would no longer support me in any financial way.

I was very disappointed at this news. Moreover, I was shocked at the ignorance. I understood that Willamette was an academic institution, and that athletics are not a priority for them, but I felt abandoned by my alma mater. I had earned the school *seven* national titles. My family had given them over one hundred thousand dollars for my education, and this was how the school wanted to end our relationship? By pulling out every bit of support when I needed it most?

Not knowing what to do, I called Coach Sam. On the verge of tears, I explained to him that I had to be out of my rental by the end of the week and had no idea where I was going to live during the weeks that led up to the USATF Championships. The always generous and hospitable Coach Sam suggested that I move into his home until after the season was over. That was beyond his call of duty, but I was very grateful. I can honestly never thank him enough for all he has done for me. With that, I drove home to finish packing.

With my coaching and living arrangements set, there was only one last piece to figure out: how to pay for the travel. I once again called Mom and Dad. As always, they came to my rescue, agreeing to cover my expenses that summer. Mom likes to joke that she was my first official sponsor. And, in a sense, she and Dad were. I was very lucky to have them help me financially, and doubt I ever would have made it this far without their support.

My last bit of preparation for the USATF Championships was to fly to Palo Alto, California to race a 1500 at a "last chance" meet at Stanford University. This meet was set up to help people attain their qualifying marks in the 1500. I was not interested in racing the 1500 at the USATF Championships, so was simply in the race to try to run for a new personal best time.

The Nike Farm Team, a small developmental team coached by legendary distance coach Frank Gagliano, put on the meet. "Gags" as everyone called him, was a large, ex-football coach who had been thrown into the sport of track and field several decades earlier when Rutgers cancelled their football program. Unsure what to do, they suggested he coach the track team. When he tells the story his reply to Rutgers is always, "What the hell do I know about running?" Hearing him tell the story today is quite comical, as he has coached more track and field Olympians than almost any other coach in America.

I had heard a lot of stories about the legendary Gags. He had just entered his eighth decade of life and had an old school mentality. I heard that he could be very tough on the men and women he coached, but that you couldn't find a man who loved his athletes more. I walked up to the big guy with the kind face and introduced myself. I mentioned that I had just graduated and was looking for a coach. I was surprised that Gags had heard of me, and he even let me in on a rumor that Nike might be moving the Farm Team to Eugene, Oregon at the end of the year. "Keep improving and we may have a spot for you," he said before slapping me on the back and walking off.

I laced up my shoes and began my warm up, happy that the legendary Coach Gags knew who I was and, more importantly, was considering coaching me. With adrenaline pumping through my veins, and knowing exactly what was at stake, I ran the race of my life that evening. I finished third, but shaved another five full seconds off of my personal best in the 1500 meters.

After the race Coach Gags gave me a giant bear hug. "I'm proud of you kid," he whispered in my ear. In three years of running for Coach Kendrick I had never once heard those words. As I was cooling down, Gags talked with Coach Bean, and with my dad, who had flown down to watch the race. Gags explained that the rumor of Nike creating a team in Eugene was really closer to fact, and that after tonight he very much wanted to coach me. Everything was falling into place, but I still needed to have a good showing at the USATF Championships if I was to secure a sponsorship with a shoe company.

In the world of professional track and field, "shoe contacts," as we call them, are often the largest source of income for an athlete. In many other nations, the government provides ample support for their Olympians. However, here in America, there is little financial support from the government and athletes are dependent on corporate partners for income. I was aware of this from the start and knew I needed to draw attention from the various shoe manufacturers if I wanted to fund the next two years of my life as I trained for the 2008 Olympic Trials.

As I packed my bag for Indianapolis I thought about the various companies: Nike, Adidas, Reebok, etcetera. Then I looked at the mismatched selection of branded running apparel I had acquired over the years and realized I had no idea what to race in. I didn't want to wear a Willamette University singlet, as they no longer supported me. Also, I wanted to remain brand neutral so as not to scare off any potential partners.

Finally, I decided to wear a beat up, black Bishop Kelly High School singlet and plain black running shorts manufactured by Brooks Running. The singlet had been manufactured back in the 1970s and was quite worn, but it was one of my favorite possessions. Wearing the black and gold singlet was my way of paying homage to my parents, who were funding this adventure, and to Coach Shanahan, who was writing my workouts.

My dad and Uncle Ed had already committed to coming out and supporting me in Indianapolis. Uncle Ed is my mom's brother-in-law and had always been supportive of my career. I think he was equally as excited to watch me race as he was to play several rounds of golf with my dad in Indiana. It was a great way for them to kill time before my races. Though Mom and Lauren had school obligations back in Boise, they promised they would be watching on the television.

Coach Sam was going to be there too, but would arrive two days after I did. I was grateful and eager to have him along, because nerves overwhelmed me as soon as I stepped out of the plane in muggy Indiana. The greatest meet I had ever known was the NCAA Division III nationals, and this meet was many levels higher than that. *Am I in over my head here?*

As we stood in line to get my race packet, I glanced around the room and saw many Olympians. All around me were track and field royalty. Olympic medalists Bernard Lagat, Allison Felix, and Jeremy Warner were standing just feet away from me. *I need to get autographs and pictures with them!* I had looked up to these athletes for years and wasn't sure if I would ever have an opportunity like this again. But, afraid of looking like a dopey, out of place, Division III kid, I left them alone and remained patiently in my place in line.

Nearby there was a list of competitors for the men's 800 meters. Thirty-two names were listed. This field of thirty-two would be narrowed down to sixteen in round one. Those sixteen semi-finalists would then be narrowed down to eight in round two. The eight finalists would then race one last time to decide who would be that year's national champion. My qualifying time of 1:47.3 put me at the bottom of the list of competitors. I tried not to let this psych me out, and reminded myself that I had not lost an 800 meter final in seven years. This weekend I would be pushed to my limit and would finally find out just how fast I could cover two laps of the rubber oval.

Going into the first of the three rounds I had trouble controlling my nerves. I hadn't slept well the night before and felt flat in round one. I failed to earn one of the automatic advancing spots that were given to the top finishers in each heat, but managed to run fast enough to advance to round two on time. As I cooled down after that first race I worried that I had peaked several weeks before and would be left in the dust in round two.

However, I came back the next day feeling much better. Going through the motions in the first round had primed my legs and adrenal system, and I felt much more comfortable as I warmed up for my semi-final race. When the gun went off I went to the back of the pack, content to go for a ride for 700 meters. When I reached the homestretch I gave everything I had and, to my amazement, found myself hitting the finish line in first place. I had won my semi-final race and was, therefore, guaranteed a spot in the final. The other semi-final winner was the defending national champion, and number one ranked, Khadevis Robinson.

Khadevis or KD, as he was affectionately known around the track, had been our nation's best half-miler for several years. He had won this event several times and was built like the quintessential middle distance runner. Tall, long, and lean, he had an impressive stride and relatively high arm carry. I had looked up to him for many years. KD's personal best at 800 meters was close to four seconds faster than mine, an eternity in our event. I knew it would be almost impossible for me to beat him. However, I thought that if I ran a smart race, I could perhaps out kick one or two of the other finalists in our race.

I had become known for my kick in college. The "kick" is an athlete's ability to push through the pain and lactic acid in the final stretches of a race, and is one of the most important parts of a runner's arsenal of weapons. In a good "kick," a runner should lift and drive his or her knees to keep the impulsion going.

Now, I toed the start line wearing my old BK singlet, looking very out of place, like a high school kid stumbling around the court at an NBA game. The race began and I went straight to the back of the eight-man pack. The pace felt faster than anything I had ever known, but I hung on for dear life. I knew if I could maintain contact with the pack, that they would tow me to a fast time, just as had been the case in Tennessee. I hoped that even if I finished dead last I would run a fast enough time to impress a sponsor or two.

Coming off the last bend I moved to the outside of lane two in order to have a straight shot at the finish line. As I swung wide, I dug deep to find my trademark kick. Despite the fast pace of the race, I found that I had much left in my legs. I began to quickly move up alongside the pack of runners. With each couple of steps I was able to pick off one of my competitors. I went from last place to seventh, to sixth, to fifth.

The lactic acid began gripping my legs and I closed my eyes and dug as deep as I could. I could hear and feel the other runners laboring around me. I opened my eyes just before the finish line and lunged for it. I had finished in a dense mass of runners and wasn't completely sure where I had placed. I stood, hands on knees, gasping for air while I looked up at the video board to see the results. The board read: 2nd SYMMONDS 1:45.83. I shook my head in disbelief.

I had not lost an 800 meter final in more than seven years, but if the streak had to go down, I am very glad it went down like this. Though I had lost, I had just become the second best 800 meter runner in the entire country, and had shaved another one and a half seconds off my personal best.

In the media zone I was bombarded with questions: "Who are you?" "Where are you from?" "Did you know you could run 1:45?" "What are your plans for the summer?" "Who are you going to sign with?" "What is BK?" I did my best to answer all of the questions while at the same time taking business cards from men in suits who called themselves "agents." I knew I would now be able to get a sponsor, but apparently I needed one of these people to help me do so.

Overwhelmed, I threw the cards in my backpack and looked for the national champ. Sitting across from me in the tent was my long time role model, Khadevis Robinson. "Excuse me KD," I said. "Could I trouble you for a photo?"

"Yeah sure, kid," he said. "But just this once, cause you're getting too fast." Then he gave me a big grin before stepping next to me to pose for a picture.

I spent the rest of the day hanging out with my dad and my uncle. I also talked with Coach Sam who had watched the race with Coach Gags.

Sam told me that right after the race Gags was clapping and shouting, "We gotta get the kid to Eugene!"

In the interviews I did that weekend with the media I mentioned two things: one, that it had been a very long season and I would be taking a break from racing for the rest of the summer, and two, I very much wanted to run for Coach Gags in the fall. Unbeknownst to me, saying these things hurt my leverage with the shoe companies. In speaking with the agents afterward, they told me that by not running a full summer season I was not giving any potential sponsor exposure through racing, and that by committing to Coach Gags, I was locking myself into a Nike contract. As the coach of the new Nike funded, Eugene based team, Gags was employed by Nike and unable to coach anyone who had a deal with any different shoe company.

The agents went on to tell me more. Despite the negotiating leverage I had lost with my comments to the press, the agents shouted out big figures. They also tossed around names of well-known athletes they worked with. Impressive as it was, it all sounded like a lot of bullshit to me. Not sure who to believe, I turned to a guy I knew had my best interest at heart, and who had been involved at all levels of the sport, the new Oregon State University women's track coach, Kelly Sullivan. On the phone with him shortly after the meet I explained that I had been contacted by several agents and had no idea who to sign with. Glancing through the business cards I had been handed, I listed off the names as he listened.

Coach Sullivan paused, cleared his throat, then said, "Sign with Chris Layne. He's a good guy and is in this sport for all the right reasons."

Most athletes spend weeks or even months meeting with agents, choosing one the way they would a college, but that didn't appeal to me. Coach Sullivan's word was gold in my book, so I called Chris Layne. He answered on the second ring. "I'd like to sign with you and your company, Total Sports Management," I began in all ignorance. "But I don't want you to take 15 percent of my base. Another agent is offering to take only five, and I think I like that better."

Chris laughed and asked who the other agent was. He then said he would only be interested in working with me if he got 15 percent of the contracts he negotiated for me. He explained that was standard among all reputable agents in track and field, and promised that with him, I would get what I paid for.

I thought this over for a few moments, then told him that I respected his honesty and that I would like to sign with him. Chris was perhaps a bit surprised at how easily this deal was taking place. Nonetheless, he said he would send over some paperwork and start negotiating my shoe contract.

"What do you think we can get?" I asked, cautiously optimistic.

"After what you accomplished at the USATF Championships, I'm thinking something around seventy thousand a year," was his response.

With my hand shaking, I thanked him and hung up the phone. *Seventy grand a year?* At the time my net worth was roughly a thousand dollars. I felt like I had just won the lottery.

8

I had worked hard to make my pro career happen and now that it had, I wanted to reward myself with a vacation before everything kicked into gear. So, I headed to Spokane, Washington. Cooper had just moved back to his home there. It was the Fourth of July weekend, and he and I spent the entire time drinking beer, wakeboarding on Liberty Lake, and flirting with girls.

After that I drove to Boise to visit my parents. We own a cabin eight hours from Boise, near Big Sky, Montana. It's a tradition on my dad's side of the family for everyone to meet there in August, and some of my fondest memories are from weeks spent at that cabin, which is just a few hundred yards away from the Gallatin River. After all the hard work I had put in at college it was therapeutic for me to relax with my family, fish, hike, fish, swim, fish, play board games . . . and fish.

I actually love everything about fishing. I tie my own flies and will fish for anything that swims, particularly trout, salmon, and steelhead. I was wading along the river trying to fool some rainbow trout when I got a call from Chris, my new agent.

"I know you have shut it down for the summer," he began, "but there are a couple of exhibition meetings taking place at the end of August and early September." Overseas, track meets are called meetings.

Curious, but eager to get back to the fishing I replied, "Thanks Chris, but I haven't run in almost a month and really want to focus on slowly getting back into shape for next season."

I was about to hang up when he said, "These are races where you will represent Team USA. You will receive two giant boxes of official Team USA gear if you agree to race."

Almost before he could finish his sentence I said, "I'm in!"

Though I was out of shape, I wanted that Team USA gear very badly. To sweeten the deal, the races were in Birmingham, England, and Moscow, Russia—and all of my travel expenses would be paid.

In shape for almost nothing except drinking beer and fly-fishing, I began putting in a few miles every day. I knew I was going to be far from race ready for these meetings, but I didn't want to totally embarrass myself. By the time we returned to Boise, I had two weeks of training under my belt, which included several intense interval sessions on the track.

As promised, waiting for me on our front doorstep were two large cardboard boxes. I dragged them into my room and opened them like a kid on Christmas morning. There were dozens of items all individually wrapped in plastic. Shirts, shorts, tights, backpacks, all colored red, white, and blue, emblazoned with "USA" across them. I opened up every item and tried them on. With my new crisp white USA singlet on I ran to the backyard to show my parents. They applauded, and dad even grabbed his camera for an impromptu photo shoot.

The next day I passed through security at the Boise airport with a ticket to London. Although I had traveled internationally a few times on vacation with my family, I had never done so for work. I had always dreamed of having a career that took me around the world and here I was, just a few months out of college, headed for Europe on official business.

I connected in Denver, then spent ten hours crammed into a tiny seat at the back of the plane. My all expense paid business trip did not include a business class ticket. I wasn't upset, however, as my excitement overwhelmed any sense of disappointment. I did my best to drink a lot of water and get up to stretch my legs as often as possible, but still felt tired and beat up when we touched down at Heathrow International Airport in London.

It was late in the afternoon, and after dealing with the notoriously strict Heathrow customs officers for twenty minutes I was waved through to baggage claim. I exited into the main terminal expecting to find someone waving an American flag with a sign that read SYMMONDS. However, I found no such person.

I nervously walked up and down the terminal for thirty minutes trying to find anyone associated with Team USA or the meeting. I had no international cell phone and no way of contacting my agent, so I put on one of my Team USA jackets, sat down on my luggage in the middle of the terminal, and proceeded to read one of the books I had brought with me, *Sophie's Choice*. Now that I was no longer obligated to read biochemistry text books I was pouring through all the literature that I had been wanting to read for years.

As I opened up my book and pulled out the boarding pass I had been using as a bookmark I shook my head and laughed. *Well, this is an amateur set up*, I thought. As it turned out, this was the first of a thousand times during my career when I would say this exact phrase with regard to our governing body, USA Track and Field.

I sat reading my book, occasionally glancing up to look for someone from USATF. An hour later I finally saw a few other people come through customs wearing Team USA gear. They looked like athletes, so I ran up to introduce myself. These veterans told me it was not uncommon to show up to a destination and wait hours for someone to arrive to transport them to the meet hotel. They suggested we find a restaurant and get something to eat until someone showed up.

Eventually, someone with the meeting found us, and led us to a bus that took us on the two-hour ride to Birmingham. Overcome by jet lag I sat by myself and allowed myself to sleep. Before nodding off I looked around at my new teammates. Surrounded by many of the world's best athletes I felt I was exactly where I had worked so hard to be. However, in the back of my mind I wondered if my teammates looked at me as something of an imposter. I imagined them asking each other, "Why is this D3 kid here? He doesn't look like a runner, does he?" Whether they thought these things or not, everyone was friendly and did a good job of making me feel welcome.

The event was a quad meet comprised of teams from Great Britain, China, Russia, and the USA. Each country had two representatives per event. The other male American half-miler here was Khadevis. I felt a huge sense of pride knowing that I represented America alongside him.

While this was the first time I had competed on Team USA, the actual race does not stand out vividly in my mind. What I do remember with stunning clarity, however, is how great I felt being around my teammates, and how awesome I felt putting on the USA singlet to compete for the first time. I remember that Khadevis won the race and that I was fifth, with the relatively slow time of 1:48. I was disappointed, but cooling down with KD afterwards, he told me that I was the future of 800 meter running in America. That made me feel a lot better.

That night we all proceeded to get fairly drunk. I stumbled around the streets of Birmingham with a friend who was a fellow athlete, and we shared our views about which girl on Team USA was the prettiest. My friend and I asked if I was headed home and I told him I had another race in Moscow in two weeks. He wished me good luck and we drank some more.

In the morning, still slightly inebriated, I grabbed my bags and jumped on a bus bound for Heathrow. Earlier in the week Chris asked where I wanted to stay during the two weeks between races. He suggested I stay in Great Britain, given that there would be very little language barrier. I had toured Great Britain with my family when I was younger and felt like seeing someplace new. "I speak a little Spanish and have always wanted to see Madrid," I said. Chris said okay and booked me a ticket to Spain's capital city.

Flying over Spain, I was amazed at how dry it was. Madrid is the highest capital in Europe and is surrounded by desert. The climate reminded me very much of southern Idaho. When I exited through security, this time I was thankful to be greeted by a man with a SYMMONDS sign in his hands. Chris mentioned that he had a contact in Madrid who would transport me to a hotel where he had reserved a room for me. I practiced my Spanish with my driver as we navigated the narrow highways and streets of Madrid. When we arrived at our destination I stepped out onto a crowded sidewalk on a busy street. There were tables and chairs set up outside various restaurants, and despite the fact that it was almost ten o'-clock at night, the city was very much alive.

A tall gentleman in a hotel uniform helped me with my bags and led me into a beautiful lobby. I rolled my Team USA suitcase across the well-polished marble floor toward the reception desk. As I stepped up to check in, dollar signs were beginning to flash in my mind. I was told that the rooms were 100 euro a night and that I would have to put a credit card down. My heart jumped when I heard the room cost more than a hundred dollars a night. As I had zero credit at the time, much less a credit card, I instead put down my debit card. This debit card was linked to my life savings, an account that totaled approximately three hundred dollars.

Exhausted, and still hung over, I knew I needed to get a good night's rest. I could figure things out in the morning. I lugged my bags to the elevator, dropped them on the floor of my room, and passed out on top of the bed, still in my clothes.

I woke up the next day at sunrise and walked to one of the local restaurants. Once I was settled with a strong *café con leche*, I pulled out a map of Madrid to familiarize myself with where I was. My bearings intact, I found an Internet café where I sent an email to Chris explaining that I could not afford the hotel, and that I would look for alternate accommodations. He replied that I could do what I liked, and that the negotiations with Nike were going well. He was confident a deal would be reached soon.

Though I believed Chris, I wasn't interested in a one thousand dollar hotel bill being deducted from my first paycheck. Not only that, I was lonely staying in that hotel room all by myself. *What kind of European adventure is this?* I Googled "youth hostel," and found one that was highly recommended just a few blocks away. The cost per night: five euros.

Back at my hotel, I rolled my bags back up to reception. I thanked the lady working the desk, then wheeled my Team USA bag down a cobblestone path and up a giant hill. When I arrived at the hostel, there were all kinds of people my age sitting around, drinking coffee and eating stale loaves of bread. I could hear many different languages being spoken all at once. *This is much better.*

When I handed over my passport and twenty euros to the young lady at the front desk, she handed me back a fresh bed sheet, a towel, and a key to a locker. I was then led down a hall to a room that had three bunk beds. This hostel had several rooms, six beds to a room, with a living room and kitchen up front. Coffee and bread were provided free of charge.

I plopped down on my mattress, the lower of one of the bunk beds, and took my first Spanish siesta. When I woke up it was late afternoon and there was a lot of noise coming from the common room. There, I found a dozen people sitting around a table drinking beer and wine, and laughing. Although people sometimes spoke different languages in smaller circles, everyone came back to English when they addressed the group. They invited me in and a young German-looking guy put a glass in my hand and filled it with a dark, rich red wine straight out of a box. I thanked him and told him I would pay him back.

"Don't worry about it," he shouted. "This stuff costs only one euro per liter here!" Then he shouted *salud,* and raised his glass to the ceiling. Everyone else echoed this word, raised their glasses, and promptly drained them.

"I can tell I'm going to like it here," I said, and drained my glass.

The next week was pretty much a blur. Each evening started the same way. As a large group we drank wine, stumbled out of the hostel, found food, and then hit up a nightclub until three or four in the morning. I slept until noon, woke up and threw on my running shoes. I then headed into the unbearable mid-afternoon summer heat for a hung-over shakeout run.

"Man, you are crazy," my roommates said as they watched me from their bunks as I laced up my trainers.

Our hostel was situated only a mile from one of the largest municipal parks in the world, the *Casa de Campo.* This hilly, desert terrain was full of wonderful dirt trails. It was also full of prostitutes. Daily, as I entered the park through one of the main gates, I saw several women in nothing but g-strings and heels. I ran by them, shirtless, and they whistled and shouted, saying something in Spanish that I didn't quite comprehend. I kept my gaze on the road and wondered if it was rude to stare at their almost completely naked bodies. *Or is it rude not to stare?* Either way I remained nervous as I continued along my runs.

On more than one occasion I made a turn on a trail only to come across two people in what can only be called potentially embarrassing circumstances. Unabashed however, and in the midst of coital bliss, they smiled and sometimes waved. *Do I look, or not look?* I decided to just wave back and continue my run.

I relayed my stories to my hostel friends in the evenings and everyone laughed. Some of the guys adamantly wanted to see, and possibly meet, these prostitutes for themselves.

"So, you are like, a professional runner or something?" I was asked, often.

"Yeah, on Team USA," I proudly said.

"Shouldn't you maybe not drink so much and perhaps run more?" was usually their next question.

That was my opportunity to go into my pre-rehearsed speech about how I wasn't sure I would ever have this opportunity to travel again and wanted to make the most of my trip. I told them I had just graduated college and more than anything just wanted to enjoy my summer. I knew that training with Coach Gags in the fall was going to be brutal and I wanted to be mentally rested when I showed up at his practices. Though I knew I wasn't treating my body the way it needed to be treated for optimal performance, there would be plenty of time for that when I returned to Oregon.

Just as I had always loved coed cross-country practice, so did I love this coed hostel. Early on I made friends with a beautiful Argentinian girl who was staying at the hostel, too. We made out most nights, but found it impossible to find any alone time in our rooms, which were shared with five other people. On the second floor of our building was another hostel that rented out private rooms for twenty euros a night. On the last two days of her visit I splurged on a private room and finally got to enjoy some alone time with her. She didn't speak a word of English, but it didn't make too much of a difference.

Although I have been back to Europe every summer since, this first trip stands out in my mind as one of the wildest. Running fast was low on my priority list; having fun was at the very top. In fact, the only part of that trip that I remember as distinctly not fun was waiting outside the Russian embassy in Madrid for eight hours trying to get a visa to enter the country for my next race. Four hours into the wait, and not even half way through the line, I almost bagged the whole deal, but then I remembered Chris saying he had negotiated a two thousand dollar appearance fee for me if I ran in Moscow. I stayed put knowing how badly I needed the money.

When I finally had my visa in hand, I returned to the hostel to get back to the partying. Toward the end of my stay in Madrid, Lauren flew over to join me. She was studying at Gonzaga University in Spokane now, and was about to begin a semester abroad in Seville. During our lazy days at the cabin we had made plans to overlap in Europe and travel together for a few days. I met her at the airport when she landed and ran to give her a hug. Though I was enjoying my time traveling alone, I was relieved to see her. Lauren and I had already traveled together to many foreign countries, and trips were always more fun with her around. We caught a train from Madrid to Valencia where we enjoyed a swim in the Mediterranean and a large dish of *paella*, a native rice dish.

The next morning we caught another train to Buñol, a town due west of the city of Valencia. This tiny, sleepy Spanish village of approximately nine thousand people is known internationally for one thing: *La Tomatina*. This festival, which occurs on the last Wednesday of every August, brings thirty thousand people to the town for the world's largest food fight. Dump trucks full of tomatoes drive in, pressing past the crowds to the town square where they dump their loads of produce. People from all over the world come to hurl tomatoes at strangers, and to have tomatoes thrown at them.

To Lauren and me, this was the party of the decade. The fight lasted several hours and when all the tomatoes had been thrown there was a river of tomato pulp running down the streets. When there was nothing left to throw, tourists piled back into trains to return to Valencia. Exhausted and covered in tomato juice and pulp, Lauren and I crammed into one of these trains.

The next day I walked Lauren back to the train station where she would travel to Seville. I hugged her good bye and told her I was proud of her for taking on a trip of this magnitude. International travel is tough, but living in a foreign country is tougher. I then headed to my train, which would take me back to Madrid where I would catch my flight to Moscow.

My experience in Moscow was very similar to that in Birmingham. I enjoyed representing my country and being around my teammates. The results were similar as well; I again finished fifth, with a time of 1:48. Considering I had spent the majority of the two previous weeks drinking wine, fornicating, and throwing tomatoes, I was rather pleased with this result. It also made me excited for the future. *How fast can I run if I actually take care of my body?*

As I showered in my hotel room after the race, I smiled while the warm water cascaded down on me. Just then there was a knock on my door. My smile faded as I wondered who was on the other side. I stepped out of the shower and wrapped a towel around my waist, but when I went to open the door there was no one standing on the other side. I looked, left, then right . . . and then down. There, at my feet, was a white envelope that had been slid under the door. It looked rather fat and had my name written on it in thick black ink. I reached down and picked up the girthy envelope.

When I opened it, my jaw dropped. Inside were twenty crisp one hundred dollar bills. I knew there was an appearance fee associated with this race, but I never imagined it would be paid like this! With just one day of work my net worth had tripled. Having never held this much money before, I felt paranoid. I looked around the room nervously, unsure of what to do with the cash. I ultimately decided to stash it in my computer case.

When I went to dinner I asked some of my teammates if they, too, had received envelopes full of cash.

"Oh yeah, it happens all the time when you compete in Eastern European countries," said one.

"Best part is you don't have to pay taxes on it," said another.

I was no accountant, but I was pretty sure Uncle Sam was going to want a piece of this money, and said so. "I think you are supposed to report all overseas earnings to the IRS."

You would think I had suggested handing over their first-born child, the way my fellow runners looked at me. They burst out in laughter and began to tell me all of the creative ways to sneak cash back into the country. Some stuffed it in their underwear, others in the soles of their shoes. I smiled and nodded, then made a mental note to report my two grand to the government.

I have always reported my overseas earning to the IRS. I don't do so out of any moral code or sense of patriotic duty. I do so simply because of a piece of advice Coach Sam once gave me. "You can default on a loan from the bank, you can cheat on your wife, heck you can even go bankrupt and you still stay out of jail," he said. "But, if you cheat on your taxes you are gonna go to prison." Never one to take a piece of advice from Coach Sam lightly, I made it a personal policy to never mess with the IRS.

That night in Moscow I had a great time with my track and field teammates. I asked them all the questions that had been on my mind about professional running, and learned all I could from them about life on the road. They told me that most of the meets held after-parties and that they all served booze.

The after party in Moscow was no different. On a table next to the food were several hundred shot glasses, all full to the brim with crystal clear Russian vodka. Every time I approached the buffet someone with the meeting grabbed me and, in very broken English, asked me to take a shot with him—or her. Not wanting to be rude I always said yes.

Many shots later I was spinning and stumbled back to my room. I managed a few hours of sleep before waking and packing my bags again. I then caught a flight back to Heathrow and realized I had a sixteen-hour layover. My flight back to the Unites States wasn't until eight o'clock the next morning.

Tired of partying and in desperate need of a good night's rest I made some calls to various airport hotels. The cheapest accommodation I could find was three hundred US dollars per night. Even though I had an envelope of cash burning a hole in my backpack, I simply couldn't stomach the thought of spending that much money for a room I would, for the most part, be unconscious in.

I made a new plan. I was a brash, over-confident twenty-two-year-old professional athlete traveling through Europe. Surely I could find someone to share her bed with me tonight. I packed my backpack full of extra clothes, a toothbrush, and a new book, this one *The World According to Garp* by one of my favorite authors, John Irving. The two thousand dollars in cash remained tucked at the bottom of my backpack. I then put everything else in a locker that was available at one end of the terminal.

I made sure to grab my Team USA jacket as well, and then caught a train bound for downtown London. When I stepped out from the underground I found a brilliant September afternoon. The sun was shining and it was quite warm. I found the nearest park and lay down under a tree to read my book. I quickly fell asleep, but woke as the sun was setting. It was a beautiful evening, and I took a moment to watch several ducks splash in a nearby pond. I smiled and watched couples walk hand in hand as the light slowly faded.

As the sun set, the temperature began to drop. This reminded me that what I needed was food and shelter to get me through until the next morning. The first was easy to come by. I simply walked until I found a pizza parlor. I sat down and ordered a beer and a pie while I read. A few tables away a group of young people were speaking Spanish. I could pick up most of what they said, and every time I heard something interesting I picked my head up and looked their way. More often than not I caught the eye of a girl who was facing me. I smiled and she smiled back.

The table was made up of three girls and three guys, and I assumed they were all paired up. When one of the guys approached me, I expected to get chewed out in Spanish for smiling at his girl. Instead, he touched my jacket and, in perfect English asked, "Where did you get this?" I told him I was part of the USA track team, and that I was flying home from my last competition of the summer. He took a seat across from me and we chatted about running, traveling, and London. He then suggested that I join his table, and I gratefully accepted.

There was a seat free next to the girl I had been smiling at, and I grabbed it. Now, just a few feet away from her, I could see she was a classic Spanish beauty with dark eyes, dark hair, and dark, creamy skin. She was dressed in punk-ish clothes and had several piercings, including an eyebrow ring. I began to wonder if she was as wild in bed as her image suggested she was in life.

I let the group know that they should continue speaking in Spanish, that I understood most of what they said, but the guy who had invited me over said, "No. Because we are in England, we will speak English." I've always liked that policy.

To show my new friends my appreciation for their companionship, I purchased a couple of pitchers for the table. We spent the next few hours talking, laughing, and pounding pints of British beer. I worked up the courage to talk to the beautiful brunette and found her name was Lucia. She was originally from the south of Spain, but was currently living in London to learn English. She was single, and when she spoke English it was with an accent that made me weak in the knees.

Lucia suggested we head to SoHo, part of London's west side, for more drinks, and to find a club where we could dance. Although dancing is not my first choice of how to pass time, if a girl suggests it, and if I have enough drinks in me, I will own a dance floor. As if to test this policy, when we arrived at the club Lucia grabbed my hand and led me to the dance floor.

We spent the next few hours bar hopping, and downing gin and tonics. By the third club I leaned in to kiss her and she kissed me back. Making out in the middle of the dance floor she stopped, leaned into my ear and said, "*Esta noche eres mía.*" Tonight, you are mine. I had no other sleeping arrangements, but if I had, I would have bailed on them to spend the night with her. "*Claro que si,*" I whispered back. Yes, of course.

At some point just before dawn we arrived at the apartment Lucia shared with several of her friends. Fortunately, she had her own room and we made good use of the privacy until an alarm on my phone went off signaling that it was time for me to get back to Heathrow. I kissed her goodbye and we exchanged email addresses. As I stumbled down into the nearest Underground station smelling of her perfume, and with a back-pack full of Benjamins slung over my shoulder, I felt so grateful that I had chosen the sport of track and field, or rather, that it had chosen me.

9

The flight back to the United States was long, made even longer by my anxiousness to begin my new life in Eugene, Oregon. Not long after I returned home, I went to Coach Sam's where all of my worldly possessions were located. I then loaded them into my car and drove the hour from Salem to Eugene blasting music, almost giddy with the possibilities that awaited me there. I no longer had to focus on school, or work, or fraternity stuff. Every bit of energy I had could now be put toward my new career.

As I rolled into town I played Lou Reed's "Take a Walk on the Wild Side" on my stereo because in the movie *Without Limits* it's the song that plays when Steve Prefontaine drives into Eugene for the first time. I was now officially living the life I had dreamt about for years.

The dream rolled on for several months as I got to know Coach Gags and his team at the Oregon Track Club (OTC). The team was comprised of roughly twenty men and women, many of us fresh out of college. Gags made it clear that his mission was to develop all of his athletes and try to get as many of us to the USATF Championships as possible. Ultimately, he had hopes that a few of us would make it onto the Olympic Team in 2008. He knew most of us were under contract with Nike (others worked odd jobs to help pay the bills), and that running was our primary focus, so he worked us hard.

Those first few months were also confusing for me, as the paperwork for my contract with Nike still had not come through. The seventy thousand a year that Chris had estimated I was worth ended up being a far cry from what I was eventually offered. I had indeed pigeonholed myself with Nike by telling the media I was going to work with Coach Gags. Thus, none of the other shoe companies made an offer, eliminating any competition for Nike that could drive the price up. To add insult to injury, Chris found out that one of my old college coachs called Nike and told them not to sign me. According to my agent, he told them I was an arrogant little shit who couldn't be controlled. Sounds about right.

These days I am often contacted by Willamette University and asked to donate my time and money to the school. Though I am grateful for the memories, the friends, the wonderful teachers, and the degree that I received from Willamette, I am reluctant to give them anything. I feel that Willamette turned its back on me when I needed it most at the end of my collegiate career. Furthermore, one of their coaches cost me tens of thousands of dollars in lost income with his telephone call to Nike. Several wonderful people at Willamette University have worked hard to repair the damage done to my relationship with the school, but I am stubborn and have a hard time forgiving a school that employed a coach who tried to sabotage my fledgling professional running career.

Fortunately, thanks to Coach Kelly Sullivan's advice, I had chosen the best agent in the game. Despite the call from Coach Kendrick, Chris Layne was able to get Nike to commit to a contract. He was even able to get them to pay me retroactively for the summer months when I represented them in Europe. With a nice chunk of money coming my way and a loan from my wonderful parents, I purchased a small house in Springfield, Oregon, a small town just east of Eugene. I rented out my extra bedrooms to a couple of teammates and the three of us lived as frugally as we had in college.

Life was simple and I was happy. Very happy. A typical day began at eight A.M. One of us would make a pot of coffee and we proceeded to get fully caffeinated while watching a fishing or hunting show on TV. Practice started around ten and lasted several hours. Most days we covered anywhere from six to fourteen miles in our grueling morning sessions. Some days we had weight lifting after the runs. Always, we returned home exhausted and ate several thousand calories. In the evening we ran again or did some form of cross training. I had never trained like this before and seriously wondered if my body could withstand the workload.

Fatigued, I lay in bed every afternoon with a novel and read. I devoured both fiction and non-fiction at a ravenous pace. Both of my parents had always been avid readers and they kept the books arriving in the mail. I typically alternated between a Dad pick and a Mom pick. Their tastes in literature are as diverse as mine and sometimes I couldn't tell who had recommended the science fiction and who had recommended the sappy love story.

On weekends we partied. Coach Gags was smart to give us early morning practices on Saturday, so Friday nights we were on our best behavior. However, Sunday's long runs were on our own and this meant that Saturday night we were free to get wild. And that's exactly what we did. Even though it was not the best idea for professional athletes, most Saturday nights the team met at someone's house and we all drank to excess. We then called cabs, drunkenly poured out into a street, and found a bar where we could hang out until two in the morning trying to pick up women. More often than not I failed, and went home dizzy and alone.

I remember being lonely in the evenings during my first few months in Eugene. I also remember feeling guilty about how hard I was still partying. I knew that drinking to excess was not going to help me accomplish the running goals I had set for myself, but after running seventy miles each week it was how I chose to let off some steam. It was a young, dumb decision.

During the lonely times I thought about my friends and family in Boise, and how deeply I missed them. That first season I looked forward to Thanksgiving break every single day. When the time came, I went home and spent almost all of my time watching movies with my mom, and hunting with my dad. The only time I wasn't hanging with my parents was when I took a friend out on a date. Her name was Chelsea and I'd had a crush on her since high school. We had stayed in touch and were both single, so we met up for dinner. She was beautiful, and into many of the same things I was, hiking, nature, family, reading. Chelsea and I began an exclusive relationship, despite the geographical distance between us.

From the beginning it was tough. Chelsea was in school at Boise State University and not able to move to Eugene. I flew her to Eugene one weekend a month, though, and tried to get back to Boise every few weeks.

I enjoyed every minute I was able to spend with Chelsea. Given our limited time together I planned fun outings for us each trip. We went to the coast, the zoo, and to rivers to fish. We often watched movies in bed or went shopping. On one of Chelsea's trips out we were at a shopping mall in Eugene when we passed a pet store. It was just a few days before Easter and the shop had a dozen baby rabbits in stock. We picked up the tennis ball sized fluff balls and played with them for an hour. Chelsea turned to me and said, "Nick, I want one." Not wanting to disappoint her, I told her to pick out her favorite. She pulled out a little black bunny that looked more like a rolled up sock than a rabbit and said, "I want this one. His name is Mortimer." I paid twenty dollars for Mortimer and thought, *what the hell am I supposed to do with a rabbit when she leaves?*

My plan was to let Chelsea enjoy Mortimer's company until the end of her trip, at which time I would take Mortimer out to woods. There I would release him to live happily ever after with all the other critters of the forest.

Several days later I took Chelsea to the airport and returned to our new pet. But when I looked at him, I knew he wouldn't survive five minutes in the wild. So instead of a walk into the woods, I Googled, "how to house train a rabbit." What I should have Googled was, "how long do rabbits live." Though Chelsea and I unfortunately broke up later that summer, Mortimer has been by my side for more than eight years.

In Springfield, Mortimer and I were fairly happy bachelors together. Once in a while, my game was solid enough to convince a girl to come home with me. Usually, these women had a thing for runners (or rabbits) or were lured by the hot tub I owned that I had not so subtly mentioned during our conversation.

This hot tub had the unfortunate location of being just a few feet from my fence, and no more than five yards from my neighbors' bedroom window. On more than one occasion the Springfield Police were called to my house and I was issued a citation for excessive noise. Today, at thirty years of age, I feel terrible for my neighbors and what they must have heard going on in that hot tub. However, at twenty-three, I didn't really care, and kept the party going every weekend.

One day I got a call from Coach Gags. "What's this I hear about orgies goin' on in ya damn back yard?"

"Coach Gags, I have absolutely no idea what you are talking about," I said.

Gags went on to explain that my neighbors had written a letter to the president of the University of Oregon complaining about the parties going on at my house. I laughed pretty hard when I heard this, considering I had absolutely zero affiliation with the University of Oregon. When their letter, and Coach Gags's shouting, failed to put an end to my parties, my neighbors sent a letter to the CEO of Nike, who passed it down to their sports marketing department.

Years later one of the Nike employees told me that when they received the letter they all sat down to read it, laughed until tears ran down their cheeks, and tossed the letter in the trash. "I want an invite to your next party!" the employee said. "These things sound legendary!" It seemed my main sponsor was only concerned that I perform well on the track.

Though I still kept in touch with several college friends, I was becoming close to the guys on my new professional team. At college I never really felt I belonged. I felt as if I was living in someone else's world, living on their schedule, jumping through hoops they put in front of me. But here in Eugene I was my own boss, running my own business, on my own schedule. My teammates wanted what I wanted: to have fun and become the fastest person in the world. We devoted all of our conscious hours to these two things, and through our daily struggles, became very close.

My closest friends on the team were the Jefferson twins out of Indiana. Sean and John were both sub four-minute milers and nearly identical. Gags could never tell them apart and, for some reason, decided instead to just call them both Jeff. Although they both came off as shy, they had incredible wit and intelligence to go with their beach boy hair and good looks.

Another of my closest friends on the team was a guy named Christian Smith. Christian had gone to Kansas State University and had been one of the top Division I middle-distance runners during my senior year. He and I had traded better marks in the 800 and 1500 all year, and I saw him as my biggest competition on the team. However, I liked his laid back, Midwest personality so much I didn't let competitiveness get in the way of our friendship.

The final piece of this puzzle fell into place a year after OTC was created when fellow Division III stand out, Will Leer, joined the team. The five of us spent most of our free time together drinking beer, playing the music-based video game Rock Band, or going out for burgers. We all lamented how hard it was to meet women in Eugene, and started calling the town The Trenches.

"So fellas, we headed back into The Trenches this Saturday night?" I might ask.

"Damn it, guess so," my friends usually replied.

We were all relatively good looking, fit, and successful, but the tough part about being a young professional in a college town is that if you aren't a part of the college you are looked at as something of an anomaly. There were very few people our age as, upon graduation, most students left to find jobs in bigger cities. Several times I found a nice girl to date, only to have to say goodbye as soon as she graduated. This was, perhaps, for the best, as it allowed me to focus on my career and not on maintaining a relationship.

Weekly, I had dinner with Coach Gags and we talked about life, family, and running. He worked hard for all his athletes, but I think he spent extra time with me. Perhaps it was because he knew I needed someone to help keep me focused, or because he saw extra potential in me. Either way,

I very much enjoyed our weekly meetings. I loved working with Coach Gags as a coach and still love him to this day as a friend. I fondly recall him yelling at me after some of my less stellar races in a thick New York accent, "What was that? Some kinda Division IV crap?"

But, after a poor race, Gags always sat me down to go over what I did wrong. This was always followed by a giant bear hug. "I love ya kid, and you're gonna be great," he'd say before telling me to go cool down. I loved him, too.

Coach Gags was the reason we were all in Eugene. He was a legend and knew how to get people onto Olympic teams. Not everyone was ecstatic to be living in a sleepy college town, but most everyone was thrilled to be running for Coach Gags. I was certainly one of them and, though my love life was suffering, I enjoyed living in the Emerald Valley, which was what locals call the Eugene/Springfield area.

I learned pretty early on that if I was going to make this place my home, then I needed to find a hobby. I had been fly-fishing in Idaho and Montana for trout since I was old enough to hold a rod. I also knew that Oregon was legendary for its diverse fisheries, so I began to study up on the various species that ran through the state's rivers and the myriad sea life available for harvest in its estuaries and coastlines. I made friends who were fishermen and spent my free days with them talking about everything but running. We caught salmon, steelhead, trout, rockfish, crab, clams, sturgeon, ling cod, and tuna. As a result, our freezer was packed full of fresh fish year round. I can say with certainty, that without my love for fishing, I would not have stayed in Springfield, Oregon for the better part of a decade.

Track Town, USA as the area is fondly known in the running world, is truly the most supportive place for runners that I have ever known. The running community across the United States is fairly small, and in Eugene it is tiny—but dense. When I first showed up I was overwhelmed by the amount of positive support the entire team received from the community. Doctors met with us on their lunch breaks, massage therapists saw us on weekends, and nearly every person we passed on a run waved or smiled at us.

Before my big races people came up to me during the day to wish me good luck, and after the big wins they patted me on the back in congratulations. This reminded me of those first races in Idaho, when after a race I'd receive the positive affirmation and attention my insecure teen self needed. As a young man I did not need this adulation as much, but I welcomed it, as it made me feel a proud part of the community.

On one occasion a wealthy and generous man came up to me at a restaurant, put his hand on my shoulder and said, "Thank you so much for all you do for this community and this country." As he said this, he set three folded $100 dollar bills down in front of me.

I jumped up and said, "Thank you so much, sir, but this is not necessary."

He just nodded his head, patted my back, and walked out of the restaurant.

Although I was a kid from Boise who had spent the last four years in a Willamette jersey targeting Oregon Ducks on the track, the community of Track Town, USA adopted me as one of their own. At major meets, when the athletes were announced prior to the race, the crowd always erupted after my introduction. To this day the sound of their applause still gives me chills and sends a wave of adrenaline coursing through my veins.

10

I had raced at Hayward Field many times. This historic stadium sit-uated on the lush, green University of Oregon campus is known for hav-ing many knowledgeable and passionate fans. They rewarded great performance with thundering applause and I had heard it many times. On a few occasions the applause was even for my own performance. But, never had I received such eardrum shattering applause as I did on the evening of June 30, 2008. That evening I raced for a spot on the Beijing bound USA Olympic Team in front of a sold out stadium. It was one of the most amazing experiences of my life.

Coach Gags and I had prepared diligently for two years for the team selection process, knowing that it would be mentally and physically taxing. To make the USA Olympic Team in the men's 800 meters, you must do two things. First, you must have an Olympic A standard—a time set by the International Olympic Committee (IOC) that athletes all over the world must hit to compete at the Games. There is a less competitive B standard, but the United States is so deep in talent that in most track and field events this does not come into play.

Second, each American must go through three rounds of competition. The sum of this is a grueling four-day process in which more than thirty of the country's best athletes are narrowed down to just three team members. Each country is allowed a maximum of three entries per event, and we were all racing for these spots.

My training had been going well and I felt I was physically prepared for this test. Mentally, I was confident and eager to prove myself. However, on a scorching hot day in Carson, California in May, my Olympic dreams were almost crushed. I had traveled to The Home Depot Center (now called The StubHub Center) with Coach Gags and a few teammates to compete at the Adidas Grand Prix meet.

The plan was to run a 1500 meter race as a last strength test before switching our training over to prepare for the shorter 800 meters. That day the temperature on the track was well over one hundred degrees, and the meet director had allowed close to twenty people to toe the starting line. This size of a field is too large for a professional 1500 meter race. Not a fan of the heat or the field size, I considered withdrawing from the competition. Ultimately, I decided that I had flown all the way down there and might as well have a run at it.

Dripping sweat, I stepped on the line and waited for the gun to go off. I was completely immersed in elbows the first 50 meters and finally, with a lot of pushing and shoving, was able to get into position behind American miler Lopez Lomong. Just as I did though, someone's feet ahead of him tripped him up, and he went down. I never claimed to be much of a hurdler, but I did my best to jump over him. I had just about cleared him when my right knee came sliding down along his upturned metallic spikes. I could feel the steel ripping through the thin skin of my knee.

The starter fired another shot calling all the competitors back to the line. This is common practice when someone goes down in the first 100 meters of a race. As I walked back to the line I could tell something wasn't quite right. I looked down at my knee and saw a two-inch gash dripping blood. In the center of the gash was the glistening white bone of my kneecap. I knew it needed stitches, but I felt it could hold up for three and half more minutes, and got back to the starting line.

The gun went off again and this time, despite an equal amount of pushing and shoving, all competitors managed to stay on their feet. I tucked into the back of the pack and tried to move through the bodies and heat as efficiently as possible. I felt a dull ache in my knee, but no serious pain.

With each step, however, I began to wonder if I was doing serious damage to my knee. *What if this keeps me from running in the Olympic Trials,* was the refrain that echoed through my head. With one lap to go the pain and fear got the better of me and I stepped off to the inside of the track. In ten years of racing I had never once failed to finish a race—until now. To this day, that race remains the only DNF (did not finish) to my name.

As I hobbled across the track towards the medical tent I asked if there was a doctor around. The massage therapists and trainers looked at each other and then back, and assured me there was one somewhere. I sat down in the tent and waited for twenty minutes until a doctor finally showed up.

"Yep, that's gonna need stitches. Gonna have to get you to a hospital," he said after examining my knee for all of two seconds.

I was upset that I had not finished the race and terrified about what this meant for my training going into the Olympic Trials. To make matters worse, the meet did not have anyone who could drive me to the hospital a mile away, so my agent picked me up in his rental car and drove Coach Gags and me over. As we approached the entrance, Gags told me not to worry, that it would all work out. His words did little to easy my worries.

We entered the emergency room through sliding glass doors to find a horrifying scene. In a waiting room made for fifty people there must have been more than one hundred. It was hot, and the smell was rancid. There were people coughing and babies crying. Some sat in chairs while others remained standing or lay on the floor. There were people who looked sick and others who looked injured. Though I don't specifically remember anyone with a nail sticking out of his or her head, that affliction would have been quite appropriate for the scene.

I approached a receptionist who was sitting behind a shield of bulletproof glass and told her my knee needed stitches. She slid a clipboard and some paperwork under the glass and told me to fill it out and bring it back to her.

"How long do you think it will take?" I asked looking around.

"Honey, don't be in a rush cause there's a lot of people ahead of you. Could be eight hours before a doc can see you."

"*Eight hours?*" I asked in disbelief. "But I need to catch a flight out of LAX in four!"

She shrugged her shoulders and pointed at the clipboard. As I turned to walk away she shouted after me, "Wait, do you have health insurance?"

I turned back to her and said, "Yes, I do."

With that, she took the clipboard back from me and said, "Then just walk across the street to the other hospital."

With Gags by my side I hobbled out of the building, into the sunshine, and across the street. Again we entered through sliding glass doors, only this time what we found on the other side was a cool, quiet, pristine waiting room with soft jazz playing over the speakers. I approached the receptionist and explained to her what the problem was. Like the receptionist across the street, she handed me a clipboard and asked me to fill out some paperwork. Unlike, the other receptionist, however, she then asked me for a copy of my health insurance card. I handed it to her and sat down to fill out my paperwork. A few minutes later a nurse came to get me and took me back to see a doctor. Within an hour I had ten stitches in my knee, a lollipop in my hand, and was on my way to catch my flight out of LAX.

Though I'd had some previous experience with hospitals and operating rooms I did not have much experience with emergency rooms. I learned a valuable lesson that day: make sure you have health insurance. In a country where we have decided that it is every man or woman for his or herself, I feel bad for those who cannot afford the astronomical premiums charged by health insurance companies. I have sought out medical attention in many foreign countries that have universal health care and have seen first hand the way each citizen is treated with inexpensive and effective care. I am appalled at the way our health care system is run in the United States. There are very clearly two forms of health care in America: world-class health care for those who can afford it, and shitty-sit-in-a-crowded-room-for-eight-hours-with-a-nail-sticking-out-of-your-head health care for those who cannot.

Upon arriving back in Eugene I scheduled a visit with our team physician, Dr. Olson. I liked Doc Olson a lot. He had been a runner himself back in the seventies and eighties and he worked hard to keep me healthy and running well. Dr. Olson looked at my knee and prescribed both topical and oral antibiotics. "You're not going to like this, but you need to take a week off of running," he said.

Tears welled in my eyes as I saw my Olympic dreams fade away. "With every bend of your knee you stretch this wound open, allowing bacteria to enter and increasing the likelihood that it will develop an infection. An infection at this point would put you out of commission for a month."

I looked at Gags and he explained that we could bounce back from a week off, but that with the trials only five weeks away, a month off would definitely end our season. I thanked Dr. Olson and decided to follow his advice.

With my knee in stitches and my butt relegated to the couch I took the opportunity to continue work on my mental preparations. Though I had been through high-pressure situations like this before, never had I been to a competition where, if I made a mistake, I would have to wait four more years to have another try. To make matters worse, I knew there were potentially hundreds of thousands of dollars riding on whether or not I finished in the top three. As the day approached I felt less and less prepared mentally to deal with the pressure.

Unsure of how to talk to Coach Gags about these feelings, I once again put a call into my longtime friend and trusted confidant, Coach Kelly Sullivan. Coach Sullivan had steered me right many times before and I knew he would have some words of wisdom for me now.

"The pressure is killing me, Coach," I said. "It's all I can think about. It keeps me up at night and I'm worried that I'm wasting all my energy on worrying about the outcome."

In his calm, reassuring voice Coach Sullivan said, "Nick, this is normal. All your competitors are doing the exact same thing. What you need to remember is that in a championship race like this, the cream always rises to the top. Don't ask me how, but the rounds and the pressure somehow always set the cream apart. And, you have proven time and time again that you most certainly are part of the cream."

His words helped calm me down and for the next few days whenever my heart started to race and I felt my nerves taking control again I said in my head, *You are the cream. The cream always rises.*

A week later my stitches came out and I was allowed to start training again. Knowing that I had lost strength, I began to spend more time with my lifting coach, Jimmy Radcliffe. Coach Rad, as we called him, is the head strength and condition coach for the University of Oregon. He is also world famous for his ability to make strong people stronger and fast people faster. Though we had been working hard in the gym all year there were a few things we could improve on. We lightened the loads I had been lifting and focused on form. Everything I did became faster, more dynamic, more explosive.

In our last few practices, just days before the event, I began to run strides as though they were the final 50 meters of the Olympic Trials Finals. Having been beaten by Khadevis in a lean across the finish line just a few months earlier, Coach Rad and I worked on an improved lean that could end up being the difference between my making the team or staying home.

Given that KD had defeated me at the USATF Indoor Championships and again at the Prefontaine Classic just ten days before the Olympic Trials, he was, in most peoples' eyes, the number one seed going in. He also had the fastest personal best and Olympic experience to his name.

There were more than thirty other competitors in my event at these Olympic Trials, which were to be held in Eugene at Hayward Field. Just as in a USATF Outdoor Championship, these men would be narrowed down to sixteen semi-finalists in the first round, and those sixteen would then be narrowed down to eight finalists. These first two rounds are run back to back, and then the eight finalists are given a day off to rest up for the final.

KD and I both advanced fairly easily through our first two rounds. Joining us in the final were some usual suspects, plus a few new characters. KD loved a fast pace and was sure to appreciate the other sprint-based 800 guy in the final, Jonathan Johnson. Johnson was the defending Olympic Trials champion, and the only other guy in the race with Olympic experience. I knew that these two would get out fast, and try to control the race from the front.

One of the new faces in the final was a young, talented sophomore from the University of Oregon, Andrew Wheating. He had been coming off a phenomenal collegiate season where he had finished as runner up at the NCAA Championships. The six foot five white kid from Vermont was rounding into shape perfectly for the Olympic Trials, and had a kick that deserved serious respect.

The other finalist I paid close attention to was my training partner, Christian Smith. I was not so concerned that he might beat me, but rather that he was the only athlete going into the finals without the Olympic A standard. Christian was one of the last athletes to be invited to the Olympic Trials and he'd had to run a season's best just to make it there. Christian was still a very good friend and I badly wanted him to do well. The cruelest part of the selection process was that unless he ran the A standard in the finals it was extremely unlikely that he would be selected for the team.

The night before the finals I studied the list of entries closely and imagined how the race would unfold. Given that Wheating and I were distance runners known for our kicks, there would be sprinters who would try to take it out fast and sap our strength. Khadevis and Johnson were both known for their front-running styles and I was sure that one of them would go to the front early. But exactly how fast would they take it out? Where would I find myself at 200 meters into the race, and how could I navigate traffic to get to the front? As the various permutations played out in my mind my adrenal glands pumped adrenaline into my system and sent my heart racing.

As is common for me before most of my competitions, I lay in bed staring at the ceiling trying not to think about the race. Eventually, I was able to nod off and have the nightmare I have before all big races. In my dream I have slept through my alarm clock and missed the race. Of course, in the real world this is impossible, as most of my races take place in the evening and were I to fall asleep, a teammate or coach would surely come wake me up. But in the dream I am not woken until it is too late. When I am finally shaken awake in the dream, I simultaneously awake in real life, sitting straight up in bed with my heart pounding in my chest and sweat beading up on my forehead. After my breathing had returned to something close to a normal, I lay back and did my best to fall back asleep.

When I awoke in the morning I felt somewhat rested, but almost sick to my stomach from nerves. So, I made a cup of coffee and went for a walk. Most athletes like to do a shake out run the morning before a race, but I often prefer a walk. A shake out run might only last ten minutes whereas a slow walk could last up to an hour. With the race set to take place in the evening I wanted to kill as much time as possible.

With my coffee in hand I walked down to the Willamette River and sat on a bench and watched fisherman chase steelhead. Part of me wished that I were one of them, transfixed by the rushing, crystal clear water, without a care in the world. Another part of me realized that today presented a life altering opportunity, one that I had trained ten years for.

Back at my house, I did what I always do to kill time before a big race: watch crappy TV. I usually try to find the dumbest programming possible; something that is riveting yet mindless, to keep my attention away from the race. The hours leading up to a big competition are their own battle. Many athletes are defeated before the gun even goes off by wasting energy in these pre-race hours. I didn't want that to be me.

Fortunately, I had Coach Sam with me. When Coach Gags and I first started working together he asked what I needed to be successful. The first thing on my list was Coach Sam. As my best friend and mentor I felt infinitely more at ease when he was around. We had been through a lot in six years and now we were about to attempt to make our first Olympic team.

Coach Sam and I sat on the couch together, flipping through the channels to find some trashy programming. I'm sure he was just as nervous as I was, but you wouldn't know it looking at him. Lounging on the couch with a water in his hand, Coach Sam cracked jokes all afternoon to lighten the mood.

Despite my best efforts, the afternoon dragged on. I'd look at my watch, note the time, and go back to sipping my watered down sports drink. I've never loved the sugary stuff, but watered down it is palatable and a good way to get electrolytes. Finally, the alarm on my watch went off signifying that it was time to get ready. As was my usual pre-race routine, I began with a hot shower to warm up my muscles. When I stepped out and toweled off, I then slipped into my skin tight, black half tights. I blasted gangster rap through my bedroom speakers while I packed my backpack. Oddly, something about heavy beats and angry lyrics has a calming effect on me before a race.

I double-checked my backpack to make sure everything I needed was in it. Then, panicked that I had forgotten something, unloaded everything and repacked it. I'm not typically this neurotic, but before a big race my mind never feels as if it is working quite right. Finally, convinced that I had all that I would need, I stepped out of the house and joined Coach Sam, who was waiting in his truck.

Sam and I had been through this process many times before and he already had the rap blaring at a deafening level. The three-mile drive from my home to Hayward Field crosses the Willamette River and again I found myself wishing I were in the river, fishing.

As we approached the stadium I glimpsed the thousands of people who had paid to watch tonight's event queuing up to enter historic Hayward Field. As I had never been to an Olympic Trials before, I wondered what it would be like for these people to watch someone race for a spot on the Olympic team. Did the fans know how important this race was? What it meant for an athlete's career financially? Did they know that for some, this meet might be the very last of their career? Those thoughts hit me like a punch to the gut, and I tried to put them out of my head.

Coach Sam pulled up next to the athletes' entrance and dropped me off. He told me he would park the truck and find me shortly after. Once again, I felt so lucky to have Coach Sam on my side. As I approached my team, Coach Gags walked to meet me. He put his arm around me and asked how I was feeling. "Pretty good, nervous," was all I could say.

"Good," he said. "Use the nerves. You are a champion, you hear me?"

With that he let me walk to a spot where most of my teammates were lying on the ground with their headphones on and their feet up. I joined them in this most relaxing position, rested my head under my backpack, and watched as the other athletes warmed up. Lying on a plush bit of grass under a brilliant blue sky I was awed by the many amazing athletes who surrounded me. Truly the best that America had to offer were here. I smiled, finally acknowledging that I was one of them, though at times I still felt like a Division III kid who didn't belong.

Several of the 800 meter women walked by and I felt testosterone mix with the adrenaline already in my system. I had been celibate for the month leading up to this event. Not so much out of choice, but due to how focused I had been. Seeing these phenomenally fit, beautiful women walk by in nothing but Spandex was equal parts exhilarating and tormenting. I closed my eyes and tried to focus on why I was here.

With just over an hour before race time, Coach Sam asked if I was ready to warm-up. I stripped off a couple items of clothing and headed out to Pioneer Cemetery, an old cemetery adjacent to Hayward Field where I usually warmed up before practices. I remember feeling so grateful that these Olympic Trials were in my backyard and I took a lot of comfort in going through the exact routine I had gone through for every practice during the two years leading up to this event.

I jogged at a very easy pace for just over two miles. As I ran along a gravel path under magnificent ponderosa pines I was a surprised at how good my legs felt. Given that I had already raced twice in the previous three days I expected to feel tired and heavy. Instead, I felt fresh and bouncy! I allowed myself to pick up the pace a little, but tried to keep it under control. *Save it for the race.*

Back at the warm up area, Coach Jimmy took me through a series of stretches and drills that were designed to make my muscles and ligaments feel even better and work more efficiently. I switched to a lightweight pair of shoes and ran a few fast strides. At the accelerated pace my legs felt even better. The warm up process left me feeling unbelievably smooth and I smiled, realizing that most of the pre-race nerves I had felt were now gone. I ran up to Coach Gags and gave him a big hug.

"I am totally ready for this, Coach," I said, meaning every word of it.

"Damn right you are," he replied. "Make sure you are up front with 100 meters to go!" he shouted as he slapped me on the back. I nodded and jogged off.

As had been my pre-race ritual for years, the last person I saw before heading into the call room was Coach Sam. He, too, gave me a big bear hug, then said, "I love you. Now go and get this. You've earned it."

"Love you too, Coach," I replied. And with that I walked into the call room.

The call room is a weird place. Typically, it has a dozen or so folding chairs set up in a small tent. The competitors are asked to come in and sit down, then they must allow a stranger to rummage through their backpacks. Everything about this is uncomfortable for me before a race. I don't want to be around my competition, I really don't feel like sitting down, and seriously, stay the hell out of my backpack.

Apparently, meet officials are instructed to go through our stuff to make sure we don't have any logos that might not fit into their rigid set of rules and guidelines on where and how logos can be displayed during competition. They also typically confiscate all electronics for some reason.

Fortunately, at Hayward Field there is a 50 meter section of track that an athlete can use to continue his or her warm-up whilst their rights are being violated. Wanting to keep my legs warm and feeling good, I did some drills along this stretch of rubber, then was given two #1 stickers, my "hip numbers," and told to put one on each leg. The hip numbers tell the athlete what lane they will be starting in and are not necessarily based on ranking. The call room official finally announced that we had five minutes until we headed out to the track. My heart jumped. I sat down to calm my pulse and breathing down, and to change into my spikes.

I could feel the nervous, jittery energy from my competitors, and tried to ignore them. I could also hear the crowd cheering wildly for the women's 800 meter race, which was being run while we waited. The knowledgeable Hayward Field crowd was going nuts and, as always, their cheers sent a fresh wave of adrenaline through my veins. At the conclusion of the women's race we lined up and walked out onto the track.

The crowd, though fresh off of cheering loudly for the previous race, erupted once again when we took our lanes. This race had been hyped up quite a bit, given the fact that there were three Eugene-based men in the race. Some had talked about the potential of a Eugene medal sweep, but I knew the odds of that happening were very slim. Each of us ran a few strides in front of the 23,000 person crowd, stripped off our sweats, and took our places a few feet back from the starting lines of our respective lanes.

The voice of the announcer boomed over the loud speakers as he presented us to the crowd, one by one. I was in lane one and the first to be introduced. "In lane one, four time NCAA Division III champion at this distance while at Willamette, now representing the Oregon Track Club and Nike, *Nick Symmonds!*" The crowd gave me a loud and heartfelt welcome, and I appreciated every decibel.

My training partner, Christian Smith, was to my right and was the second to be introduced. As the names of my competitors and their accomplishments were announced I jumped up and down and stretched, trying to keep my muscles warm and limber. I listened as the announcer read out each name, not to hear each runner's accolades, but to hear how the crowd responded to each. I was not surprised to hear the largest applause come for Andrew Wheating, the local college kid, and for Khadevis Robinson, the defending US champion.

I heard the announcer give the stats for Jonathan Johnson, the defending Olympic Trials champion. He was in lane eight and I took a deep breath knowing that the gun would be fired in seconds. "*On your marks!*" the starter shouted from his stand on the infield.

I took several choppy steps to the start line and placed my right toe as close to the white line as possible without touching it. I lowered my body into an athletic crouch and expected my entire body to collapse under the weight of the pressure that I had placed on this race.

11

I was only at the starting line for an instant, but it seemed a lifetime.
And, during that instant all the pressure I felt melted away. I felt light and
strong, and supremely confident. I had played this exact moment through
my mind thousands of times and each time I always imagined that here,
crouched at the starting line of an Olympic Trials final, I would experience
the greatest feelings of dread and anxiety. But that is not how I felt at all.
Instead, my body felt like it was in perfect balance, ready to do what it had
done so many times before. This feeling of total readiness is something I
had experienced before, but never on such an intense level as this.

My muscles ached to fire as I remained there, crouched for what felt
like an eternity. Finally, with a loud "bang" we were set free. The first few
steps felt difficult. Just as a car uses up gas at a much faster rate when it
accelerates, my body uses up more of its energy reserves in these first few
meters than at any other point in the race.

There is a common phrase in distance running coined by the
Kenyans called "stealing time." The idea is that your legs are so fresh at
the beginning of a race you can take off at a pace much faster than you

would be able to hold for the entire race. The energy stored up in your legs is meant for this monumental burst of speed, and you can tap into it without greatly affecting the latter stages of your race. By using this method you can supposedly "steal" a second or two in the first part of a race. I'm not a physiologist, but in my personal experience this theory is complete crap. As much as I would like to believe it, I have tried it in many races and practice sessions and never found it to be true. Any acceleration performed in the race results in a quicker accumulation of lactic acid, and it will ultimately grip your muscles and slow you down.

As my spikes dug into the track and my legs fought inertia to bring me up to race pace this thought was at the front of my mind: *fast, but relaxed.* This race mantra was given to me by Coach Shanahan nearly ten years prior to this event. It was still the best way to describe how the first part of a race should be run and I repeated it in my mind over and over again.

The strain from the first few steps of acceleration was visible on my face, but 20 meters into the race my expression changed to total relaxation, just as we had worked on in practice many times. *Arms loose, jaw relaxed, lower lip bouncing.* These are the thoughts that trigger my body to stay relaxed and I repeated them to myself.

I began to wonder if I was too relaxed, however, as I watched my competitors quickly pull away from me in their lanes. American half-milers are notorious for taking races out fast, and many subscribe to the notion of stealing time. I looked to lane six to see where Khadevis was. As he was the favorite to win this race I knew I had to keep him in my sights at all times. By the time we had covered the turn, he had put close to 10 meters on me and was flying down the backstretch. The other six members of this race were doing everything they could to stick with him as we broke out of our lanes and headed to the rail.

What is going on? We were moving faster than my legs had ever carried me through the first 200 meters of a race, and I started to panic. I picked up my pace just to maintain contact. I was running in my first Olympic Trials final and was in dead last doing everything I could just to stay with the pack. *Is there something wrong with me, or are we really running as fast as I think we are?* I tried to run as effortlessly as possible, but knew that if I hit the 200 meter mark and saw a split, a running time, of 26 seconds, I was in big trouble.

At both the 200 and 400 meter marks on the track there was a clock positioned on the infield that gave the runners their splits. Though I don't always check to see what the time is (it can be a distraction to focusing on staying relaxed), I knew that what I saw when I came through the 200 meter mark would effect how I ran the next three-quarters of the race.

From the back of the pack I peered around to the front and saw Khadevis pass by the clock. It read 23.9. *Is he serious?* If Khadevis held onto that pace he would run a world record by over four seconds. In an event where it might take an entire year of training to shave off one-tenth of a second, Khadevis wasn't just stealing time, he was trying to pull off the heist of the century.

I kept my eye on the clock as I came through the 200 meter mark and saw it roll over to "25" as I flew by, still bringing up the rear of the pack. Directly in front of me were Andrew and Christian. Though I try not to key off too many people in a race, knowing that they too were struggling with the hot pace helped me relax as we came to the home-stretch of the first lap. Normally, the pace would slow down considerably here and I would start to move up closer to the front of the pack. Today, however, the pace didn't slow much at all.

To move up now, I would have had to slow down, move out to lane three, and reaccelerate. *Suicide.* I glued myself to the rail and thought: *Patience. Shut your mind off for a while.* I stared at the back of Christian's singlet and allowed my mind to quiet down. *Maintain contact. Maintain contact.* This was all I allowed myself to think for a couple of hundred meters.

Though it might seem silly that I would need to turn my mind off in a race that lasts a little over one hundred seconds, I do it to allow my body to simply run free. The constant panic that the mind creates for itself during an 800 leads to tiny shifts of body weight and acceleration that can sap energy. By sitting on the inside of lane one, putting things on cruise control, and allowing my competitors to break the air for me, I was not only running the shortest distance, but also expending less energy than the race leaders. *The pace is hot and it* will *string out.* I told myself this right before I shut my mind off.

For me to move from eighth place to first over the second and ultimate lap of this race would take every bit of cunning and physical prowess I had in my body. I knew I would have only one shot at getting to the front of the pack, and that the decision to move would have to be made in a fraction of a second.

I missed seeing the 400 meter split and could not hear the announcer call it out over the noise of the crowd. My body told me it must be around 50.25 give or take a quarter second. After ten years of doing this I could usually hit a quarter-mile within a half-second, no mater what the pace was. Whether that is an impressive feat or a troubling sign that I had run way too many laps, I'm not sure.

As I rounded the top bend my eyes were still transfixed on the back of Christian's jersey. When we hit the backstretch for the second time I woke up and started to panic once again. We were only 300 meters from the finish line and I was still in last place.

I tried to follow Christian along the inside rail, but ran out of room. Though I was now in sixth place, I had no way to get to the front. I looked through the pack and tried to find a gap. *There is none.* I glanced to my right and considered going around everyone in an outside lane. *Impossible.* For one, Wheating had moved up onto my outside shoulder and trying to move the six foot five giant would have taken a forklift. The runners ahead of me were bunched too tightly to move through them. *What do I do? There is no good way to get through this pack! Why hasn't it strung out yet? My patience has defeated me and now I will never be an Olympian.*

I remained in the back of the pack, certain that I had made the most costly tactical error of my life. I had no choice but to continue to be patient, and hope a gap would open up in the last 100 meters of the race. I knew I probably would not win this way, but thought perhaps I could at least sneak in for a top three finish and punch my ticket to Beijing.

My legs felt good still, in fact, they felt amazing, but there was just nowhere to go. This is 800 meter racing. I shouldered my way along the rail almost certain I had screwed myself out of a spot on the US Olympic

Team. However, with 150 meters to go a narrow gap opened up between Jonathan Johnson and Christian Smith. It was a narrow gap and I knew it would only last for a half second. Going through it could mean getting tangled up with someone and getting tripped. No victory, no more chances, no Olympics.

Not going through it could mean being too far back from the leaders when everyone started their kick. This would result in me being left behind simply because I was too scared to get out with the leaders. These thoughts all passed through my brain in less than a quarter of a second and I knew I had less than that before the gap would close. *Take it!*

As I pushed my foot on the accelerator I knew this decision would be one of the greatest or worst of my life. I closed my eyes and visualized driving my knees forward, as Coach Radcliffe had taught me in the gym. I needed to have perfect form to make it through this tangle of legs; a long back kick and I would be sure to get clipped and go down. I leaned lightly into Jonathan and my bulk shifted him to the outside of lane two. My six-inch gap nearly doubled and I was free.

I now had a clear view to the front and could see that Khadevis still led the pack. Though I was now running in lane two, there was nothing separating me from him. With each step I thought about squeezing the trigger of a rifle. I was trying to exert as much pressure on the trigger without actually pulling it, and releasing the firing pin. This thought helped me accelerate at a controlled rate. Suddenly, I was closing in on the leaders.

As we left the last turn and hit the home stretch I had pulled up even with Khadevis. I looked up and could see the finish line in the distance. I took one final analysis of my legs and knew I had enough energy left to get me there. I went back to the rifle in my mind and allowed myself to finally pull the trigger. The firing pin in my soul ignited every bit of energy I had stored in my muscles and I exploded from the pack. As my legs clawed the rubber I pulled farther and farther away from my competitors. I was separating myself from the best half-milers in America and was less than 80 meters away from realizing a ten-year dream.

The crowd had been steadily getting louder as I made my move through the pack, and now that I was home free, they were going wild. I tried to listen to my breathing or the sound of my spikes hitting the track, familiar sounds that often comfort me and take my mind off the pain that is gripping every fiber of my body, but I could not hear anything. The roar of the crowd was deafening. I was giving each step everything I had and could see the finish line only a few seconds away when I thought, *this noise cannot be for me . . . it's for* Wheating!

I had run at Hayward field many times, and even had the opportunity to hear a Hayward Field crowd cheer me down the homestretch against the defending Olympic champion to win a Prefontaine Classic, the greatest non-championship race held on US soil. The crowd had never sounded like this. For the final time in this race my body was sent into a panic and I was sure that the sophomore from the University of Oregon was just steps away from passing me. I dug deep one last time. This last bit of energy was the kind that can only be accessed in incredible situations. It is born from natural adrenaline that no drug could ever replicate.

I hit the line and threw my right shoulder as far out in front of me as I could without falling to the track, as Coach Rad had taught me. I had no idea where my competitors were, but I knew I had done everything humanely possible to get to this finish line first. I glanced to my left and right and could not see any of my competitors. *You have done it. You are an Olympian. Not only that, but you have won the Olympic Trials. How exactly does one celebrate something like this?*

The moment I realized I had won the race, made the team, and accomplished a goal that was ten years in the making, a wave of testosterone hit me. This is similar to the feeling of adrenaline, but a different high. This feeling was not associated with a sense of panic, but rather with absolute joy and relief. I felt like a prizefighter who had just knocked someone out in the twelfth round to win a world title.

The only way I could demonstrate the euphoria I felt was to throw my arms up and flex my biceps. My momentum from the final meters of the race had not yet died and I was able to get a good couple of seconds out of this pose before my cement-filled legs brought me to a halt.

This last demonstration of bravado was almost my undoing, as it drained the final ounce of energy left in my body. I could no longer hold myself upright and was fortunate to turn around and find Wheating right behind me with his arms in the air. He had kicked hard down the final stretch in lane three to finish second. We leaned into each other and embraced as much to congratulate the other as to keep from falling down. I stepped back and felt fatigue grip my body. I fought the urge to hunch over or collapse to the track. *Enjoy this moment proudly, not hands on knees, begging for oxygen.*

As I drew in each breath I realized there was one more person on this track that understood the way Wheating and I felt. The top three finishers make the Olympic team and I looked up at the video board to see who had finished third. There, right below Wheating's name was CHRISTIAN SMITH. I could not believe what I had just read, and did a double take. Sure enough the board read:

1 NICHOLAS SYMMONDS 1:44.10

2 ANDREW WHEATING 1:45.03

3 CHRISTIAN SMITH 1:45.47

4 KHADEVIS ROBINSON 1:45.53

5 LOPEZ LOMONG 1:45.58

6 DUANE SOLOMON 1:45.78

7 JEBREH HARRIS 1:46.21

8 JONATHAN JOHNSON 1:48.11

8:29.45 P.M. UNIVERSITY OF OREGON 1:44.10

It was the Oregon sweep that I thought could never happen. I ran to Christian and helped him up off the track. He had dived for the finish line to out lean Khadevis for the final spot on the Olympic Team. He had beat Khadevis by five one hundredths of a second, about one inch. In doing so, he had run the A standard that he so badly needed. He was Beijing bound.

The three of us were handed water and American flags and told to take a victory lap. As I turned to the crowd the first person I saw was Coach Sam, standing on the other side of the three-foot tall fence that ran around the perimeter of the track. As Coach Sam had perhaps played the largest roll in my making this team, it seemed very fitting that he would be the first person to congratulate me. I ran over to him and gave him a huge hug. "*I love you, man!*" he screamed into my ear.

"I love you too, Coach!" I said back to him before continuing on my victory lap.

A few meters down I saw Mom running down the stadium stairs. Tears were streaming down her face. I hopped the short fence that separated us and climbed up to hug her. "My boy, my boy!" she screamed as we embraced.

The entire victory lap took close to half an hour as Christian, Wheating, and I stopped every few feet to hug a friend or sign an autograph. It seemed that everyone who had helped me along the way was here and I wanted to share this moment with each one.

When we had completed this final lap we were taken to team processing and drug testing. This tedious but necessary process takes place at every US Championships. All I wanted to do was be with my friends and family, but instead I was forced to sit in a crowded room drinking water until I could pee.

When we were finally released it was late, and most of the fans had left the stadium. I quickly found my family and coaches. We spent the next few hours taking pictures, catching up, and getting dinner at Track Town Pizza, a local pizza parlor that runners frequent after meets.

After dinner we walked across the street to Villard Street Pub where track fans had been meeting each night for beers. My dad snuck in two bottles of champagne and some glasses for us to start the celebration off right. Surrounded by my family and best friends we popped the bottles and toasted to an amazing day.

To my surprise, when I walked into the pub people began to cheer. As I worked my way to the bar they slapped me on the back and asked to take pictures with me. One guy I didn't even know came up to me, shook my hand, and said, "Tonight, you don't pay for a single drink. Anything you want is on me."

I accepted his gracious offer. Eventually, the party began to die down and my family decided to head back to their hotel. I hugged them goodbye and thanked them for everything. Those who still wanted to drink went back to my house where my roommates already had a pretty good house party going. We didn't stop celebrating until sunrise.

Later the next morning I woke up exhausted and hung over. I was in desperate need of electrolytes, so I walked to the corner store. With my shades on to hide my bloodshot eyes I walked up to the store and saw the cover of that day's paper on display in the dispenser. To my surprise, a picture of me crossing the finish line was front and center. The headline read: HALF-MILE HEROS. I chuckled, purchased a copy along with my sports drink, and sat down on the curb to read the article.

Coach Gags had given me the next few days off, so I spent them sleeping and partying. Having been through two Olympic Trials now, I can say that the hardest toll they take on your body is not from the running, but from the incredible parties that occur each night. With hundreds of your closest friends all in town, and something to celebrate every night, it is hard to turn down the festivities.

One day during the 2008 Olympic Trials, after I had made the team, I was issued my Olympic Team USA jacket. I threw the beautiful blue and white top on and admired the Olympic rings that were sewn into it. I was interested to see what kind of reaction this jacket would get from the public, so several of my teammates and I headed to Taylor's Bar & Grille. This local "meat market" is where many college kids go when they are looking to make a new friend. As a rule I avoided the place, but tonight I had my new jacket on.

Outside of Taylor's there was a short line and we waited our turn to get in. The place looked crowded, which we decided made it worth waiting for. This particular evening I had Christian and the Jefferson twins with me. Inside, the place was packed. John Jefferson was competing in the 1500 in a couple days so he was not drinking, but couldn't pass up the chance to celebrate with the rest of us. Sean was coming off an injury and would not be competing at these Olympic Trials.

I had known these guys for almost two years and we had been through a lot. John was my roommate in Boston in 2007 when I had won my first USA indoor title. Sean once had my back in an argument that got out of control at a bar down the street called the Indigo District. That night at Indigo, an ex boyfriend was harassing the girlfriend of one of our teammates. When I saw him shove her I had to step in. I'm not one to provoke confrontation in a bar, but I became enraged when I saw him shove our friend's girl.

The ex grabbed my shirt and pulled me close. Never before had I been in a fight, outside of sports that is, but I pulled back and punched him hard. We fell to the ground and I was fortunate enough to end up on top. One of his friends jumped on my back, however, and began to punch me in the back of my head. Sean came running across the bar to even up the fight before the bouncers came to break things up. When the bouncers got there, they told us they had seen everything and kicked the two hot-headed college kids out of the bar. Sean and I had been pretty tight ever since.

Now, at Taylor's, surrounded by drunks, I was thankful to have him with me and we bought a couple of pitchers. The four of us were all single and hoping to not go home alone, as was often the case.

That night, though, was definitely our night. Many of the guys in the bar were at the meet earlier and recognized me. They all wanted to say congratulations. Soon, word spread throughout the bar that Christian and I had just made the Olympic Team. Lots of girls came up to take pictures with us, or to ask what it felt like to be on our way to the Olympic Games.

As I was chatting with one girl I noticed several other girls behind me.

"Dude, the chicks are forming a line to talk to you," Sean whispered to me.

I smiled. "Guess I now know how Oregon's quarterback must feel!"

I was doing my best to be polite and get to know each girl. I had met one special girl a few months earlier when I introduced myself to her in the student athlete weight room, but never had the nerve to ask her out. It turns out when you have just made the Olympic Team you don't have to do the asking, the girls come to you. I was fully aware that the attention I was receiving was both shallow and fleeting, but that didn't hinder me from enjoying that night.

Two A.M. came around pretty fast, and we all left Taylor's as they closed the doors behind us. My female friend from the weight room was still by my side and the two of us got into a cab. She told the cab driver her address, then leaned into me. When we pulled up outside her place she invited me in, so I paid the cabbie and continued to play the part of college quarterback.

The next few days at the trials were a tough mix of easy running, drinking with friends, and sleeping next to a kind, beautiful woman. Granted, this is probably my favorite way to spend a day, but maybe was not the best way to prepare to compete at the Olympic Games. By the time the Olympic Trials were over I was extremely grateful to get back to my training program.

Though I had lived in Oregon for six years I had never once spent the month of July there. During college I had usually returned to Boise, and as a pro, I traveled to Europe to race each summer. Now, with the Games just a few weeks away, I was finally able to remain in Eugene for the best month of summer. I was very glad, because I truly do not think there is a more enjoyable place in the entire world during the summer than Eugene, Oregon. The lush green river valley explodes with life as the clouds part and the sunshine pours down. Salmon and steelhead work their way up through the crystal clear rivers and everything smells fresh and alive.

During this month I fell into a perfect routine. I woke up every morning to a cup of coffee and small breakfast before I headed to Hayward Field to work out. After the run was complete I enjoyed lunch, then headed to my new lady friend's house where we spent a few hours together before I went out to run or fish in the warm evening air. It was paradise.

For a month I enjoyed this idealistic existence, but of course, all good things must come to an end. All too soon I boarded a plane for San Jose, California where the Team USA processing would be done. Once on the San Jose State University campus I met up with Andrew and Christian. We were eager to see what awaited us at team processing.

We were initially disappointed to find a great deal of paperwork, but ecstatic to find a giant warehouse full of Olympic gear. We were given a shopping cart and told to check in at each of ten stations to receive our official Team USA items. By the time I was done making the rounds, I had two shopping carts full of clothes from Ralph Lauren and Nike. We were also given gold watches and fitted for Olympic rings. I overheard someone say that the estimated value of all we were given that day was around ten thousand dollars.

We each pulled out several pieces that we wanted and needed with us in Beijing, and shipped the rest back to Eugene. That night we tried our best to get some rest, but I struggled to sleep. I was way too excited. The next day we boarded a plane bound for Beijing, China.

12

This wasn't my first trip to Asia, but it was my first time in China, and I was glad to have Andrew and Christian with me to share this experience. We were constantly making jokes, and stopping to take pictures along the way.

My lack of sleep from the night before was a blessing in disguise, as I was now able to sleep much of the flight from San Francisco to Beijing. When we touched down I peered out the window and saw a hot, red orb trying its best to shine through the thick brown smog that enveloped our plane. I had been told that the air quality in Beijing was bad, but this was like looking through chocolate milk.

Team USA collected their bags and we were taken through customs and then on to the athlete village. Each Olympic athlete village is different, but they are all constructed for the same purpose: to house and protect each country's competing athletes. The athlete village in Beijing was brand new and had been built specifically for these Games. There were row upon row of apartment buildings, each decorated with flags that represented the nationality of citizens they housed. We would call these apartments home for one month (until the conclusion of the Games) at which time Beijing citizens who had purchased apartments in these buildings would move in.

We received our credentials and were set free to explore the village. It was extremely hot and humid, and I remember the hiss of the cicadas in the trees as almost deafening. Almost all Olympic athletes must share a room, and Christian and I had requested to be roommates. We found our building and settled into a tiny apartment that we shared for the duration of the Games.

When we first walked into our building we almost bumped into Michael Phelps as he was leaving for the pool. He had been all over the media leading into these Games, as he was expected to do very well here. And he did, winning eight medals in Beijing. Christian and I looked at each other wide eyed.

Our "apartment" was small and simple, with sparse furnishings similar to a college dorm room. Christian and I didn't care about our simple accommodations much, as we planned to spend the majority of our time in the cafeteria, or by the 50 meter outdoor pool that had been built in the middle of the village.

Lounging by this pool was surreal. Like most pools, there were girls in bikinis, but these weren't your average girls; they were the fittest, most athletically talented women on the planet. There were also people swimming laps, but they were not doing so recreationally. These were the finest swimmers in the world, gracefully pulling themselves through the water. I was interested in the prospect of getting to know some of the foreign beauties, and wondered how I could make that happen. But, I also knew I needed to remain focused on the job I was here to do, and tried to put girls out of my mind for the time being.

Opening ceremonies were that night and the next morning Christian and I were going to fly to Dalian, China, where the USA Track and Field team was based until track and field competitions began. The entire summer Olympic Games lasts almost four weeks, and track and field is usually toward the end. To make matters worse, the men's 800 meters is usually one of the last events to be contested.

That night most members of Team USA dressed in our beautiful Ralph Lauren designed outfits and congregated outside our apartment buildings. Both men and women wore white slacks with a navy blue blazer emblazoned with the Olympic rings. The outfit was completed with a white beret. Though many people had warned me how strenuous the opening ceremonies would be, it was an event that I did not want to miss. However, five minutes in a full suit in ninety-degree weather and I was beginning to have second thoughts.

Fortunately, Team USA was quickly escorted to the gymnastics arena where we could wait in air-conditioned coolness until it was our turn for the parade of nations. It was incredible to be in this building with all of the best athletes from the United States. While we waited, we took turns posing for pictures and taking them for our friends.

Just as we were beginning to get tired and anxious, two doors opened and several tall gentlemen with dark suits and glasses walked in. I recognized them right away as Secret Service agents, and moments later President of the United States George W. Bush walked into the gymnasium. He had several of his family members with him, including his father, the former President Bush.

Most of the athletes jumped to attention and rushed over to shake the president's hand and get pictures with the first family. The president did his best to accommodate all the requests of Team USA, but must have felt overwhelmed as athletes crowded around him. As if to save the president just in time, the USA Basketball Team entered through the back door. One girl screamed, "Oh my God, it's Kobe!" and all the Team USA members turned in unison.

I thought the mobbing of the president had been impressive, but the way the USA Basketball Team was being mobbed took the cake. I had never been a big fan of professional basketball, but I wasn't going to miss a chance to get a picture with Lebron James. He and the rest of his teammates were very polite, and accommodated as many photo requests as they could before it was time for Team USA to walk into the Olympic Stadium.

I am told that the 2008 Olympic Games Opening Ceremonies were truly a sight to behold, but I really didn't get to see much of them. There had been no live feed in the gymnasium and by the time we entered the stadium the ceremonies were almost over.

However, I can't imagine that anything would have been able to top the sight I beheld as I entered the stadium and set foot on the track for the first time. The "Bird's Nest," as people had begun calling this Olympic Stadium, held more than ninety thousand spectators when it was at capacity, as it was that night. On the infield were the teams that had entered prior to Team USA, along with hundreds of drummers pounding out a rhythm in unison.

We took our time walking around the track and waving at the crowd. People around me were pushing and shoving to get near a basketball player, knowing that they were more likely to be broadcast on television back in the states if they walked next to a "star." Christian and I walked in together and enjoyed every minute of it.

By the time we took our places on the infield the magic of the moment had started to wear off, replaced by sheer exhaustion. Most of us had completely sweated through our suits and were desperate for a seat and a drink of water. Just when I thought I was moments away from passing out, though, the lighting of the torch began and I got a jolt of adrenaline. That carried me through to the end of the ceremonies.

As soon as we could, Christian and I sprinted out of the stadium and stripped our soaking wet clothes off. We walked shirtless in the warm, still summer air back to the athlete village, where we collapsed in our beds.

Our next two weeks were spent in Dalian, China. This major seaport was just over an hour from Beijing by plane. It was still very hot and humid there, which made it difficult to train, but the air quality was better than it had been back in the Olympic Village. Coach Gags and Coach Radcliffe were with me to make sure my training went as well as possible, and I was so happy to share this journey with them.

With just three days to go before my first round, I flew back to Beijing. I was excited to return to the athlete village. However, the village I came back to was quite a different place than the village I had left. During the first few days everyone had been on his or her best behavior. The vast majority of people in the village were coaches and athletes who had spent most of the four previous years preparing for these competitions. As events were contested and athletes set free from their rigorous schedules, the village turned into one giant party.

Though it was difficult to get non-credentialed people into the village, most athletes at some point left to attend one of the parties sponsored by a beer company, and then stumbled back into the village late at night. I desperately wanted to go out with them, but I wanted even more to get decent rest so I could compete at the top of my abilities. I went to bed early each night and wore earplugs.

As the day of my first round approached, I began to get nervous. Coach Sam and my family had flown in from the states and I spent as much time with them as possible to take my mind off the race. Christian and I explored Tiananmen Square and frequented the Nike hospitality suite that was located across the street from this famous Chinese attraction.

I woke up on the morning of August 20, 2008 and went through my usual pre-race routine. I had coffee, went for a walk, ate a small breakfast, and showered. Then I loaded my backpack with everything I might need for the competition and caught one of the buses that left every fifteen minutes to shuttle athletes to and from the track.

I had drawn a decent first heat and knew that if I executed my race plan I should be able to finish in the top three and advance to the semi-finals. I jogged around the warm-up track visualizing how the race would play out. Coach Sam and Coach Gags were forced to wait outside the track, as they had not been given official Team USA coaches passes. These passes instead went to the personal coaches of "serious" medal contenders and the glorified babysitters who were selected as official Team USA coaches.

Just before the race, I jogged to the fence to get some last minute words of wisdom from Gags.

"Stay close to the front, you hear me?" he said looking me dead in the eyes. I nodded and he said, "Good luck," as I shook his hand.

Coach Sam gave me a fist bump through the fence and a "Love ya, brother."

I turned and jogged up to the call room where I took a seat next to my competitors. These preliminary heats are not particularly exciting, as they rarely eliminate any real medal contenders. Given this fact, the stadium was only half full. I was grateful to have a relatively quiet stadium, and knew that if it had been like the night of the opening ceremonies, I would have had real trouble controlling my nerves.

We were led out to our lanes and asked to strip down to our race attire. I tried to imagine I was back home in Eugene, doing what I always tried to do: win in front of my home crowd. This mentality worked and I went on to win my very first Olympic race in a somewhat uneventful first round. I tried to keep things in perspective and remind myself that I had a long way to go to win a medal, but allowed myself to revel in pride and joy at crossing that finish line in first place for Team USA. Doing so earned me a spot in the semi-finals the following night. Christian and Andrew had not been so fortunate and were eliminated in round one. I was now Team USA's only hope for a medal in the men's 800 meters.

The semi-finals in my event were extremely brutal, as the field was narrowed from twenty-four to just eight finalists. To achieve this, three races of eight competitors were pitted against one another with only the top two in each race advancing. The two fastest men who did not place in the top two of their heat filled the last two finalist spots. The heats were drawn evenly, so that each race was guaranteed to have several men who all deserved to be in the finals. But, at almost every World and Olympic Championships I had watched, these semi-finals had managed to eliminate at least one of the favorites.

I was not a favorite by any means, but I also did not want to be eliminated in the semis. I returned to the athlete village after the first round and spent the entire day in bed relaxing and reading, trying to let my legs recover from the day's earlier efforts. The semis would take place the following evening, so I had ample time to recover.

The next day was torture. I woke up early and realized I had twelve hours to kill before my next race. Just as it had been at the Olympic Trials, dealing with the anticipation proved to be as much of a challenge as the competition itself. I spent the day chatting with Christian, hanging out in the cafeteria, and lying in bed. The hours dragged on.

Most of our races as professionals take place at night, so I was used to this. In fact, the evening time slot helped me get into the right frame of mind, as it made this race feel like something I was used to. When it was finally time to go to the track, once again I felt ready, both physically and mentally.

Again, my coaches were not permitted inside the warm up area so I was forced to run laps with them watching from 30 meters away. Every few minutes I stopped to check in with them to see what they had to say. Gags looked nervous, and reminded me to stay out of trouble. "Be close to the front with 100 meters to go," he reminded me again. Both coaches wished me luck, and with that I was off to the call room.

Inside, I sat down and took a good look at my seven competitors. On paper I wasn't expected to make it out of this round, but what the paper said had never stopped me from winning races before. When we were led onto the track I kept my head down and stared at the rubber in front of me. I was afraid to look up into the stands and see ninety thousand people staring down at us. I was certain that doing so would paralyze me with nervousness.

I again tried to imagine that I was at Hayward Field, racing in front of my home crowd. I imagined that everyone in the stadium wanted me to win, and wanted me to put on a show for them.

When the gun went off I intended to do just that. I fought for space and positioned myself well the first lap. The first lap of 53 seconds wasn't terribly fast, three seconds slower than at the Olympic Trials, and I knew I would need perfect positioning in the second lap to out kick everyone. Coming down the backstretch for the second and ultimate time, I could see that everyone else had the same idea. We all pushed and shoved, jockeying for position. As the final curve approached I knew that I absolutely had to beat everyone to the corner. If I couldn't get to the rail by the end of the straight away I would be forced to run the last turn in lane three. Doing so would add several meters to the length of my race.

I looked down at my legs and smiled. My legs felt incredible and I knew there was a great deal of speed stored up in them. I started to accelerate and called upon my signature kick. *Let the show begin.* I moved to the outside of lane three and surged as hard as I could. Soon, I began to inch ahead of the rest of the field. Very aware of what was happening, each of my competitors responded.

My kick, which was so efficient at pulling away from American half-milers, was well-matched by these more talented foreigners. I began to panic as they moved right with me down the backstretch, keeping me in lane three. As the turn approached I realized there was no way for me to get back to the rail. I was stuck there for the final 200 meters. By the time we exited the turn I was completely sapped of all energy and faded to fifth. I had failed to advance to the final.

I collapsed on the track, my Olympic dream crushed. I gasped for air, fighting back huge tears. When I felt that I could finally stand again, I got to my feet and stumbled off the track. I did my best to answer all of the questions that I was asked by the media, but I really just wanted to get out of there. Finally, I collected my gear and walked back to the warm up track.

Outside the fence I could see Coach Sam and Coach Gags standing where I had left them. They had watched the race from inside the stadium and rushed back to be there when I returned. I approached them with tears in my eyes.

"Tough one brother," Sam said.

"I'll say!" added Coach Gags. "I mean what the hell was that? Why were you ever in lane three? Where were your damn race tactics? That was a disgrace!"

I turned around and started my cool down before they could see me cry. Coach Gags was right; it was a disgrace. Tactically, I had run a very poor race. As I cooled down, though, I couldn't help but feel as if I had made the right decisions, just in the wrong setting. I was twenty-four and this was only my second semi-final at an outdoor global championship. I made a promise to myself that I would learn from this mistake and be better for it.

After the cool down I talked to Coach Sam. He said that as soon as I walked off, Coach Gags had turned to him and said, "I was too hard on the kid. But he's gotta learn a lesson!" Coach Gags was right, and learn my lesson I did. I was glad when he came up to me before I got on the bus and gave me a huge Gags' bear hug.

"I love you like a son, young man," he said.

"I love you too, Coach," I replied.

I showered, changed, and then went to find my family. With my mom, dad, sister, and coaches around me I felt loved and supported, despite the cloud of depression settling into my mind. We found an incredible restaurant with outdoor seating and sat down to drink wine and share all of our stories from Beijing.

When the night finally wound down, Coach Sam, his son AJ, and I went in search of a party. I had been very stressed over the last few weeks and needed to blow off some steam. We hit up several sponsored parties and a few clubs before calling it a night. Then I stumbled back into the athlete village and collapsed in my bed, alone.

The next two nights were similar and I found myself boarding a plane on the final day of the 2008 Olympic Games, proud that I had stayed so focused on my running but disappointed that I had not enjoyed some of the extracurricular activities that the athlete village was infamous for. I decided that I would just have to train hard and make the London Olympic team in four years.

13

The rest of the summer of 2008 was a blast. Despite my massive disappointment in not making the finals in Beijing, I look back on that summer as one of the best of my life. When I finally returned to Eugene in September, I took a month off to let my body recover, and so I could catch as many fish as possible. One day I met up with Christian and Andrew, who had also just gotten back to town. Over the summer we had talked about getting the Olympic rings tattooed on our backs when we returned home. Now that we were all together we wanted to see who was really serious about it.

Before this I never had an urge to get anything tattooed on my body. But, I always said that if I ever did get any ink, it would have to really mean something to me. I knew that up to that point in my life, the accomplishment I was most proud of was making the 2008 Olympic Team. I had a feeling I would not regret this particular tattoo.

With that, I called a local tattoo parlor and made an appointment for the three of us to go get inked. I was nervous the entire time, both about the pain and the thought that what I was doing to my body was permanent.

I had the tattoo artist draw up a sketch of how I wanted the rings to look. He transferred his drawing to stencil paper, placed the stencil on my back, and fired up his electric tattoo gun.

The buzz of the gun sent my heart racing, and I braced for the pain of the needle to enter the skin of my right shoulder blade. To my surprise, it did not hurt much. Certainly, it was less than the physical pain I had gone through to make the team, or the emotional pain I had gone through in Beijing. When the tattoo was finished I stood up and admired the artwork in the mirror.

The tattoo was beautiful and exactly what I had asked for, but when I looked at it I felt an overwhelming sense of regret. *What did I just do?* This was permanent. I had just marked up my skin, marring the body I had worked on hard in the gym—and on the track—for more than a decade. I began to panic and threw on my shirt, trying to put it out of my head. Then I watched in silence as Christian and Andrew got their tattoos. The knowledge that they were also permanently marking their skin, that we were sharing the experience, calmed me down.

When the tattoos were completed we posed for a picture together with our tattoo artist, then said good night to each other. When I woke up the next day I peeled off the plastic wrap that covered my tattoo. Then I looked at it in the mirror for a while.

Though my new tat was red and puffy, I thought it looked pretty damn cool. My fears finally subsided. One day this chapter of my life would come to an end and I would be a much older, slower, hobby runner. I imagined that people would get a kick out of seeing an old guy in a race singlet hobbling down the street with the Olympic rings tattooed on his back.

Now, whenever I catch a glance of the ink on my back, I look at it with pride. It reminds me of the hours spent with Coach Gags and my teammates. It reminds me of the selfless love that my family and Coach Sam showed me. And, it reminds me of a special night with Christian and Andrew, of when we walked into a tattoo parlor. It also reminds me that I should probably never get tattooed again.

When my legs were well rested I began training for another season. My contract with Nike was up at the end of the year, but Chris thought that with my successes in 2008 I should have no problem getting another contract.

Chris was right, because not long after, the offer came through. It was much less than what we had expected, and we were again pigeonholed into taking it if I wanted to stay a part of OTC. I signed the contract, but made a note to never have such little negotiating power again.

To that end I began to work hard at something Coach Sam had suggested I do from the very start: build my own brand. First, I incorporated my running business, registering Nick Symmonds, LLC with the state of Oregon. Then I set about building my own website, nicksymmonds.com, and I worked hard to build up my friends and followers on social media.

I have always been a private person, but I had realized that the people who got paid the most in this sport were the ones who were willing to put themselves out there publicly. I also began to tweet more frequently.

Before Twitter came along I resented doing interviews. *Why would I help you create content for free?* That was the thought I always had when I was asked to do one. However, once Twitter went live, things changed for me. Now there was a very real way to measure public exposure. There was a way to keep score. With each interview I did, I visualized it being published and my Twitter followers increasing, thus making me more attractive to potential sponsors.

Companies pay close attention to social media and whenever I contacted a potential new sponsor, one of their first questions was, "How many Twitter followers do you have?" Twitter was obviously going to be a big part of building my brand.

As I trained hard and traveled around the world I also worked hard to create a public image. This image was one of a well-educated young man from Boise, Idaho who loved to train hard, loved the outdoors, and loved to travel. Another part of this was that I was single, and I played up this angle in the media. It was not a hard angle to play up, as the majority of time I was, in fact, single. That's not to say I was without female companionship. There is actually, a lot of sex that takes place on the circuit.

I imagine sex plays a large role in any group, but it does especially among high-strung, stressed out athletes who are among the fittest people on planet Earth. We are often on the road for months at a time, in some of the most beautiful cites in the world, and stay in magnificent hotels at no cost to us.

Often the athletes hook up with each other. I have experienced my share of this, but I always felt uneasy about doing so. I do not like to mix business and pleasure and prefer to find companionship away from the track. Some of my more adventurous colleagues feel the same way. Others prefer to keep things strictly professional and hire companionship.

The amount of prostitution available on the circuit might surprise you. From Amsterdam, where one can visit the government regulated brothels of the Red Light District, to Monaco, where high-end prostitutes will happily spend a night with you in exchange for approximately one thousand dollars (US), there is always action if you are willing to pay.

Perhaps the least well known "paid for" attention can be found at the Shanghai Diamond League meeting. I had heard rumors about this over post-race beers many times. In 2009 I ended up being invited to the meeting and flew from Europe to Shanghai to investigate for myself.

The meet hotel was a beautiful building in the heart of Shanghai, and was constructed around the track where the event was held. Most of the rooms looked down onto the lush, green soccer field and the eight-lane track that is protected by the hotel.

Rumor had it that there was a spa next to the lobby where you could get a fantastic massage for about forty US dollars. The beautiful young masseuses working at this establishment were all young Chinese women. Apparently they would take great care of you in whatever way you fancied, as long as you were willing to pay. I had no idea what all that meant and my curiosity got the better of me.

As I dragged my bags into the hotel after a twelve-hour flight, I thought that a relaxing massage would be wonderful for my sore muscles.

I put my bags in my room and walked down to the spa. When I walked in a lovely, small Chinese woman greeted me. In broken English she asked where I was from and what I was looking for. "Just a massage," I replied, looking at the menu that was displayed next to the register.

I chose a hot oil massage and paid up front. Then I was led to a private room complete with shower, hot tub, and massage table. The lady who greeted me told me to make myself at home, and that the masseuse would be in shortly. I stripped down and got in the shower to wash off the travel. Once I was clean, I wrapped myself in a towel and lay down on the massage table.

As soon as I was prone I could feel the jet lag wash over me. Just before I nodded off to sleep there came a knock on the door. Another pretty woman walked through the door and greeted me. In broken English she asked where I had flown in from, then she told me to lie face down, and that she would make me feel much better.

She was right. When she was done, I had never felt so relaxed. Her hands had done a *very* thorough job of working out all the stress and tension in every part of my body. All I could do was return to my room, crawl into bed, and have one long, peaceful sleep.

I have never trusted myself much around temptation. In many ways, I am a person of great mental and emotional strength, but in other ways I am quite weak. I recognize this part of my character, and it is one of the reasons I have remained single for the majority of my athletic career.

Early on I could see that on the circuit there were three ways to survive a lifestyle that kept you on the road for over half the year: you could bring your partner with you (an expensive option that few had the means for), you could cheat on your partner (an option I saw many choose, but one I did not feel comfortable with), or you could remain single.

When I saw a teammate or competitor cheat on a spouse while on the circuit I struggled to understand how they could do such a dishonest thing. I see how the temptation and frustration could be overwhelming, but I wondered why they got married so early. Granted, we are all human and we make mistakes, but cheating on a spouse is a mistake I feel should never be made, and it is one I never want to make.

Though I have spent many lonely nights on the circuit, I have had my share of amazing moments as well. The women I have met taught me much about life and love. And, following the advice my mother gave me when I was young, I always did my best to be upfront and honest with my intentions, and to practice safe sex.

Through most of my twenties I knew I was not ready to commit to someone for the rest of my life, and now, as I enter my thirties, I am just beginning to appreciate all the amazing things monogamy has to offer. I am glad that I listened to my inner voice when I was young, and did not give into societal pressures to settle down before I was ready. I believe too often we are pressured into choosing the person next to us to be our life partner due to pressure we receive from others, even if the person is not right for us, or we are not ready to make such a serious commitment.

As each year passes and I leave my youth behind, the pressure to find a mate and settle down becomes much greater. As I have done so many times before, I ignore those who would have me leave the path my instincts tell me to take. For now, I know my primary focus must still be running as fast as I can. That said, I look forward to the day when my primary focus will involve being a great husband and father.

There is another aspect of the circuit lifestyle that is also omnipresent: drug testing. As much as the media portrays our sport as one of cheaters, of athletes who hide in corners to inject themselves full of performance enhancing drugs, I believe that professional track and field is actually very clean. Sure, we have our share of doping violations, but what sport doesn't? In reality, professional track and field is many times cleaner than other professional sports, such as the NFL. The punishment for a first time doping violation in track is usually two years. In the NFL it is four weeks. Add to that the fact that the NFL doesn't even test for one of the most common performance enhancing drugs, human growth hormone.

Whenever someone in track and field cheats, and subsequently tests positive, the sport of professional track and field dies a little bit. The entertainment value of our sport comes from watching people test the boundaries of their own human limits. This entertainment value goes to zero if competitors test the boundaries of drug amplified superhuman limits.

However, in eight years as a professional runner, I can honestly say that I have never personally witnessed anyone using a banned performance-enhancing drug, nor have I ever used such a drug myself. Many of these drugs destroy your internal organs and shave decades off your life. I have always felt that temporary glory and success are not worth the subsequent long-term health effects. Furthermore, what sense of personal achievement can a person get when he or she knows they only won with the help of pharmaceuticals?

Perhaps I should take a minute to clarify something. Cocaine is not typically thought of as a performance-enhancing drug, but it can give an athlete a sudden burst of energy, a surge of confidence, and a loss of inhibition. For those reasons, the World Anti-Doping Administration (WADA) and the United States Anti-Doping Administration (USADA) lists it as a banned substance in competition. I would be lying if I said I had never personally witnessed people using this particular drug.

Perhaps the most memorable instance of this was in the spring of 2007. That year I had just won my first US national title indoors, and my star in the world of track and field was rising quickly. After my win, I was asked to go to Los Angeles for a few days to shoot some photos for an advertisement. The company that had asked me to come even put me up in an expensive Hollywood hotel. I was excited to explore the city and to see a few college buddies who had recently moved to the area. One of those friends was my usual partner in crime, Cooper.

The shoot went well, and after, Cooper and I decided to celebrate. One of our good friends had just moved into a beautiful apartment building in Marina Del Rey, a few blocks from the beach. That night he was having a barbeque, followed by a little get together with some European girls he had met in his building.

Cooper and I showed up at the apartment with beers, rib-eye steaks, and an eight-ball of cocaine. I have never purchased drugs and had not bought them now. Cooper, on the other hand, had developed a taste for the bitter white powder on the Costa Rican trip we had taken together during college, and he occasionally still made the financial transaction to acquire the illegal substance.

Once at the party, we popped open the beer and shared college stories. Our host then began to tell us about the women we would hang out with later that evening. They lived a few floors up and attended a local college. As dinner wound down, Cooper pulled out the small plastic bag of white powder. The powder was dumped out on the polished coffee table in the middle of the living room. Some people then proceeded to take turns passing around a rolled dollar bill, snorting the powder up into their nasal passages. I watched as the small white lines were greedily inhaled, one by one. The curious part of me wanted to join in the fun, but the responsible side of me said no.

When the cocaine was gone I grabbed all the beer I could find and the party headed to the elevators. We made plenty of noise as we walked through the apartment complex—to the huge frustration of the neighbors, I'm sure. Our host led us to a door that appeared identical to the others in the complex, and knocked. Before long a tall, stunning woman answered the door. She introduced herself and then welcomed us inside before introducing her roommates, who were equally beautiful.

We spent the next few hours chatting up these lovely foreign neighbors, but eventually the cocaine wore off of all who had taken it, and we returned home.

I had a restless night and woke up after just a few hours to the rising sun. I felt as terrible as most of my friends and a buddy and I decided to sweat out the effects of the night before. We laced up our trainers and stepped out into the bright California sun.

Outside, the light seemed overly bright and harsh and slammed into my retinas. I took my first few tentative steps. As my foot struck the cold, hard pavement I felt the concrete reverberate through my bones. My dehydrated muscles fought me each step, even though I tried to focus on the beauty of the marina as I plodded along. Eventually, my body warmed up and I felt more like myself. I started to sweat and felt very good about that. Not knowing about my night's activities, Coach Gags had previously suggested I run twelve miles that morning. Wanting to punish myself for the night before, I figured I would do at least that.

As we clicked off the miles, my body adjusted to what was being asked of it. I made it to mile seven feeling pretty good, but that's when things took a turn for the worse for my friend. He had been overly enthusiastic with the Bolivian marching powder and reached for his nose. When his hand came back, it was covered in blood. We stopped running, as he pinched his nose and tipped his head back.

We walked for a few minutes and then resumed running. Blood, however, continued to pour out of his nostrils. He stripped off his white cotton t-shirt and held it to his nose as we walked and jogged back toward the marina. For the next thirty minutes we did our best to jog back to the apartment while the T-shirt held to my friend's nose slowly turned from white, to pink, to deep red. As we passed people on the bike path they looked at him like he was a leper. A few asked if he was okay. He nodded and we pressed on

When we finally got back to the apartment the bloody shirt was tossed in the garbage, and my buddy's nose was packed with tissue. When it was my turn to use the bathroom I stripped down and stared at the mirror. *What a stupid drug!* I thought to myself. I looked at myself and realized that if I wanted to become one of the best in the world drugs like that could not be a part of my life. I made a promise to myself to avoid that dangerous, corrosive white power, and it is a promise I have kept.

Later that day I said goodbye to my friends and boarded a plane for Eugene. I was grateful to be going home and excited to get back to my routine. As the plane cruised over California at thirty-five thousand feet I looked out the window and replayed the events of the weekend. There

had been some really fun moments, but I knew that the Los Angeles party scene was not for me.

The plane touched down in rainy Eugene, and I caught a cab back to my home. As soon as I saw my front door I was reminded that I needed to update the USADA of my whereabouts. I am required to do this at all times to keep in good standing with the various federations that hold professional track and field competitions. Once inside I pulled out my laptop and sent an email to alert them that I would be at my Springfield, Oregon residence for the next week.

Back at home I fell into my normal routine of training hard and eating healthy. It felt good to be back home, living the pure lifestyle I had come to love. When a DCO (doping control officer) caught up with me several weeks later, I provided him with the samples he requested. As always, I breathed a sigh of relief when the samples came back negative––for everything. In the course of my eight-year career as a professional runner I have been tested more than one hundred times, and I have never once tested positive for a banned substance.

The procedure of collecting a sample from an athlete is rather invasive. First, I am required to tell USADA where I am at all times. There is a website where I list my place of residence and my training location. I must do this for all 365 days in the year. I am also required to provide them one sixty-minute time slot every day, with an exact location of my whereabouts during that slot. If a DCO comes to this location and I am not there, it is an automatic missed test. Athletes are only allowed three missed tests in an eighteen-month period. Three missed tests results in a doping failure and typically a two-year ban from the sport. When a DCO does find and identify me, I am required to provide them with a sample of urine, blood, or both. Failure to provide them with the samples they are after also typically results in a two-year suspension.

When the DCO arrives, he or she asks for a form of identification, and then tells me what samples he or she is required to collect. If they need blood, the rep will have brought along a phlebotomist to draw several vials of the precious red blood cells I have been working so hard to build. If they want urine, then a DCO follows me into the bathroom and asks me to wash my hands. The DCO then asks me to pull my pants down to my ankles and lift my shirt up to my armpits while he stands inches away to watch the urine leave my body and enter the little plastic cup they have provided me with. Needless to say, this can take some getting used to. I absolutely hate this part of my job. I find it to be a huge invasion of my privacy.

I frequently list my sixty minute time slot as being from six to seven A.M., typically because that is the only hour I know where I will be: at home in bed. When the knock on my door inevitably comes it jolts me awake and I know that my peaceful night's rest has been ruined. I am not the most chipper person in the morning, but when I am woken up by a DCO I am even less pleasant. I'm sure they dread coming to test me as much as I do seeing them in my doorway.

Drug testing is a necessary evil though, and I try to remind myself that it is not their fault that they barge into my home uninvited. Rather it is the few dirty, cheating people in the sport who rob us all of privacy. I continue to subject myself to the monthly tests because I know that one day I will no longer be a professional athlete. Regaining my privacy will be one of the sweetest parts of retirement.

There are, however, loopholes in the policies and protocol of the anti-doping agencies that make it incredibly easy for a cheater to dope undetected if he or she decided to do so. The many ways that crafty cheaters have beat the system are legendary.

There is a story of Russian women who put clean urine into a condom and inserted it into their vaginal canals before being tested. When it came time to provide a sample, the women broke the condom with a fingernail, and one hundred milliliters of clean urine flowed into the cup.

Men have been equally clever. I have heard of men who put flakes of soap under their fingernails, then flick the flakes into the sample to throw off the tests. There are also tales of athletes who use a product called The Whizzinator to beat drug tests. A Whizzinator is a fake penis attached to a plastic bladder via a catheter. This bladder can be filled with clean urine, which is then dispensed through the fake penis for a waiting doping control officer.

Cheaters will always find ways to beat the system. The cat and mouse game between the anti-doping agencies and these fraudulent crooks will always be a part of professional sport. To keep ones sanity, a clean athlete must try to ignore this unfortunate side of sports.

There are times when I lament the fact that I have never been ranked number one in the world, but never once have I considered cheating to get there. I take pride in the fact that at night I can collapse onto my bed after a hard, honest day's work. I also take much joy in the fact that when I lie down in my bed, I don't have a fake penis hidden in my underwear, along with a bag of someone else's urine strapped to my leg.

14

I was enjoying life as a professional runner. I loved the travel, the lifestyle, and the sense of adventure. I had even grown to love the training. But in the year that followed the 2008 Olympic Games, something happened that I didn't love. Coach Gagliano retired. It was very difficult to say goodbye to the man who had coached me to my first Olympic Team, but he promised he would always be in my corner. He also promised that Oregon Track Club would find a great replacement.

To the credit of OTC and its visionary president, Vin Lananna, they hired the perfect man for the job. Mark Rowland had been coaching professional athletes in the United Kingdom for years, with great success. Frustrated with the politics of United Kingdom Athletics, he made it known that he was interested coaching abroad. OTC was renamed the Oregon Track Club Elite (OTCE), they hired Coach Rowland, and he and his family relocated from their home near London to Eugene, Oregon.

Coach Rowland had been a professional runner and Olympian himself. He had even won the bronze medal at the 1988 Olympics in the steeplechase. He talked with a heavy British accent and used slang I had never heard before. To be honest, at first I could barely understand him, but what I did understand conveyed his vast knowledge and passion for coaching distance runners.

In my first year with Coach Rowland I won the USATF Outdoor Championships and qualified to represent the United States at the world championships that summer in Berlin. With some great coaching on Mark's part, I went on to make the finals in Berlin where I finished a disappointing sixth. I had learned from my mistakes in Beijing, and now knew what it took to make the finals at a global championship, but to learn how to finish in the top three would take even more experience.

My next chance came in the summer of 2011. That year I was in fantastic shape. As usual, I had made many sacrifices to ensure that I was ready for the summer racing season. I had recently attempted to maintain a serious relationship, but the stresses of my career put an end to it. I had only been home perhaps two months in the previous eight, and had spent the vast majority of the winter and spring at training camps building strength. The result was that I entered the 2011 outdoor season in the best shape of my life.

The world championships that year were set to take place in Daegu, South Korea in September. This placed the pinnacle of our season much later than usual. Coach Rowland and I expected that many of our competitors would be tired by the time the championships took place, so we decided to race sparingly during the summer season. Doing so cost me a lot of income in the form of appearance fees and prize money, but I decided it was worth it, as I desperately wanted to win a medal.

In the sport of track and field there is a very distinct separation between those who have won medals and those who have not. Those with medals get special perks, such as increased appearance fees, rooms to themselves when traveling, and a lasting legacy. Those without a medal are often quickly forgotten.

I knew going into Daegu that I was finally in the kind of shape it would take to finish top three and win a medal. Though I did not go into these championships as one of the top three ranked athletes, I was in the top ten, and usually did better than my ranking at championships meets.

At this event my body propelled me through the first two rounds with relative ease. I qualified for my second World Championship finals feeling that I had wasted very little energy. Most of the medal favorites all made it into the finals along with me, but I was still confident I could be one of the first three across the finish line. It was now just a matter of running the race to see who would come out with the hardware.

When the race went off, I positioned myself well during the first lap, tucked into the middle of the pack in fourth place. I was content to rest here, with my brain shut off, until I reached the last turn. As I approached this bend I started to make a move to get closer to the front, as Coach Gags had taught me. Just as I began to inch my way up, my friend and frequent competitor from Poland, Marcin Lewandoswki, came around me in lane three and elbowed me, nearly stopping me in my tracks. This kind of bumping is legal in middle distance racing, but is usually avoided as it often costs both runners momentum. I was unable to recover the lost momentum and faded down the home stretch to a gut wrenching fifth place.

Despite all his effort, Marcin only managed to finished in fourth place, one spot out of the medals. He and I both walked off the track with our heads hung low. It would be one full year before we had another chance to win a medal.

To say I was crushed was an understatement. I was so devastated that I was unable to watch a replay of that race for more than a year, due to the hopelessness it made me feel every time I tried. It wasn't just that I had come that close to a medal, but rather that I knew I had the power in my legs that night to kick with the leaders. Watching a replay of that race now, two full years later, I still shake my head and wonder what I could have accomplished had I not been bumped. Alas, that is part of 800 meter running. I have been on both the giving and receiving end of many elbows and shoves in my career, and do not hold any hard feelings toward Marcin.

After the race I sulked around the hotel for a day, and then begged my agent to get me on the first flight out of South Korea, despite the fact that there were several days of competition left. I just couldn't stand being around athletics one minute longer. This time, the disappointment hit me even harder than in Beijing.

I suppose what frustrated me the most was that I put in all that work and made all those sacrifices to finish fifth in the world. I was extremely proud of this accomplishment, but worried I would go down in history as just another guy who got close, but ultimately couldn't get the job done and win a medal for his country.

It hurt to think that this might be how I would be remembered. When I touched down in Eugene, I stepped out into the lush, green city of Track Town, USA and decided that although I may never be a medalist, I was damn sure going to leave a legacy. I also knew exactly what I wanted that legacy to be.

From my very first days of running, my running idol had always been the late Steve Prefontaine. As a kid, as soon as I started to learn more about the sport of distance running, his name came up. Pre, as people called him, had lived a brief, but brilliant life as one of America's greatest distance runners. He had been raised in Coos Bay, Oregon and had attended the University of Oregon where he set numerous school and American records. Pre finished fourth at the 1972 Olympic Games, but while preparing for the 1976 Games, he died in a car crash at the age of twenty-four. Pre never had the chance to win his medal, but he left a legacy of records, and of challenging the sport's governing bodies that were treading on the rights of American athletes.

Nearly three decades after his death, I looked at the sport of "professional" track and field and realized we still had a long way to go toward realizing Pre's dream, even though the Amateur Athletic Union that Pre had battled with was no longer in existence. The United States of America Track and Field (USATF) and the International Association of Athletics Federations (IAAF) had replaced it. These were the entities that now governed track and field.

For years, many of my colleagues and I had been frustrated with how these governing bodies controlled our sport. In particular, we were adamantly opposed to restrictions placed on how athletes were able to market themselves to potential sponsors. The way the IAAF had written the rules were as follows:

3.1.1.2 Any other Advertising on or by or otherwise associated with an Athlete is prohibited, including but not limited to body painting, tattoos, jewelry, hair dying, hair shaving, the use of any flags, banners, T-shirts, hats and any other form of display of Advertising.

3.1.1.3 No advertising or display of Sponsors of the Athletes in the form of "an Athlete x sponsored by company y" or similar may be displayed or appear on the Athletes or otherwise anywhere in the Competition Site.

Along with these international rules, our domestic governing body, the United States Track and Field Association, had drawn up the following guidelines:

The USATF Athlete uniform policy (hereinafter "Guidelines") allows club names and a manufacturer's name/logo to be displayed on an Athlete's competition and warm-up attire. The size of all logos must comply with the below Guidelines.

The competition and warm-up attire of Athletes may only have advertising and/or identification as permitted under these Guidelines. Any advertising or other identification on such attire not specifically permitted under these Guidelines is strictly prohibited and will constitute a breach of these Guidelines. Any other advertising on or by or otherwise associated with an Athlete is prohibited, including but not limited to, body painting, tattoos, jewelry, hair dying, hair shaving, the use of any flags, banners, T-shirts, hats, and any other form of display of advertising.

These rules and guidelines essentially made it impossible for any athlete to represent a company that didn't make a piece of his or her racing attire. Many times I had approached potential sponsors and pitched to them how I could help market their products. But invariably, I was asked where they could put their logo on me during competitions. When I said that current rules prevented me from doing so, negotiations ceased. There had been a few athletes who had attempted to wear non-compliant logos in the past, but they were always forced to cover the offending logo with tape.

Over the years I had heard this exact same story from many of my colleagues. It seemed that everyone knew of at least one company that could offer them free product, or even monetary compensation, if only the partnered corporation could place some form of advertising on the athlete during competition. During my first five years as a professional I thought, *Someone is going to have to do something about this.*

That sunny September afternoon, I decided that I was going to be that someone. Having no idea where to begin, I figured I would try to make a scene on the Internet, and see what kind of attention it drew. I logged onto my Facebook account and created a group called "I'm tired of USATF and IAAF crippling our sport." The group info read:

> *This group is dedicated to changing the antiquated rules that govern the type of advertisements track and field athletes are allowed to wear when they compete. Currently, the IAAF is damaging our sport by making it next to impossible for athletes to gain corporate sponsors because of their regulations on where and how a logo can be displayed. It's time for these damaging rules to be changed so that badly needed dollars can once again flow into our sport!*

I shared the group with a few friends, and they shared it with a few of their friends. Within forty-eight hours the group had more than four thousand followers. Suddenly, I was inundated with media requests. People wanted to know why I was speaking out so loudly against these rules. Many people also wanted to know how my main sponsor, Nike, felt about all of this. Although I knew that Nike's sponsorship of Team USA made up almost half of USATF's annual operating budget, I was not sure how much influence they had on the enforcement of the guidelines. I expressed this in a blog that I wrote for a popular running website, flotrack.com:

> *The only advertising allowed on an athlete's body is that of their club and clothing manufacturers, and even these have absurd rules limiting where*

they can be placed and how large they can be. Do Nike, Adidas, ASICS,
Puma, New Balance, etc. care that the USATF and IAAF are bullying
them? Or, perhaps, I am being too naïve: It could be that the shoe compa-
nies agree to have their logo shrunk down to the size of a postage stamp
so long as USATF and IAAF ensure that it can be the ONLY logo
there.

As it turned out, I was being far too naïve. As I recall, Nike was the
only company to go on record regarding the issue, saying they preferred
the IAAF to set all rules regarding logo restrictions.

Through all of this I managed to capture the attention of the Track
and Field Athletes' Association (TFAA), a fledgling athletes' union that
hoped to empower athletes by giving them a unified voice. I joined their
organization and encouraged other athletes to do the same.

The TFAA had a lot going for it. Its organizing members included
both Olympic medalists and business school graduates. It also had one
very powerful ally in attorney David Greifinger. David resides in the beautiful city of Santa Monica, California, and represented runner Carl Lewis
during his career. David was incredibly well versed in the laws surrounding
track and field, and pointed out to us that the "guidelines" that USATF
enforced did not appear anywhere in their rulebook. He went on to say
that by the very definition of "guidelines," they were not mandatory and
we did not have to follow them.

David also felt that if USATF continued to enforce their "guidelines," they could run the risk of violating US anti-trust laws. Armed with
this knowledge and emboldened by David's presence, many of us at the
TFAA booked our tickets to the 2011 USATF annual meeting to voice
our concerns. This meeting was set to take place in St. Louis, Missouri the
first week of December.

I had many other meetings during my three-day trip to St. Louis, but
the most interesting one was an Athletes Advisory Committee (AAC)
meeting that included athletes, agents, and representatives from Nike. I
was asked to speak at this meeting to give the room an athlete's perspective.
That day I wore jeans and a gray, USATF T-shirt with the giant USATF

logo covered in tape. The logo would have been considered noncompliant with their own guidelines. I stood at the podium, wearing my ridiculous looking taped shirt, in front of several hundred people. There were a few Nike representatives sitting in the first row, and as I spoke, one scowled at me and shook his head.

I understood very well that I was still under contract with Nike, and tried to keep the conversation directed at the relevant party, USATF. "I am extremely grateful for everything that Nike has done for me," I began. I went on to say that I felt that USATF had confiscated advertising space that belonged to me. They then sold it to *their* sponsors for the highest dollar, and kept the vast majority of that money for themselves. I argued that there was nothing wrong with one company having exclusivity with regard to advertising space on an *athlete*, but that a company should have to pay the athlete for that exclusivity, not the governing body.

That is what happens in many other sports. Take golf, for example. Nike typically has exclusive contracts with their athletes, and Tiger Woods is not an exception. However, to have that exclusivity, Nike pays Tiger tens of millions of dollars. Nike pays for the logo on his hat, ball, clubs, shirts, and on his shoes. They do not pay the United States Golf Association for this exclusivity. I felt that it should be no different in track and field.

Shortly after I concluded my speech, a Nike executive got up to say a few words. Several minutes into his speech he was approached by a colleague and told that someone in the room was live streaming the meeting on the Internet. The executive and his companions said this was unacceptable, and left the room.

We athletes were then chastised by AAC president Jon Drummond for our "unprofessionalism" for posting a video feed of the meeting on the Internet. Jon went on to tell us that he had promised the Nike representatives that this would be a closed door meeting. Unfortunately, Mr. Drummond failed to mention his Nike promise to the rest of us. In the end, the situation made the athletes look bad when it was Jon Drummond who, in my opinion, had acted in an unprofessional manner.

These absurdly amateur moments, which AAC meetings are notorious for, continued when I brought up the point that, in AAC operating protocol, to have a closed-door meeting required a vote among the members. As I brought this to the attention of the room, a former AAC leader stood up and verbally threatened me, swearing at me in front of the entire room. She said that I was new to these meetings and had no idea what I was talking about (even though David Greifinger had pointed out that what I had said was correct). After several minutes of verbal abuse, someone finally escorted her out of the room.

As an athlete who was trying to run a business in a "professional" environment, I was flabbergasted. In my mind, these meetings were anything but professional. The only real professional part of the sport seemed to be the relationship I had with Nike, which was only professional because we had entered into a legally binding contract together.

That, however, is where good relations stopped with regard to me. Shortly after the AAC meeting, my agent, Chris Layne, received a call from a Nike staffer. According to Chris, the Nike rep said if I wanted to get out of my contract, they were happy to let me go. The process of negotiating a sports contract like mine can be long, intricate, and difficult, and the experience is not always pleasant. That's why I am glad Chris has my back. Chris explained to Nike that, for the most part, I enjoyed working with them very much, but felt that Nike should pay me for my exclusivity, not USATF.

Needless to say, it was a long weekend and I left St. Louis drained of energy and motivation to stay in this very poorly managed sport of track and field. Just as I was about to end the fight, and maybe my professional running career, I received a call from David Greifinger. He had great news. In its final meeting, USATF had tabled a vote on logo restrictions, and for the time being, the guidelines would no longer be enforced. The athletes had won the battle.

What this amounted to was that domestically, in all meetings governed by USATF, athletes could now run around looking like a NASCAR driver if they chose. However, the more high profile international meetings, such as the Prefontaine Classic or the New York City Diamond League, were still governed by the IAAF and we would still be subjected to their rules.

Armed with this exciting new knowledge, I flew home to Eugene and plotted how I could use it to my advantage. I first tried to reconnect with some of the sponsors who had shown interest in the past, but for the most part, I did not hear back from them. As is typically my move when I'm at a dead end, I decided to do something radical.

Aware of how Nike felt about me putting other logos on their products, I started to think of other ways I could give a potential sponsor a return on their investment. One cold, rainy night as I sat in front of my TV, I had an idea. I was going to put the advertising space of my left shoulder up for auction on eBay. The advertisement would take the form of a temporary tattoo, which I would display on my left deltoid during all of my competitions in 2012.

Initially, I was curious what something like this would go for, and did not expect it to fetch me much money. For this reason, I decided to auction off the space as a place for someone to advertise their Twitter handle, rather than a corporate logo. This also allowed the average fan to take part in the auction, as not everyone has a logo but almost everyone has access to his or her own Twitter handle. I figured worst case scenario it would be a fun way to interact with my fans. My plan also could bring more attention to the struggles many Olympians face when they try to gain corporate support.

On the evening of January 7, 2012, eBay auction #180789582037 went live. The auction was titled, "Your Twitter Name on an Olympian in 2012." I began the auction at 99¢, but set a reserve price of fifteen dollars to cover the cost of having the temporary tattoos made. I then posted a link to the auction on my various social media accounts.

Within minutes, the auction shot up to over one hundred dollars, as friends and fans took part in the excitement of an auction of this nature. Within twenty-four hours the auction was up over a thousand dollars, and I realized I needed to draw up some form of legal contract to protect myself, lest I end up having to advertise something inappropriate on my shoulder all season.

I was in need of legal advice, so I contacted the brilliant David Greifinger once again. We worked together to come up with a disclaimer and legal contract that was added to the auction listing. The disclaimer and contract read:

Thank you to everyone who has checked out this auction and to those of you who have bid on it. In the days since I began this auction I have done interviews with ABC, CBS, Wired.com, The Wall Street Journal, *and a host of other media outlets. Many of these media outlets will be covering the conclusion of this auction. Whose Twitter handle will they be reporting as the winner? It could be yours! I did not anticipate this auction gaining so much attention. Due to the fact that this auction is now about an athlete-sponsor relationship that is worth thousands of dollars it is in both parties best interest to have a contract. By placing a bid on this auction you are agreeing to the terms set forth in the contract below. I believe you will find that these are the same terms as outlined above, but present more clarification as to the terms of the agreement. That said, rest assured that I will make sure that the person or company who's Twitter name appears on my arm gets much national and international exposure through the entire 2012 season. As stated in the contract below, no American has a guaranteed spot on the 2012 Olympic Track and Field Team until after the Olympic Trials. For me to make this team I will need to finish in the top 3 at the USA Olympic Trials. I am the current defending Olympic Trials Champion at 800 meters and in 6 years of competing at the USA National Outdoor Championships my lowest finish has been 2nd.*

Thank you,
-Nick Symmonds

The Contract

This is a contract made and entered into by and between Nick Symmonds, LLC ("ATHLETE") and _____ ("SPONSOR"). In consideration of the mutual promises, terms, and conditions set forth in the contract below, the parties agree as follows:

A. CONTRACT PERIOD: The contract term shall begin upon the execution of this contract and will expire at 12:00 A.M. on January 1, 2013.

B. ATHLETE'S Responsibilities: ATHLETE agrees to wear a temporary TATTOO of the SPONSOR's NAME on his left deltoid during all running competitions in the 2012 season. This includes, but is not limited to, all distances located on a 400 meter track or road race. The TATTOO shall take the form of decal, henna, or stenciled marker and will be subject to athlete's discretion so as to maximize the TATTOO'S ability to remain legible during strenuous exercise. ATHLETE also agrees to TWEET the support of the SPONSOR's NAME on the first of every month during the Contract Period unless specifically prohibited to do so in the book of regulations published by governing bodies. If SPONSOR is a business or corporation, ATHLETE agrees to endorse the SPONSOR'S Products after a thorough review of the Products' quality, and provided that the endorsement does not interfere with the terms already set forth in contracts with the ATHLETE'S other sponsors, which include, but are not limited to, NIKE and Melaleuca.

C. SPONSOR'S Responsibilities: SPONSOR agrees to provide ATHLETE with monetary compensation based on SPONSOR's winning bid at EBAY auction of item #180789582037. This monetary compensation shall be paid as a lump sum payment via check or wire transfer to Nick Symmonds, LLC within ten days of the execution of this contract. SPONSOR also agrees to provide a logo, which will be used to design and produce the TATTOO.

D. Mutual Understandings Between ATHLETE and SPONSOR: ATHLETE and SPONSOR understand that in some cases, governing bodies including IAAF, USOC, and IOC may require ATHLETE to cover the Tattoo in accordance with the rules outlined in their rules books, and the Team Member Agreements (TMA). In these instances, ATHLETE agrees to place a strip of TAPE over TATTOO during the time the regulation requires, and shall remove the TAPE the moment the rules permit. In all interviews before and after a competition, ATHLETE agrees to mention SPONSOR'S NAME when asked about the TAPE covering the TATTOO.

ATHLETE and SPONSOR understand that no American athlete has a guaranteed spot on the 2012 Olympic Track and Field Team until after the 2012 Olympic Trials. This agreement shall be legally binding whether ATHLETE makes the 2012 Olympic Team or not. ATHLETE and SPONSOR understand that injuries are an unfortunate part of professional sports and this agreement shall be legally binding even in the event that ATHLETE is unable to compete in any competition in 2012 due to injury.

E. Exclusivity: No other form of advertising shall appear on ATHLETE's left deltoid before, after, or during competition, during the Contract Period. SPONSOR understands that this is the only form of exclusivity that shall be granted by ATHLETE.

F. Contract Territory: This contract shall be enforced throughout the World.

Definitions of Terms

(a) "ATHLETE" means Nicholas Boone Symmonds, Owner of Nick Symmonds, LLC.

(b) "NAME" means the Twitter handle of SPONSOR.

(c) "TATTOO" means a temporary tattoo in the form of a decal or ink impression, not to measure less than two square inches.

(d) "SPONSOR" means winning bidder of EBAY auction of item #180789582037.

(e) "TAPE" means a strip of adhesive in the form of duct, athletic, or kinesio tape.

(f) "PRODUCT" means any item sold by SPONSOR.

(g) "WORLD" mean all countries on planet Earth.

(h) "TWEET" means an online posting created by a Twitter user.

Athlete	Sponsor
_____	_____
Date_____	Date_____
Address_____	Address_____
_____	_____
Email_____	Email_____
Phone_____	Phone_____

Although I was nervous that the contract would present a barrier to potential bidders, it did not seem to slow the bids down. Over the next few days I continued to do local and national press interviews regarding the auction. I was often asked if I saw the auction as a distraction from my training. Yes it was stressful, but I also got a big kick out of playing this chess game with the people who currently controlled track and field.

The pinnacle of all of the media attention came one morning when I woke up and flipped on my TV to watch the news. I was flipping back and forth between CNN and HLN, when I saw a picture of my shoulder pop up on the screen. HLN, the national news outlet, was covering the story. My story! Here I was lying in bed in my home in Oregon, watching a national news story about myself. *This is too weird!* Talk about getting a kick out of it all. I could not stop smiling, it was too much fun.

The fun continued when I got a call from my agent, Chris Layne, who told me he had gotten a call from Nike. According to Chris the exact words used were, "That little shit just lost his contract." Chris had to remind the people at Nike that while there were often terms in Nike contracts that forbid an athlete from wearing another corporate logo on a Nike product, there were no such terms that forbade an athlete from wearing a logo on his or her own skin. For now, my Nike contract was safe.

I received a much better call the next day after an employee of a marketing company, Hanson Dodge Creative (HDC), contacted me. This marketing firm based in Milwaukee, Wisconsin had seen my auction and was interested in placing a bid, but wanted to ask a few questions first. Soon, I was speaking to HDC co-founder Tim Dodge.

Tim and I had a great chat, in which we discussed why I was doing this and how we could help each other if HDC was to ultimately win the auction. Toward the end of the conversation he asked if I would be interested in partnering with HDC even if they did not win the auction. I told him that yes, I would be interested, but that I would feel a sense of obligation to the auction winner for taking a chance on something new and radical like this. I wanted to focus the majority of my energy on getting a great return for my new partner, the eventual auction winner.

On the final day of the auction I watched the computer screen from my home nervously. By noon the auction was up to just over five thousand dollars. However, in the final five minutes it skyrocketed, and made thousand dollar jumps in seconds. When the auction finally ended, the winning bid was by a user going by the name of alvink7. The winning bid: $11,100.

I clicked on alvink7's name and saw that the user was based in Milwaukee, Wisconsin. I jumped out of my seat when I read this. *Hanson Dodge Creative!* Not only did I earn over eleven thousand dollars, I had just picked up an entire marketing team that would invest thousands into helping me grow my brand. I couldn't believe my luck. I stood there in my living room shaking my head and was reminded, once again, that when you are willing to take big risks, incredible rewards can follow.

Left: My parents, Andrea and Jeffrey, were all smiles on their wedding day in 1981. Photo courtesy of Andrea and Jeffrey Symmonds.

Below: Amazing shades! Here I am at our Rochester, Minnesota home in 1986. Photo courtesy of Andrea and Jeffrey Symmonds.

One of our many family camping trips. This trip was to Trinity Peaks, just north of Mt. Home, Idaho. Photo courtesy of Andrea and Jeffrey Symmonds.

Another camping trip. Here we with our dog, Jake, at Lincoln City on the Oregon Coast. I still love camping to this day! Photo courtesy of Andrea and Jeffrey Symmonds.

Halloween 1990. Lauren dressed up as Tiger Lily and I was Peter Pan. Our costumes (as always) were made by our parents. Photo courtesy of Andrea and Jeffrey Symmonds.

Jake, Lauren and me, catching dinner in Big Sky, Montana in 1991. Photo courtesy of Andrea and Jeffrey Symmonds.

Above: Lauren and I did not seem all that excited to go back to school, although Mom and Dad looked pretty happy. Photo courtesy of Andrea and Jeffrey Symmonds.

Right: I loved running cross-country for Bishop Kelly High School. Photo courtesy of Andrea and Jeffrey Symmonds.

Lauren and I both did well at the 2000 Idaho State Cross-Country Championships! Photo courtesy of Andrea and Jeffrey Symmonds.

With Coach Shanahan at the 2002 Idaho State Track and Field Championships in Boise. Photo courtesy of Andrea and Jeffrey Symmonds.

Dad and me after a fifty-mile backpacking trip through the Sawtooth Mountains in central Idaho. Photo courtesy of Andrea and Jeffrey Symmonds.

With Mom and Dad in May 2006 at my graduation from Willamette University. Photo courtesy of Andrea and Jeffrey Symmonds.

Fresh caught lingcod for dinner, thanks to Captain Nate Stansberry and the rich fisheries off the Oregon coast. Photo from the collection of Nick Symmonds.

Lauren and I had fun riding the train from Valencia to Buñol for La Tomatina. I am so proud of my sister and am not surprised that she has gone into a profession that makes a difference in the lives of children and families. Photo from the collection of Nick Symmonds.

The famous temporary tattoo I had to fight for. Photo by Donald Gruener and courtesy of Hanson Dodge Creative.

I ptoudly support the NOH8 Campaign, a charitable organization whose mission is to promote marriage, gender, and human equality through education, advocacy, social media, and visual protest. Photo by Adam Bouska and courtesy of the NOH8 Campaign. (noh8campaign.com)

Above: I loved hanging out with Lebron James during the Opening Ceremonies at the 2008 Olympics in London.

Above right: My faithful friend Mortimer riding shotgun in my truck in 2009.

Right: Kobe Bryant and I posed during the Opening Ceremonies at the 2012 Olympics in London.

Photos from the collection of Nick Symmonds.

Standing at the top of Humphreys Peak near Flagstaff, Arizona in April of 2012, 12,637 feet above sea level. Photo from the collection of Nick Symmonds.

Above: Coach Sam and I were ecstatic after we won our fifth straight US title, and qualified to be on the 2012 USA Olympic Team. Photo from the collection of Nick Symmonds.

Left: Coach Shanahan helped me with with my final tune-up race (in Dublin, Ireland) before the 2012 Olympic Games. Photo from the collection of Nick Symmonds.

Above: My official head shot for Brooks Running! Photo courtesy of Brooks Running.

I am all smiles standing on the medal stand in Moscow, Russia in 2013. Photo from the collection of Nick Symmonds.

Below: One of the stunning photos shot by Stephen Wayda. (stephenwayda.com)

15

The storybook relationship between Hanson Dodge Creative and Nick Symmonds, LLC grew over the next few months. Initially, Tim Dodge flew to Eugene and called a press conference where we announced our new partnership. There were many interviews that followed and I did my best to field them all, but could feel my energy being sapped. I knew I needed to get away from distractions for a while. I needed to get back to training.

I had a good friend who lived in Sydney, Australia who had an extra bedroom for me, and there were several races down there where I could show off my new @HansonDodge temporary tattoo. I boarded a flight from San Francisco, and fourteen tortuous hours later was in the southern hemisphere for the first time in my life.

As excited as I was to be in sunny Australia representing my new corporate partner, I raced poorly in my two competitions there. The hectic months leading up to this trip had been too much. Between the training, the interviews, and the fight with the governing bodies, I had over extended myself. My body was totally fried.

Despite my poor results on the track, Hanson Dodge Creative continued to invest in me. By the time I got back to the states, HDC had done a complete redesign of my web page, and had created an infographic for me to share via social media. Hanson Dodge Creative even went so far as to hire a camera crew to follow me around for two days to film a small YouTube series that chronicled my life as I trained for the Olympic Games.

As a top notch marketing company, HDC realized that winning the auction was only a small part of the story to be told. The much larger part was how a world-class marketing firm could help an athlete grow his brand and create incredible original content.

Though the partnership with Hanson Dodge Creative was better than I had ever hoped, the partnership with my girlfriend at the time was on the rocks. She and I had been in an on and off relationship for most of the past two years. Though our relationship was a bit tumultuous at times, we always gravitated back to each other.

This girl was stunningly gorgeous. I loved her personality and, despite the fact that my job kept us apart frequently, very much enjoyed being in a monogamous relationship with her. As hard as the distance was on us, it was the looming Olympic Trials and my disenchantment with the sport that took the heaviest toll on our relationship.

Following my poor showing in Australia I returned to the states and then flew across several time zones to spend time with my girlfriend. She and I enjoyed running together, lying by the pool, and catching up over meals. However, my frustration and anger toward the world of professional running was still burning hot within me, and I struggled to keep these feelings to myself. The result was that she and I fought often during that trip.

When we weren't fighting, she told me about a man she had met through her job. Hal Lifson was a publicist based in Beverly Hills, California, and they had been working on a project together for several weeks. She thought Hal might make a good publicist for me. My bullshit detector is very sensitive, and this time it was going off like crazy. I didn't trust any shifty Los Angeles publicist and told my girlfriend that I wanted to have a chat with this Hal Lifson.

Not too many days later I found myself on the phone with Hal and I have to say it was one of the most entertaining conversations I have ever had. Coming through the phone was a fast talking guy who was equal parts salesman and stand-up comic.

I laughed and played along, listening to him as ideas poured out. Most of Hal's ideas seemed out there. However, some were really good. I felt that all his ideas were made up on the spot and I had to wonder what this guy could do with some serious time to devote to a project. I waited for him to give me the shake down, to tell me how much it was all going to cost, but that part never came. Rather, Hal switched gears and began to talk about his love of track and field, and distance running in general.

Over the course of several conversations I learned that Hal had been an avid runner most of his life and closely followed the sport of professional track and field. He shared the same frustration I had with how the athletes were marketed, or rather, not marketed, and thought he could help. We stayed off the topic of compensation for his help, but each time we spoke he said to not worry about the money, that we would work something out eventually.

By the time I headed home I was curious about the potential that lay with my new acquaintance. I also felt uneasy about my relationship with my girlfriend. I could see where our relationship was headed, and it spelled trouble for both of us, as we devoted all of our time and energy to our careers. And, I was in the middle of my final push toward the Olympic Games.

On the flight home all I could think about were the Olympic Trials, set to take place in a few short months. Given the way things were going, I had an overwhelming feeling that the stress of our relationship was going to hinder both of our abilities to succeed in our goals. When the plane touched down I found a quiet corner of the airport and called her. As I tried unsuccessfully to choke back sobs, I told her how I felt, then ended our relationship. It was an incredibly hard thing to do, but I felt it was necessary for both of us. As soon as the conversation was over I felt a sense of relief. Now we both could devote all of our energy toward our careers. And that is exactly what I did.

With my relationship woes over, I continued to streamline my life and put my fight with the governing bodies on the back burner. Then I packed my bags and headed to Flagstaff, Arizona with my team to train at altitude for a month. As is often the case, I am unable to maximize my training unless I am in a remote location that has minimal distractions. The small town of Flagstaff, tucked away in the Sierra Nevada range of northern Arizona, fits this description well. Coupled with this is the fact that at seven thousand feet of elevation, there is much less available oxygen to fuel the muscles. As a result, the body builds more red blood cells and these oxygen-transporting cells stay with an athlete for weeks after returning to sea level, allowing for increased performance.

While I was there, Hal and I had several conversations. During one of these chats he and I came to an agreement that would bring him on board as my publicist. I knew I wanted to take full advantage of my run up to the 2012 Games and felt that the investment was worth the risk. We also talked about the end of my relationship and Hal suggested that it was better for me from an emotional standpoint, as well as a public relations standpoint. He continued to help me create my public image as a world traveling, outdoor loving, bachelor.

Hal is a bright, out-of-the-box thinker who has spent much of his life in southern California. He has been around long enough, and seen enough marketing campaigns, to know that sex sells. The fact that I was now single made his job much easier, as I could now be presented to the public as "available."

Almost daily Hal and I chatted on the phone to brainstorm various PR and marketing ideas. He was adamant about going outside the tiny world that professional track and field exists in. "We have to go mainstream," he said over and over before following up with, "Think pop culture." I respected his out-of-the-box thinking, but many of his ideas were too outrageous for me to feel comfortable putting into practice. We bounced ideas off each other frequently, trying to come up with just the right idea to get the media on our side going into the Olympic Trials. I enjoyed my conversations with Hal very much and quickly formed a friendship with my new business associate.

In May I returned from Flagstaff in great shape. To celebrate all my hard work I treated myself to a day of fishing on the McKenzie River. I had just finished hauling in a twenty-pound king salmon when my phone chirped. It was a text from Hal that read:

I HAVE IT. YOU ARE GOING TO ASK PARIS HILTON OUT ON A DATE. I HAVE ALREADY COMPOSED A LETTER FOR YOU TO SEND TO HER DAD, RICK HILTON, EXPRESSING YOUR INTEREST IN TAKING PARIS OUT. GET BACK TO ME ASAP. THIS IS BIG!

I laughed out load, put my phone back in my pocket, and continued to fish. But, text after text began to come in and my phone never stopped chirping. I tried my best to ignore it, but realized there was no use. Finally, I picked up the phone and called Hal.

I did my best to be patient, and let Hal explain how he had come up with this crazy idea. Really, I just wanted to hang up and get back to fishing. I expressed the concerns I had regarding the idea, but Hal was adamant we pursue it. Frustrated that Hal wouldn't let the idea go, I responded, "This is not a brilliant publicity move, this is harassing the Hilton family!"

Hal laughed, and then explained that he knew the assistant to Paris's father, Rick Hilton, and that he could get an email to him. Finally, tired of saying no to his ideas and eager to get back to fishing, I told Hal to run with it and that I would play along. However, as I placed cast after cast into the deep, dark pools of the McKenzie River, I began to let my mind wander and wondered what it would actually be like to go on a date with Paris Hilton. I wasn't sure how realistic this plan was, but I knew that if she was interested I certainly was.

When I returned home that afternoon Hal helped me compose an email to Rick Hilton. In it I expressed my respect for Paris's stunning looks and business acumen, and formally asked Rick's permission to take his daughter out on a date. I certainly never expected a response, but Hal told me that a response wasn't the important part. The important part was that we would copy a friend of his on the email. This friend, Joe Battaglia, was a writer for the NBC Olympic web page and could guarantee that a story about this would be published. Response or not, we'd get mileage out of the email to Rick Hilton.

True to his word, Joe published the story on NBCOlympics.com and people started to talk. Most people asked why I was no longer dating my girlfriend. Others asked why I chose to ask Paris Hilton (of all people) out on a date.

I answered a few of the questions, and had a good time reading through the rest of them. My Twitter following, I saw, had jumped a few hundred since the story was published, so Hal had done his job.

A few days later I was looking through the list of my new followers and saw something that made my jaw drop. Next to a little blue check mark was the name "Paris Hilton." I clicked on the account, which was verified and had several million followers. It was definitely Paris Hilton's Twitter account. Next to her name was: FOLLOWS YOU. *Paris Hilton is following me on Twitter!* I was just about to compose a tweet to brag about this when I remember that many celebrities don't actually manage their own social media accounts. I assumed one of her team had seen the article and followed me, either to go along with the game, or simply out of pity.

I put it out of my mind and refocused on preparing for the Olympic Trials. I was able to do so until the evening of June 4, 2012. That night, while eating dinner at a restaurant, I pulled out my phone and started to check emails. One caught my eye that simply had PARIS listed as the sender. I looked over both of my shoulders, expecting to see one of my friends watching as he or she played a joke on me. When I opened the email it listed the sender's address as coming from Paris Hilton's management company. *Holy crap.* The email read:

HEY NICK,

MY GIRLFRIEND JUST SENT ME AN ARTICLE SHE READ ONLINE.
SO I CALLED MY DAD'S OFFICE TO ASK FOR THE EMAIL YOU SENT.
JUST WANTED TO SAY HELLO AND ALSO THANK YOU FOR YOUR
KIND WORDS ABOUT ME. I WAS VERY TOUCHED AND IT MADE ME
SMILE. ☐

XO PARIS

I nearly fell out of my seat. I looked around the restaurant to see if anyone could see the shocked look on my face. As much as I wanted to walk around the restaurant and tell my fellow diners that I had just received a personal email from Paris Hilton, I decided to play it cool and forwarded the email to Hal. Within seconds I had a response:

ARE U KIDDING ME??? I AM AT THE TRACK AND ABOUT TO RUN. HOW CAN I RUN??? THIS IS INCREDIBLE!! DO NOT REPLY YET. WAIT TIL WE TALK. PLAY IT COOL. DON'T ACT OVER ANXIOUS. DON'T STEP IN THE TRAP. WE'LL DISCUSS. THIS IS AMAZING!!!!

My head was spinning as I drove home, writing and rewriting, in my head what I would say back to her. In the morning, Hal, continuing to prove that he was worth every dollar I was paying him, had already composed a response for me. I edited it and put my personal touches to it before sending it on to my new heiress pen pal:

HI PARIS,

WHAT A SURPRISE TO HEAR FROM YOU! THE PERFECT FINALE TO A DAY OF TOUGH WORKOUTS. I AM VISITING BEVERLY HILLS TOMORROW JUST FOR THE DAY. DOING AN INTERVIEW FOR THE INSIDER AT BEVERLY HILLS HIGH SCHOOL IN THE MORNING AND THEN A 7 MILE RUN AFTER. MY MEDIA GUY IS ONLY ALLOWING ONE STORY AS I HAVE TO GET BACK TO EUGENE FOR PRACTICE THURSDAY MORNING. I WOULD LOVE TO MEET UP IF YOU HAVE TIME. THIS WILL BE MY ONLY TRIP TO L.A. BEFORE THE OLYMPIC TRIALS. I HEAR THEY HAVE A KILLER GRILLED CHEESE SANDWICH AT THE BEVERLY HILLS HOTEL COFFEE SHOP AND ITS VERY LOW KEY THERE. I LIKE LOW KEY. THANKS FOR THE EMAIL. HOPE YOU ARE A TRACK AND FIELD FAN!

RESPECTFULLY,

NICK

OH AND BTW YOU LOOKED INCREDIBLE THE OTHER NIGHT AT THE MTV MOVIE AWARDS! :)

Fortunately, I had booked a flight to Los Angles after Hal had arranged for me to appear on CBS's, *The Insider*. During the interview I would be filmed training at Beverly Hills High School, and speaking about my intense desire to meet the girl of my dreams, Paris Hilton. I was nervous about going on a trip just two weeks before the Olympic Trials, but I knew that this was the kind of exposure I couldn't pass up, and that the distraction might actually be a good thing. Afraid that my coach would say no if I asked for permission to leave, I booked a ticket that would have me back in twenty-four hours. That way I would not miss a scheduled practice.

I felt guilty about sneaking behind Coach Rowland's back and eagerly checked my email for a response from Paris that would confirm I was making the right decision. My heart raced each time I looked at my emails, and it felt good to feel nervous about something other than my upcoming races. Was this really going to happen? Had Hal, Joe, and I somehow convinced Paris Hilton to meet me? I tried to not get my hopes up as I headed to the Eugene airport. As I sat on my flight to Los Angeles I knew that worst-case scenario, during this trip I was going to appear on national TV and give my sponsors incredible exposure. Best case scenario: I would appear on national TV and meet Paris Hilton.

The next day I woke up early and grabbed a strong cup of coffee before Hal came to pick me up at my hotel. As we drove to Beverly Hills High we talked about how to best answer the reporter's questions. Covered head to toe in Nike gear I ran laps, conducted the interview, and at the end, looked into the camera and officially asked Paris to come watch me make my second Olympic Team at the 2012 Olympic Trials. As soon as the interview was done I checked my email and saw what I had so eagerly been waiting for:

HEY NICK,

IN NEW YORK ABOUT TO BOARD A FLIGHT BACK TO LA. I HAVE A COUPLE MEETINGS RIGHT WHEN I LAND, BUT AM FREE IN THE LATE AFTERNOON. YES, I LOVE THE BH HOTEL, REALLY CLOSE TO MY HOUSE. AND YES I AM A TRACK AND FIELD FAN, I USED TO BE

A RUNNER IN SCHOOL. THANK YOU AGAIN FOR ALL THE NICE THINGS YOU SAID ABOUT ME. IT'S NICE TO HEAR WHEN PEOPLE SEE AND ACKNOWLEDGE ME FOR THE BUSINESS WOMAN I AM AND NOT THE CHARACTER I CREATED IN MY REALITY SHOWS. HAVE A GREAT INTERVIEW AND RUN. LOOK FORWARD TO MEET- ING YOU TOO.

XOXO PARIS

I shot back a response:

HI PARIS,

THE INTERVIEW AND WORKOUT WENT WELL. IT'S A BEAUTIFUL DAY IN BEVERLY HILLS! NOW WITH WORK ALL DONE I GET TO ENJOY SOME FREE TIME HERE. I DON'T HAVE TO LEAVE FOR LAX UNTIL 6 PM. NO DOUBT YOU ARE BUSY TODAY, BUT IF YOU HAVE THE TIME IT WOULD BE MY PLEASURE TO BUY YOU A DRINK. HARD TO BEAT THE BH HOTEL AND I'VE ALWAYS WANTED TO SIP A GIN N' TONIC IN THE POLO LOUNGE, PREFERABLY WITH AN IN- TELLIGENT, BEAUTIFUL WOMAN FOR COMPANY ;) TRAVEL SAFE AND HOPE TO SEE YOU SOON,

NICK

As the day went on she continued to keep me updated on her meet- ings and when she thought she would be free. While we waited for her, Hal and I toured the Beverly Hills Hotel. The iconic building opened in 1912 and has seen many celebrities come through its doors. It is beautiful and classy, the perfect place to meet a beautiful heiress.

Late in the afternoon I received the following email:

HEY NICK,

JUST GOT OUT OF MY LAST MEETING FOR THE DAY. IT'S IN BUR- BANK, SO THE TRAFFIC IS BRUTAL, SO I WILL BE RUNNING A LIL LATE. LLL SEE YOU AROUND 430 XO

Hal dropped me at the Polo Lounge in the Beverly Hills Hotel where I explained to the hostess that I was meeting Miss Hilton for drinks and that we would prefer a private booth somewhere outside in the back. The hostess led me to a booth she had selected and I took a seat. Then I looked around the magnificent courtyard, and at the white linen covered tables and flowering plants that were hanging everywhere. *I don't belong here,* I thought. I felt like everyone in the lounge was looking at me and saying to each other, "That guy over there is an imposter." It reminded me of my first trip to the USATF National Championships, and my first time overseas, traveling with Team USA.

Before long my heart started to race uncontrollably. *Calm down.* I then did something I often do when I'm nervous in a social setting. I closed my eyes and imagined myself on the starting line of the Olympic Games final. I imagined looking into the crowd, as one hundred thousand people looked back at me, and I told myself that my success depended largely on my gaining control of my emotions. As I did this I felt my heart rate slow, and my breathing become more relaxed. Then my phone went off:

HEY I'M HERE AT THE POLO LOUNGE, WHERE ARE YOU? XO

I jumped out of the booth, re-tucked my shirt, and walked to the front of the restaurant. Standing near the doorway was exactly what I expected: a slender, graceful, blonde woman in a form-fitting dress with a big hat and giant sunglasses. What I didn't expect was to find her standing there alone. *Where was her publicist, her best friend, her bodyguards?* More important, where was the little Chihuahua, Tinkerbell? To my pleasant surprise Miss Paris Hilton had come to the hotel alone. I walked up with a big grin on my face, introduced myself, and gave her a hug. She kissed me on the cheek and took my hand as I led her back to our table.

I allowed myself five seconds to appreciate where I was and with whom I was sitting. I then tried to put it all out of my head. This was simply a first date with a beautiful girl, something I had done before.

Paris sat across from me, took off her hat and glasses, and set them next to a gift basket Hal and I had put together for her. It was neatly wrapped and she examined its bow. I blushed and said, "That, of course, is for you. One cannot show up to a date with Paris Hilton empty handed." She giggled, looked into my eyes, and smiled. I noted that she was even prettier in person than she was on television or in print. We ordered drinks: a mojito for her and a gin and tonic for me. Then we talked about things any two people would talk about on a first date: family, travel, jobs, etcetera. The conversation was easy and I did my best to make her laugh.

We had a lot more in common than I expected and was pleasantly surprised to find how attracted I was to her. I felt Paris and I had chemistry, and that, in my opinion, is the most important part of any relationship. As we talked about our pets, her dog, Tinkerbell, and my rabbit, Mortimer, I wondered what it would be like to date her regularly.

We ordered another round and talked about what had led us to this meeting. Her friend had forwarded her the article that Joe had written, and said I was cute and should read the kind words I had said about her. I told her that I meant every word, and that I was genuinely impressed with her business acumen, which I was. We talked more about the incredible world she came from and then I looked at my watch. I realized if I didn't leave soon I would miss my flight back to Eugene.

"I can't believe I am going to do this, but I have to end this date early. I have a flight to catch," I said, feeling like a complete idiot.

As I escorted her to her car I had a feeling that everyone was looking at us. I was sure they were all asking, "Who's the clown with Paris Hilton?" The clown then put his arm around Miss Hilton's lower back as the valet rolled up in her bright red Ferrari. I kissed her on the cheek and said good-bye, and she climbed behind the wheel of her sports car and blew me a kiss before driving away.

Strutting like a rooster I smiled at the valet, and walked into the hotel lobby. When I was sure no one was looking, I ran like an idiot to the back of the hotel where Hal had pulled up with his wife Brigitte to take me to the airport. As Hal drove, I replayed the entire event for them. Despite some terrible afternoon traffic I made my flight and right before I had to turn my phone off read the following email:

HEY NICK

JUST GOT HOME AND OPENED THE PRESENTS YOU GOT ME. THANK YOU, THAT WAS SO THOUGHTFUL AND SWEET. I REALLY ENJOYED MEETING WITH YOU TODAY, YOU ARE A VERY NICE GENUINE PERSON. I HOPE THE TRAFFIC WASN'T TOO BAD AND THAT YOU MADE YOUR FLIGHT. GET SOME REST AND GOOD LUCK WITH YOUR TRAINING TOMORROW.

XX PARIS 310-XXX-XXXX

Sweet baby Jesus, Paris Hilton had just given me her phone number!

16

Paris and I continued to exchange emails and texts over the next several weeks. Though my heart raced every time I got one, I did my best to keep it all in perspective and remain focused on my primary goal of making the Olympic Team. As my final preparations for the 2012 Olympic Trials wrapped up, I felt confident that I would be able to do so. My training had been going very well, and in my final tune up workout, an all out 600 meter sprint, I ran a time of 1:13.9. That was considerably faster than I had run it before winning the 2008 Olympic Trials.

However, I realized that this time there was much more at stake than whether or not I was going to make the trip to London. This time I had set it up so that all eyes would be on me. I knew there would be people in the stands and at home who hoped I would fail. No doubt I had made some people angry with my antics.

On the other hand, I knew there was an entire team of people cheering for me in Milwaukee, Wisconsin who knew that their investment largely rested on me making this team. And, there was a stunning young blond woman in Beverly Hills who I hoped would follow the results. The question was whether or not I could deal with the pressure I had put on myself.

When the competition finally began, I felt much more prepared to handle the nerves than I had in 2008. This time I was the favorite going in, and the mantra Coach Sullivan had given me again played through my head. *The cream always rises to the top.*

I advanced through the first two rounds of the 2012 Olympic Trials with relative ease. As is often the case in Eugene, it rained every day I competed and the finals were no different.

The days and hours leading up to the finals passed just as slowly as they had during the 2008 Olympic Trials. Now, however, I had Camala and Maci Lapray, Coach Sam's two daughters, hanging out at my house each day to keep me company. I had known them both since they were little girls and having them with me, watching trashy TV, took my mind off the importance of the upcoming race.

When the evening of the finals finally came, Coach Sam once again picked me up from my house, rap music blaring through his speakers. The windshield wipers were working over time to clear the warm June rain that pelted his windshield. But this time, as we crossed the Willamette River on our drive to Hayward Field, I saw no fisherman for me to envy.

Warming up in full rain gear I was surprised at how good I felt. The reduced workload that Coach Rowland had given me in my training in the previous two weeks had left me feeling light and powerful, similar to how I had felt in the Olympic Trials final of 2008. Full of nervous energy and confidence, I grinned during much of my warm up.

Once we were finally led out to the track I took a moment to look at each of my competitors. I knew how nervous they must all be. I remembered back to 2008 when I ran my first Olympic Trials final. The cruelest part of this race is that if it doesn't go your way, you have to wait four more years to have another chance at proving you are Olympic material. In a country where you either have made an Olympic team, or are largely regarded as an amateur, this race was perhaps more important than any other for these gentleman. Fortunately for me, I was able to take much comfort in knowing that even if I failed to make the team, I would always have the Olympian title next to my name. That helped ease my nerves greatly.

As the announcer introduced the athletes, I paced back and forth in my lane trying to stay loose. When he called out my name the crowd roared loudly. As always, their applause gave me goose bumps and sent a fresh wave of adrenaline through my veins. I was again grateful that the Olympic Trials were taking place here in my hometown. I also was proud to sport the green and black Oregon Track Club Elite jersey that the crowd had come to know and love.

On my left shoulder I wore a piece of white tape that covered my Hanson Dodge Creative tattoo, as per the United States Olympic Committee regulations. Needless to say, I had been asked about the tape many times during the week and had been able to plug my new corporate partner many, many times.

The crowd was hushed and we were called to the starting line. I got into an athletic crouch and waited for the gun to go off. With a loud *crack* we were set free and took off sprinting. As we rounded the first bend I could tell I was losing ground quickly, just as in 2008. However, this time I remained calm and kept the panic at bay.

As we broke from our lanes down the backstretch and fought for position I settled next to the rail, right behind my old rival, Khadevis Robinson. Khadevis had overcome the pain and frustration of missing out on the 2008 Olympic team to resurrect his career. He was ranked number two coming into these 2012 Olympic Trials.

Tucking in tight behind him, I found myself in sixth place of a strung out, single file race as we approached the second turn. As we moved down the homestretch for the first time, the crowd got to their feet and cheered loudly. Khadevis moved to the outside of lane one, which allowed me to move past him on the inside.

Now moving up into fifth, I watched as the leader, Charles Jock, a young kid from Irvine, California, came through the first lap splitting 49.86. This was faster than we had split the first lap in 2008, and the race showed it. In 2008 the pack was all bunched together, and that made it hard to move up in the race. However, now the competitors were lined up single file making it simple for me to move up on the outside of lane one.

I was a little over a half second back from the leaders at the bell and had let a small gap form between fourth place, Ryan Martin, a young runner from UC Santa Barbara, and myself. I quickly worked to close this gap and by the 500 meter mark was ready to move hard down the backstretch to catch the leaders.

As is my usual race strategy, I knew I needed to be on the leader's shoulder with 100 meters to go. This was the Coach Gag strategy that had been reinforced into me over and over again, and the one that had worked so well for me in the 2008 Olympic Trials. I was confident it would again work here.

Coming around the final turn I peered around Charles Jock as he began to fade, and set my sights on the new leader, Duane Solomon. Duane was a former Division I standout from USC. He was immensely talented, but had yet to really thrive as a pro. Watching him leading with his long graceful stride several meters ahead of me I wondered if this would be the moment that things clicked for him. I dug deep and pumped hard to get even with Duane. With only 90 meters to go in the race I pulled up shoulder to shoulder with him. Duane's breathing was controlled and his stride going strong. It was going to come down to a drag race as to who would be the 2012 Olympic Trials champion.

All the hard work, sacrifice, thousands of miles, and days in the gym paid off. I was able to lift down the home stretch, maintain my form, and gap the field by several yards. As I took the last few steps I knew what I had just accomplished. I had proven the doubters wrong, and overcome the immense pressure I had felt going into this race. In an unplanned show of relief I threw my arms wide and stuck my tongue out.

Khadevis also moved well down the home stretch and was able to out lean Duane for second place, securing a spot on his second Olympic team. Duane hung on for third and collapsed to the track with fatigue and overwhelming emotion. When I turned to congratulate my competitors on a fine race I first gave Khadevis a big hug and then went to help Duane to his feet. I grabbed his hand and said, "Get up buddy, you're an Olympian."

As had happened in 2008, the three of us were given American flags and asked to take a victory lap. Remembering how incredible this moment was in 2008, I took extra time to savor it again. I was saddened, though, that this time I was unable to take the victory lap with my fellow Oregonians Christian Smith and Andrew Wheating. Christian had struggled with injuries since 2008 and was contemplating retirement. Andrew, on the other hand, had moved up to the 1500 and would go on to make the London Olympic Team in that event.

As I passed the Nike hospitality tent I looked up to see several Nike executives among a group of high-level execs. I wondered if they were happy for me, or if they were still frustrated by the fight I had picked with USATF. On one hand, an athlete of theirs had just won the Olympic Trials in the men's 800 meters. On the other, doing so was going to give me a fantastic amount of press to further my fight with our governing body.

To address this point, the next morning the front page of MSN.com had a picture of me crossing the line, tongue out, with the caption, TEAM USA'S OFFICIAL PAIN IN THE BUTT. Truly flattered, I tweeted a link to the article and said something to the effect of, "We all knew I was a pain in the butt, but now it's finally official!"

Unlike in 2008, where I had read the news hung over from behind a dark pair of shades, this time around I kept things more under control. Maybe it was the fact that I was older and more mature now, or maybe it was because I knew I had a good chance to win an Olympic medal, either way I was responsible and kept the partying to a minimum during these Olympic Trials.

As had come to be standard protocol under the guidance of Coach Rowland, the Oregon Track Club Elite would be based in Teddington that summer. This beautiful little suburb of London is right on the River Thames and is home to Saint Mary's University, a school with a lovely track and great training facilities. Coach Rowland had coached at this university before coming to America, and he felt at home here. I had been spending summers in Teddington since 2009, so I, too, felt at home.

Upon our arrival there was little time to prepare for the upcoming Olympic Games. Coach Rowland and I chose a few key prep races to hone my fitness and prepare me for international competition. All around us, London was consumed with Olympic excitement. I fielded media requests from many sources, both domestic and international, while doing my best to remain focused on my training.

More than anything, I wanted to see the brand new Olympic Village and participate in the Opening Ceremonies. Though I had been to the Olympic Opening Ceremonies in 2008 and knew how stressful they where, I didn't want to miss out. With only thirty-six hours before the start of the 2012 Olympic Games I began to work my way toward the village.

I had navigated the London public transportation system many times, and now I caught a train into central London. Then I took the London Underground to Stratford, where the entire Olympic Park had just been constructed. I traveled light, with just a small bag, and was dressed in plain clothes.

On the train I kept my eyes open for fellow Olympians who might be traveling in from Heathrow. I didn't see any, but as I climbed out of the underground station several beautiful, slender, blonde women joined me. They were wearing the blue and yellow team issued jackets from Sweden. As we approached the entrance to the village I asked if they were athletes, and if so, what sport they competed in. "Cycling," they responded in beautifully accented English.

As we waited in line to get our credentials we conversed some more and I discovered that, for each of them, this was their first Olympic Games. I committed their names to memory and made plans to find them after we were all done competing.

The credentialing process took about thirty minutes and when I was done I had a laminated pass with my picture on it that listed my country and event. Athletes must have this credential with them at all times, as it is what gets them into the village, cafeteria, and all venues. It actually is impossible to get into the village without it. There are a few guest passes that can be checked out from your federation, but they are extremely hard to get your hands on.

With my credential hanging around my neck, I walked into the athlete village. It reminded me much of the village in Beijing, rows of apartment buildings all decorated with team flags. However, here in London the weather was much more to my liking, and there was no deafening hum of cicadas to keep me awake.

I walked around aimlessly for ten minutes trying to find an apartment building with USA flags on it. Finally, I found a volunteer who worked with the Local Organizing Committee (LOC) and she was able to direct me to my building.

Inside the apartments, the set up was just as it was in Beijing, dorm-style living. I was staying in a three-bedroom apartment, with two guys to each bedroom. The bedrooms were quite small and the beds were even smaller. My roommate, a javelin thrower and fellow Eugene resident by the name of Cyrus Hostetler, had already moved in, so I took the other bed. I plopped down on it, felt the hard, uncomfortable pillow and comforter, and rolled my eyes. Different city. Same story.

Unlike Beijing, where I had been ignorant enough to not be bothered by the sparse accommodations, I now looked around the sad little room and thought about the five billion dollars that were exchanging hands during these Games. The athletes would not receive a single cent for the paramount role they played in making the Games what they are, and the IOC couldn't even provide us with a decent blanket.

I didn't want to let negativity creep in, so I stood up and walked to our balcony. When I slid the door open I walked out to one of the most beautiful views I have ever seen. We were up several floors and faced west, and had an incredible view of the Olympic Village. I sat down on one of the chairs and watched as the sun began to set over it all. This spot, I knew, would be my refuge from the madness and frustrations that were bound to come during my two week stay here.

That evening I went to the cafeteria with a few of the other members of the track team, to see what kind of food we would be eating for the next few weeks. I soon realized that if the IOC skimped on the room furnishings, it was so they could spend money on quality food. For this I was very grateful.

The cafeteria was the size of a super Walmart and had seating for several thousand. There were rows upon rows of food vendors preparing cuisine from all around the world. Tucked in the back corner was a Mc-Donald's, open twenty-four hours a day—and everything was free!

After dinner I walked around the village to familiarize myself with where everything was. I found a very nice gym close to my building, and a beautiful grassy quad in the center of it all. After my evening stroll, I returned to my room and did my best to rest up for the long day ahead.

The next morning I threw on my trainers and began a running tour of the Olympic Park. I kept the run short though, as I knew that evening's festivities would be strenuous.

In the late afternoon all of Team USA put on our Ralph Lauren Opening Ceremonies ensemble. Just as in Beijing, my sense of patriotic pride surged as I put on each piece of clothing. Unlike in Beijing, where the team assembled in the gymnasium, here we assembled in the streets of the athlete village. Most sports congregated together using this amazing opportunity to snap pictures. I took a lot of photos with my fellow track team members, but was not particularly pressed to search out other Olympians for a photo op.

I spent most of the evening with American miler, Matt Centrowitz, talking about racing and of course, the girls we hoped to meet during these Games. As we exited the village and began the mile-long walk toward the Olympic Stadium the USA basketball team joined the rest of the USA athletes. As had happened in 2008, Team USA went nuts when our more famous colleagues showed up.

As we approached the Olympic Stadium the majesty of the moment began to sink in. The beautiful stadium was lit up and we could hear the roar of the crowd from a mile away. After more than an hour of walking, we finally approached the entrance to the stadium. For many of us, this was our first time to enter the Olympic Stadium, and it did not disappoint.

As music blared, people cheered for the various countries entering alphabetically. The United States of America was, therefore, one of the last to enter and by the time we took our lap around the track, there were already thousands of athletes standing in the center dancing, and taking pictures.

As exciting as the Opening Ceremonies are, they drag on (and on) for the athletes. We had been on our feet for several hours and had a long while to go, now that we were on the infield. Near the end we were given the option to leave early, to beat the crowd. Matt and I took it appreciatively.

My legs ached, my back ached, and after the two Big Macs I greedily devoured in the cafeteria, my stomach ached. When I finally made it back to my room I collapsed and slept for twelve hours. I awoke the next morning feeling physically beat up and emotionally drained. This was definitely not how I wanted to feel going into the biggest race of my life. I knew I needed to get out of the village and back to my quiet apartment in Teddington so I could rest. I grabbed a small lunch and headed to the Underground to work my way back across the city.

Back in Teddington I was able to get in a short run before becoming too exhausted to go on. I returned to the apartment, ate dinner alone, and crawled into bed. That night I woke up several times shivering and sweating. With dawning horror, I realized the enormous stress of the opening ceremonies had weakened my immune system and I had caught a virus. Terrified that I had ruined my shot at an Olympic medal, I called Coach Rowland. I was beyond panicked. He told me not worry; we'd just push my workout back a day or two. The most important thing, he urged, was rest and hydration. That I could do. I spent the entire day in bed watching episodes of a hilarious British comedy, *The Inbetweeners*, and sipping coconut water.

I recovered quickly from my illness and spent the next week fine-tuning my speed on the track with Coach Rowland, and in the gym with Coach Radcliffe. Just days before my first round was set to go off I warmed up on the track, expecting a fairly easy session. When I got there Coach Rowland told me what he had in mind. Listening to the session he had planned, I wondered if what he was asking was too much this close to competition.

As I warmed up for this workout I was nervous and worried. *Certainly this is too much work right before a championship race.* I expressed my concern to Coach Rowland. He nodded and replied, "Fella, you can do what you want, but I know this set of intervals is what you need." With that he walked toward the starting line.

I was nervous for two reasons. The first was that I might not be able to complete the workout and it would wreck my confidence. The second was that I *would* be able to complete it, but not recover in time for my races. I decided to once again put my trust in Coach Rowland and give his workout everything I had.

When I finished the last interval I collapsed to the track, all of my energy spent and unable to support my own weight. Coach Rowland walked over and looked down at the helpless, gasping mass he saw in front of him. "Not bad," he said as he reached a hand down to help me up. With much effort I got to my feet and swayed back and forth as I tried not to vomit. All I could muster was a nod and then tried to walk towards my bag. I made it just a few steps before I needed to sit back down.

"I hope. You know. What you're doing," I said between gasps.

Coach Rowland just smiled and said, "You'll be much better for having done this one. I promise."

He was generous with the recovery for the next few days, and allowed me to do some very easy running on the grass in nearby Bushy Park. When I returned to the athlete village I was not totally recovered, but was beginning to feel somewhat normal again.

As in Beijing, with each passing day, the quiet athlete village that I left was morphing into one big party. I did my best to stay off my feet, and spent the majority of my time in my apartment watching other Olympic events on television. In Beijing the anticipation for my event had almost been too much to handle, but I felt I had it under better control here in London.

Also helping me through the anticipation and pressure of the event was the fact that many friends and family members had traveled to London to support me. My parents rented a large house a few miles away from the Olympic park, and had invited many of our family friends to join them. That house was my refuge during the Games and I frequently left the village to enjoy a meal and catch up with the people I loved most.

When the morning of the heats in the men's 800 meters finally came around I was ecstatic. I was not nervous, but rather, full of excitement to finally compete. In six years as a pro, I had never failed to make it out of the first round of a global championship, and usually advanced to the semi-final round with a win. London would prove to be no different, as I won my first race easily.

That night, as I sat in front of my computer waiting for the semi-final heats to be drawn, I had a bad feeling. I felt certain that the world record holder, David Rudisha, was going to be placed into my semi-final. I pressed the refresh button on the Olympic web page for the hundredth time and, sure enough, there he was, listed right above my name. There was also one extra competitor that had been added to our heat for some reason. To make matters worse, my old friend Marcin Lewandowski had been placed in our heat as well. I immediately had flashbacks of the flailing Pole bumping me in the final stretches of the World Championship final in Daegu.

I stared at the screen, looking at the list of competitors in my heat. *This isn't fair!* I shouted over and over in my head. I got up and began to pace back and forth in my room. I knew I was in trouble mentally, and shot a quick email to my sport psychologist, Jeff Troesh, back in America. I hoped he was free. Within minutes he responded that he was available to talk. I explained my frustration with the semi draw, how it was unfair that there was an extra guy in our race, how unlucky it was that Rudisha was in my heat, how nervous I was that Marcin would bump me again.

After several minutes of rattling off all that worried me, I finally paused to listen to Jeff's input.

"I actually like your semi-final. Having Rudisha in the race will make it more honest, and that is good for you as one of the faster guys. Also, isn't it just as likely, maybe more so, that Marcin will get in the way of one of your competitors, and not you, thereby helping you advance?"

His logic was sound. "Yeah, I suppose so," I said, still uncertain.

"And, aren't you more likely to ruin your chances of making the final by wasting energy worrying about things you can't control?" Jeff knew that this course of reason always calmed me down.

"Yes, of course." *Control the things you can control,* I thought.

We continued to chat about ways I could best channel my nervous energy. Then Jeff wished me luck and I promised to call him before the final. I lay back in my bed and tried to think about anything other than the race. Each time my mind drifted back I saw Rudisha running away from me, my heart would race, and I'd be further from sleep. Eventually, I managed to nod off.

17

In the morning I felt reenergized. Per my usual race day routine I had a light breakfast, went for a walk, took a shower, ate a large lunch, and passed the afternoon hours reading and napping. When the time came to head to the Olympic Stadium I was as ready as I would ever be. I put my headphones on, turned up the rap music, and boarded one of the shuttle buses.

The ride to the stadium took only ten minutes and I spent that time visualizing how the race would unfold. I knew Rudisha would want to lead the entire thing. If I could somehow find an easy way to get up next to him, that would be ideal. There would be a lot of people trying to do the same thing, however, so I would have to navigate traffic wisely.

Rudisha was the clear favorite in our semifinal. After him there were three or four of us who had a very serious chance of taking the second automatic qualifying spot. Though this made for a cut-throat semifinal, having Rudisha in our race meant it would probably go very fast and open up the potential for the two fastest men without an automatic qualifying spot to come from our heat.

I warmed up around the practice track playing out in my mind all the ways the race could unfold. When it was time to walk to the stadium I knew I was ready for anything that came my way. I gave a hug to Coach Rowland and to Coach Sam, and they wished me luck.

When the gun went off, the race began exactly as I had expected. Rudisha was on my right and went flying away from me. As we ran down the backstretch he put almost 10 meters on me and was easily in control of the lead. I remained second from the back trying to conserve energy.

When we came into the home stretch I felt Rudisha ease off the pace a little. I moved to the outside of lane two so I could maintain my momentum and, in doing so moved into second place. Yuriy Borzakovskiy, the Russian Olympic gold medalist I had learned so much of my race strategy from, had the same idea and we jostled for position at the bell. He won and found himself in the enviable spot right behind Rudisha. I had to settle into third, just steps behind him as we entered into our second and final lap.

I felt good moving down the backstretch, but I also felt several competitors breathing down my neck. Rudisha was beginning to pull away from the field and I knew we would all be kicking for the second automatic qualifying spot. As we rounded the final turn I felt Borzakovskiy tiring, and moved to his outside shoulder. I began to kick with everything I had and for a brief moment found myself in second place. I had the position and the momentum to hold onto my spot, but knew there were two men on my shoulders trying to get by.

I gritted my teeth, took one last look at the finish line and closed my eyes. The crowd began to get louder, and louder. I had a terrible feeling that the roar was not for Rudisha, who was gliding along easily, just steps away from the finish line. This was the loudest I had heard the crowd and I knew they must be cheering for their British national champion, Andrew Osagie.

I heard him before I saw him, but steps before the finish line Osagie managed to gain a half stride on me. With only seconds left in the race I knew he would take the second automatic qualifying spot and there was nothing I could do. I dug down to make one last push for the finish, dipped my shoulder as I hit the line, and hoped it was enough to snag a time qualifier.

I crossed the line in third and hunched over, hands on my knees, shaking my head. I had run a tactically solid race and kicked well, but it wasn't enough. I looked at the video board and saw my time: 1:44.87. The time was faster than the third place finisher of the first semifinal race, and was typically fast enough to advance to the finals. I walked off the track and sat down on the stairs that led out of the stadium. There was one more semi-final to be run, and unless four people ran faster than my 1:44.87, I would be going to my first Olympic final.

My compatriot, Duane Solomon, was in this heat and I watched him warm up as I stripped off my spikes. A female meet official walked up to me and told me I needed to head to the mix zone.

"I'm not interested in talking to the media until I know if I am in the finals or not," I said. She shrugged her shoulders and walked off. I looked at the sky and prayed for bad weather; wind, rain, anything that might slow the runners down. As if Mother Nature herself were in the stadium, the drizzle that had been coming down all day picked up, along with a slight breeze. I felt better, but would have preferred hail and gale force winds.

The race began and the last eight semi-finalists took off in their lanes. Duane shot to the front as expected. *No Duane, slow down!* I screamed over and over in my head. I ground my teeth and nervously played with the spikes in my hands as I watched for the 400 meter split. The final lap bell began to ring as the runners approached the end of the homestretch. Duane passed through the line first, and his split came up on the video board: 51.18.

I jumped to my feet. That was not a terribly fast first lap split. My chances were looking better! Duane continued to lead for the next 300 meters, but there were several athletes right on his heels that looked like they were ready to pass him. They waited behind him patiently until the final straight. Coming off the final curve, two young African runners moved ahead of Duane and sprinted to the finish line to secure their automatic berths to the finals. Duane hung on for third, and he and I were left staring up at the video board to see if either or both of us would advance on time.

Seconds passed by like hours. I could see several television cameras out of the corner of my eye pointed at me, awaiting my expression when I found out whether or not I would advance to the finals. The times began to come in and next to Duane's name was his time of 1:44.93. He had run exactly six one-hundredths of a second slower than I had. This guaranteed that he and I would be the two semi-finalists to qualify for the finals on time. For the first time in twenty years there would be two Americans in the Olympic final of the men's 800 meters.

A huge smile spread across my face and I ran up to congratulate Duane. I was then strongly urged, again, by a race official to exit the stadium. Now that I knew there was more work to be done, I happily obliged. In the mix zone I laughed with the reporters and told them how excited I was to be on my way to my first Olympic final. I talked about my chances of winning a medal, and if I thought Rudisha could be beat. I was also asked if I thought he could run a world record in the final.

"Absolutely not." I responded, and went on to say that I had been in the race in which he had set the world record previously; that the conditions that day had been perfect and that it was almost impossible for him to run faster than that without a rabbit.

Still smiling I went to the dressing room to collect my gear. When I walked outside to the warm up track, a smiling Coach Rowland greeted me. He shook my hand, then brought me in for a hug. "Bloody brilliant," was all he said before allowing me to start on my cool down.

I had roughly forty-eight hours to recover before the biggest race of my life. Back at the athlete's village I did my best to get in a good meal and some rest. The next day I jogged a little in the morning to flush out my legs, and then worked my way over to the rental house to spend some quality time with my family.

The day of my 2012 Olympic final race passed by just like any other race day. I kept to my pre-race routine and did my best to pass the hours without thinking about the competition ahead. The hardest part was not thinking about the fact that if I failed to medal that night, I would have to wait four more years for another chance.

On the bus to the track I saw many of the men I would race in a few short hours. I knew most of them well, and smiled at them as I walked past to find an open seat. *How strange for us to all sit here smiling at each other when, in just a few short hours, we will compete against each other for something we have devoted the last four years of our lives to.*

At the warm-up track, I found Coach Sam and Coach Rowland waiting for me, and they led me back to one of the USA medical tents where I could lie down. As had become the norm, my legs had felt better and better through the rounds, and despite having to go all out in the semi-finals, I felt incredible that evening. I glided through my warm-up, confident and eager to race for an Olympic gold medal. As I ran around the practice facility I played in my mind how the race would unfold—over and over again.

Some races are unpredictable and I have to imagine five or ten different scenarios, but this race was going to be one of the most predictable I had ever run. Rudisha was going to try to lead wire to wire, just as he has always done. He would take the race out in 23 seconds for the first 200 meters, and in 48 seconds for the first 400. There would be several people crazy enough to try to go with him, but they would ultimately pay the price and fade terribly down the homestretch. I would remain in the back until 6- or 700 meters, then pick off all the stragglers. Images of Dave Wottle played through my head. Wottle had won the Olympic gold medal in the men's 800 in 1972 with a thrilling come from behind victory, a feat no American had been able to match since.

As had been the case through most of our time together, Coach Rowland and I were on the exact same page when it came to our race strategy. As I stretched, he told me how he expected the race would unfold. He said exactly what I had been thinking, and then told me how he thought I should run it. "Fella, you're not going to beat Rudisha tonight, and that's okay," he said honestly and bluntly. "Let everyone else try to go with him. You are going to be 24 seconds at the 200 mark, 50 flat at the bell, and 1:16 at 600 meters. If you do that, you will run 1:43 flat tonight and be the Olympic silver medalist."

As he said that, goose bumps spread over my body and a fresh wave of adrenaline hit my system. I believed him. Coach Rowland had seen enough and been at enough races in his life to know what he was talking about. I hugged him and thanked him several times for all he had done to prepare me for this evening. Then I found Coach Sam and did the same. Finally, I headed into the call room.

We eight finalists sat in the tiny room and listened to the roar of the crowd above our heads. Then we changed into spikes and did our best to stay warm and loose in the tiny space. When it was our time to be walked out into the Olympic Stadium we all breathed a sigh of relief. As we paraded out single file, I looked up into the stands and saw eighty thousand people looking back at me.

I closed my eyes and did my best to savor this moment, despite the incredible nervousness I was feeling. Once I had set my backpack down and stripped off my warm-ups I felt better. I was free to run a few quick strides and that movement brought me back to the moment. *You are just running two laps. You have done this thousands of times before.*

This race was going to be more of a time-trial than a tactical affair, and that meant I would be pushing my body as hard as I could from the very start. It was going to hurt very, very badly, but I knew that the pain of the race, the pain and sacrifice of all the years of training would be worth it when I stood on the podium and watched the American flag being raised.

We were called to our starting lines and asked to remain still while we were introduced to the crowd and the several billion people watching this race at home on their televisions. I tried to ignore that last part. I had spoken to Jeff about how to deal with the thought that half the world would be watching me run this race, and he suggested that I just try to look like the guy who is having the most fun out there. Whether I won or lost, if I was the guy having the most fun, then who could say I had failed?

When I heard my name blare over the speakers I raised my hands, waved to the crowd and smiled as wide as I could. To my surprise, I *was* having fun.

My smile vanished when the last name was called. I knew I had only a few seconds before I ran the most important race of my life and I need to get mentally ready. I closed my eyes and took several deep breaths to calm myself.

"On your marks."

We took our starting positions. The loud *bang* of the starter's gun set us free and was followed by a deafening roar from the crowd. I worked hard to get off the starting line, pumping my arms and legs. *Fast but, relaxed.*

As we came off the curve I saw Rudisha working hard to get to the front of the pack. Several people were there with him, trying their best to beat him to the second turn. I was content to run my own pace in the back of the pack, allowing the race to unfold exactly as I expected.

Rudisha hit the 200 meter mark first and his time of 23 mid flashed on the clock. I was 10 meters behind him, bringing up the rear of the pack and hit 24 seconds, just as Coach Rowland had instructed me to do.

Typically, at this point in the race, the pace slows down and the pack bunches up. However, Rudisha knew he needed to distance himself from anyone who might be able to out kick him, so he kept the pace honest. As we came down the homestretch the race continued to string out. I could see Rudisha's time pop up on the clock as he passed through the first lap in a time of 49.28. It was about a half second slower then I had expected him to run, but still well under world-record pace. There were still several people hot on his heels. *None of them can run that pace except Rudisha!* I thought this as I came through in the back of the pack in 50 seconds even.

Just ahead of me, running in the outside of lane one, was my compatriot. Duane Solomon. Seeing him moving well in the pack in his bright red Team USA singlet lit a fire inside me. I accelerated a little to close the gap that had formed between Andrew Osagie and me. I gained a half step, and tucked in on the rail behind Osagie. I wanted to go by him, but we were still moving so fast, and in reality, I was doing everything I could just to maintain contact with the pack.

As we hit the final curve I saw Rudisha start to pull away from the field. He was clearly going to win this race, but had he taken enough kick out of the rest of the field for me to snag the silver? With only 120 meters to go I started to find out.

As we came off the final turn I pulled up even with Osagie and began to kick for the finish line. I looked along lane one and saw a mass of runners all lined up like low hanging fruit. They were losing their form, flailing, trying to reach the finish line as best they could as the lactic acid gripped their muscles.

I put my head down and drove for the finish line as hard as I ever had before. I could see and feel the runners coming back to me. There were only 50 meters left in the race and I wondered if I had enough room to make it all the way up to second place.

I passed Abubaker Kaki of Sudan, who had been the favorite for the silver. In a few more steps I passed Mohammed Aman of Ethiopia, the only person to have beaten Rudisha in the last few years. Clearly, they had gone out to beat Rudisha and were now paying for it. But where was everyone else? Why wasn't everyone else dying a similar death? I kept driving for the line despite my own muscles becoming paralyzed with fatigue.

Duane Solomon was just steps ahead of me and I lunged at the line to try to beat him. I was unable to do so, however. As soon as I crossed the line I collapsed, hands on my knees, trying to breathe and keep from falling to the ground. I had finished in the middle of the pack, my Olympic dreams once again crushed. Not only that, but I had failed to even be the fastest American of the night.

I looked up at the video board and saw that I had finished fifth. I also saw that David Rudisha had just run a new world record. *Shows what I know,* I thought as I recalled that I had told the media a new world record was all but impossible here. I felt my lower lip quivering and was moments away from bursting into tears, when I saw the rest of the field's times come up. In fifth place, it read NICK SYMMONDS with a time of 1:42.95.

*Olympic f*****g Games and they can't even get the times right.* I kept staring at the board waiting for them to correct the time. Ten seconds passed and it remained the same. I walked around to congratulate the other runners, stealing glances at the video board all the while to find out what my actual time had been. When a minute passed and the time remained the same I began to wonder if I had actually broken 1:43, a feat that only one American had ever done before tonight. *Did I seriously just run 1:42.95?* As I watched Rudisha take his victory lap I began to understand the depth and magnitude of what had happened. A world record had just been set. Seven of the eight competitors in the race had just set personal bests. And, two Americans had just joined the sub 1:43 club along with American record holder Johnny Gray.

To give you some idea of the depth of that race, my time of 1:42.95 would have been fast enough to win a medal in every single Olympic Games ever contested except this one, where it was only good enough for fifth. I shook my head with disbelief. It's very difficult for me to describe the range of emotion I felt at that exact moment. The feeling that stands out most in my mind, though, was frustration and concern that despite all I had accomplished I would forever be remembered as a guy who couldn't bring home the hardware.

I was overwhelmed with disappointment, knowing I would have to wait four more years for another run at an Olympic medal and twelve more months for a shot at a World Championship medal. However, I had just taken almost a full second off my personal best for 800 meters. I had brought the best product of my life, at the biggest stage our sport has to offer. Certainly, that was something I could be proud of. I tried to focus on that point as I walked off the track and into the mixed zone, where I was bombarded with questions.

I did my best to talk about my own race, about how it felt to run such a fast time but leave empty handed. To be honest, I was in a state of disbelief at how it had all gone down. I answered the questions as best I could, and then began to walk toward the warm-up track, shaking my head the entire time. *How could this have happened?*

I had hit the splits that Coach Rowland had given me to the tenth of a second. I had even found an extra few hundredths in the final steps, and still it was only good enough for fifth place. When I exited the tunnel that brought me back to the warm-up track I saw Coach Rowland who had the same look of disbelief on his face. I walked up to his outstretch hand and shook it. We stared at each other, both looking like we had just seen a talking dog.

He brought me in for a hug, and said, "I am so proud of you." As he let go of me he said he was honored to be my coach and to have been a part of that historical race. With tears in my eyes I told him I was disappointed, but so grateful to have been part of the race, too. "I never would have been on that starting line without your wisdom and guidance, Coach"

Coach Sam came over with a big smile on his face. He, too, gave me a big hug and said he was proud of me. The three of us walked around the track replaying the race. We all agreed that I had done everything I could to win a medal; it just wasn't in the cards for me that night. Coach Rowland assured me that I had nothing to be ashamed of and that we should enjoy the night, celebrate all that we had accomplished. With that I set off on a cool down and did my best to try to push my feelings of disappointment aside

Try as I might, I was still in a state of shock as Coach Sam and I finally exited the warm-up track. My parents had told Sam where they would be waiting when I was ready to see everyone. As we walked toward the restaurant where they were, I did my best to set my feelings of disappointment aside. There would be plenty of time to deal with those emotions later, but right now I wanted to enjoy some time with my family and friends who had traveled all the way to London to support me. When we got to the restaurant I was led upstairs to a loft, where I found close to thirty of the people I love most in this world waiting for me.

As soon as I got there everyone jumped up and applauded. I blushed, and first walked to my mom to give her a hug. I then hugged Lauren and my dad, and made the rounds as I greeted everyone and thanked them for being there. We spent the next few hours catching up, drinking beer, taking pictures, and laughing. Later that evening I looked around and realized that even without a medal I was one of the most fortunate people on planet earth.

The party spilled out of the restaurant and into the casino that had been set up adjacent to the athlete's village. We kept the party rolling with champagne and gambling until sunrise, at which point I said good-bye and walked back to my room. I quickly passed out and slept away most of the next day.

When I woke up I felt tired, achy, and overwhelmed by disappointment. But, I rounded up a few friends and went to dinner. They had all finished competing as well, and we started talking about possible parties we could attend that night. One of my good friends and teammates at OTCE was an Irish lad by the name of Ciarán O'Lionáird. He told me that a professional Irish soccer player had rented out the VIP lounge of a club in Leister Square. The footballer was a friend of his and Ciarán thought he could get me in.

That sounded exactly like the kind of party I needed to take my mind off the disappointment I felt. We all got ready for the night and started walking to the Underground station located just outside the village. As we walked, I got a text from a friend who asked what my plans were. This wasn't just any friend, though, this was a beautiful new Swiss friend I had met a few weeks earlier at the Monaco Diamond League meeting. Her name was Rachel. She worked for the IAAF, and she and I had conversed throughout the Games. Now that the business side of the trip was over I was free to meet up with her. I texted the address of the club to her, and added that I really hoped she would join me there.

As soon as Ciarán and I walked into the club we were led to a private VIP lounge that was overflowing with athletes and liquor. On each table were giant bottles of vodka next to ice buckets full of various juices and energy drinks. I made a strong Red Bull and vodka, and drank it in a matter of seconds. I then had another. Between drinks I checked my phone for a message from Rachel. The alcohol and lack of communication from her were rapidly depressing me. Finally, a text came with the information that Rachel was outside the club. I excused myself from the group and went to bring Rachel and one of her friends in. The bouncer had not wanted to let them in, so I looked at him and said with a cocky American smile, "Don't worry, they're with me."

"So?" That was the extent of his response. I frowned, and realized that the "they are with me" line was probably never going to work for me.

I quickly gave the bouncer the name of the soccer player instead. That worked much better and I was soon escorting the girls back to the VIP lounge.

Rachel and I danced until staff at the club told us it was time to get out. I took her hand and led her out into the busy London streets. We walked for a bit and then caught a cab back to the apartment she was staying in for the duration of the Games. I escorted her upstairs and spent the rest of the night with her. When I awoke the next morning I propped myself up on my elbow and admired the beautiful girl sleeping next to me. I moved close to wrap my body around hers and as she leaned into me I could feel some of the disappointment from my Olympic Games experiences melt away.

That incredible night ended my Olympic Games dry streak, though I still have yet to hook up in the actual athletes village. I am convinced, however, that there is not actually that much sex taking place in the village. The layout and logistics simply don't allow for it!

There was a rumor started during the 2004 Olympic Games that athletes were hooking up like rabbits. Apparently, a bowl of several thousand condoms had been set out somewhere in that Olympic Village. The condoms disappeared within hours, which led the media to speculate on the wild times that must be going on behind the fences of the athlete village.

Once, at dinner with some veterans who had been a part of those Games, I asked the table about the rumors. One of New Zealand's greatest runners ever let out a loud laugh as soon as I brought it up. He confessed that he and several friends had emptied the bowl of condoms into their backpacks, simply to get people talking.

18

The next morning I returned to the athlete village from my night out in London. There were only a few hours left in the 2012 Olympic Games and I spent most of them sleeping, eating, or enjoying the view from my balcony. As I sat on the balcony and felt the warm afternoon breeze blow through the village I wondered what the rest of the 2012 season had in store for me. I certainly didn't feel like racing anymore that year.

However, I was in the shape of my life and felt I might as well make some use of that. My mind drifted to other athletic challenges that I had fantasized about tackling: climbing mountains, biking across America, etcetera. But given my race fitness, and my desire to drink more beer, nothing seemed quite as appropriate as the beer mile.

Every year, at universities throughout the United States, incredibly fit and thirsty athletes sneak onto their school's tracks to compete in something known as the beer mile. This event is a time-honored tradition among distance runners. It requires each competitor to chug a beer, and then run a lap of a full sized track. Each competitor does this four times for a total of one mile—and forty-eight ounces of beer. Official rules dictate that each runner must drink the beer from an unmodified can or bottle, and that the beer must be 5.0 percent alcohol or higher. Throwing up is not allowed, and usually results in a lap penalty or disqualification.

In college I was able to run a beer mile in 5:31. Now, that mark, according to BeerMile.com, was an American record that still stood. Though the amount of beer I consumed weekly had gone down significantly since college, so had my personal best in the mile. At the end of each professional season, I found myself wondering what I could run a beer mile in now, considering I was a professional athlete. Could I improve on my American record, or could I possibly even run a new world record? Was a crack of the elusive five-minute mark out of the realm of possibility?

The current world record was held by an Australian who claimed to have run 5:09. I had eyed this record for some time and felt that the end of the 2012 season was the perfect time to break it. I had discussed the possibility of running a very public beer mile with my agent for years, but he always cautioned me against it, for fear it might upset my fans, or worse, my sponsors. I had always listened to him.

However, as I sat on that balcony in the Olympic village I felt that the time to run one had finally come. I had just devoted four years of my life to running well at the London Games. I had set a huge personal best in the final and represented my country well. Surely, after four years of hard work and sacrifice, people would understand my need to have a little fun.

The marketing gears in my mind began to turn and I started composing an email to seek corporate support. I sent the email to many breweries, but only heard back from one, Pabst Brewing Company. It seemed very fitting that the blue ribbon of beer would be interested in supporting an athlete in a race for a record. The email I sent them went as follows:

Hello,

My name is Nick Symmonds. I am writing this from the Olympic Park in London where I recently competed for the United States of America in the 800m. I finished fifth in the world record-setting race. Though I did not win a medal, I have my sights set on another goal that I am 100 percent sure I can achieve: The world record in the beer mile. If you are not familiar with this event a very quick summary is that the runner drinks four beers and runs four laps of the track as quickly as possible. I am currently the American record holder in this event. I set this time seven years ago and am sure *that I can beat the world record of 5:09.*

The reason I am writing is because I will make my world record attempt as soon as I get back to the states. I am wondering if Pabst would be interested in being a part of this world record run. What I propose is that I will drink your product in the race. I will also mention prior to the event that I would only *choose Pabst for an event like this, as it is the finest beer in the world.*

I have a marketing team and a publicist that will assist me in making sure this video goes viral once it is posted to YouTube.

To be the official partner of this world record run I ask that we enter into a contract where I am paid a few pennies for each view on YouTube. If this is something your company would be interested in, please contact me via email. Thank you so much for your time.
Nick Symmonds
nicksymmonds.com
@nicksymmonds

Within several days I had a response.

Nick,
Thanks for reaching out. This could be a lot of fun and certainly warrants more of a discussion. Are you free for a call on Wednesday or Thursday?
Best,
John

I thanked John for getting back to me and we set out to find a time when we could chat. Unfortunately, not long after, I received this email from John:

Nick,

I had a long conversation with legal about supporting the mile. Unfortu-
nately there are too many issues—primarily promoting excessive drink-
ing—that we have to deal with for it to make sense. We do wish you the
best of luck in breaking the world record!
Best,
John

Millions of people drink four or more beers on a regular basis, but
I understood why the people at Pabst were hesitant. Free from legal con-
straints, I decided to go it alone and enjoy the freedom that comes with
not being obliged to work with a corporate marketing team. I enjoyed my
last few hours in London and then hopped on a flight home. My world
record attempt would take place, in Track Town, USA.

Sitting in my kitchen with my roommate at the time, Steve Finely, I started
chugging beers while he timed me. I knew from years past that it was almost impossible to pour a beer out of an unmodified wide mouth can or
bottle faster than eight seconds, so this was the time I aimed for. I found
that I could drink a full beer in eight seconds pretty easily, but putting four
back to back was extremely difficult.

While I knew I wasn't going to have corporate support for this world
record attempt, I set about making sure that my brand got as much out
of it as possible. I took the idea to a friend who happened to work at
TMZ, the celebrity gossip and entertainment news source in Los Angeles.
I asked my friend if she was interested in covering a story like this. "If
you film it and give us exclusive access to the content," she said, "then yes,
we would be very interested." It seemed like all of the pieces were coming
into place. Now all I had to do was keep training. I cracked another beer.

I decided to make the attempt later that week. I called my agent and
explained that I was going to run a beer mile, and that I would film it and

put it on the Internet. Chris said it was probably the best time for me to do it, if I was ever going to get away with it. He also wanted to know what I was going to wear for the attempt. I decided to leave that up to my apparel sponsor, Nike, and sent the following email to the representative I worked most closely with:

> *Hi Buddy!*
> *How are you man? Are you still in Europe or back in OR? I am back in Eugene and preparing for my final event of the season. I'm taking a run at the world record in the beer mile later this week. Kind of a fun way to end the season and as the American record holder in this event I think I would be doing my country a disservice if I didn't try to bring the world record back to America! Out of respect for my partnership with Nike I want to first ask what Nike would like me to wear for this attempt. Official WR is 5:09...I think I can go sub 5!*
> *Nick*

I waited several days to hear back from him, but received nothing. Operating on the idea that no answer was a sure sign of support, I decided to run the race in a plain cut-off, dry-fit top and half tights that Nike manufactured.

On a gorgeous Oregon afternoon, my roommate Steve and I sent out a few texts alerting our friends in town what was going down and asking them to come out and support us. I went to the fridge, grabbed four Coors Original and threw them into my backpack along with my Nike Victory Elite spikes. I had considered drinking PBR as a thank you to Pabst for at least responding to my emails, but ultimately went with Coors as I am, at heart, still a boy from the Rocky Mountains.

Steve and I rolled up to South Eugene High School with a few friends, but there was a peewee football practice taking place on the infield. I was sure it was unwise to binge drink near a group of eight year olds, so we changed the venue to a nearby track at Lane Community College.

Once there, we filmed a quick "don't-try-this-at-home" intro for our film. "I'm twenty eight. Don't do this if you're not twenty-one. I've got a designated driver . . . so have fun, be safe. Beer mile; a fun way to end the season," I said as I smiled into the camera. With that in the can I threw my backpack over my shoulders and set off on a jog down to the track. Immediately, I regretted my decision to do so. Even though I had jogged to a track hundreds of times before, I had never done so with four beers in my backpack. I suddenly realized I had just shaken the hell out of my race brews. As if taking four fragile eggs out of my bag, I removed them one by one and set them to settle on a shady part of the track while I continued my warm up.

By the time I was good and warm, close to fifty people were on the track to cheer me on. I set the stage, alerting them to what the current world and American records were. I then walked to the starting line where Steve was waiting. He was going to be the official timer for the event. I reached down and grabbed one of the beers. With a loud crack, I opened the first one and Steve started the stopwatch.

Despite the fact that the beer was warm and heavy on the foam, I gulped it down in eight seconds, tossed the empty can aside, and took off.

Chugging beer is hard and running is hard, and doing the two together is almost impossible. Most people assume the alcohol is what makes the beer mile so challenging. However, the beer is not in one's stomach long enough for a runner to experience any effect from the alcohol. What stops a runner in their tracks is the volume and, to an even greater extent, the carbonation. With each successive beer there is less room in the stomach for the beer to go. An ever-increasing amount of time in the exchange zone is spent chugging, burping, and trying to breathe. One ends up looking something like a pug dog being water-boarded.

Once the beer has been consumed, the athlete can start running again, but the first 100 meters are typically at a jog as one tries to burp out as much of the carbonation as possible. Running only furthers the problem, as it shakes up beer that is in an already aching gut. I have run hundreds, if not thousands of races and can honestly say that none are as uniquely painful as the beer mile.

Though my first beer and lap were fantastic, the pace and volume got to me quickly. By the fourth beer I knew the world record was unlikely to fall, but pressed on in hopes of improving my American record. I took off on the last lap not completely sure I would be able to finish, but managed to close that last lap in 57 seconds. My final time of 5:19 was far from my goal of 4:59, but it was a major improvement on my personal best, and brought me within ten seconds of the current world record.

I stumbled across the infield doing everything I could to keep from throwing up. One friend ran over with the camera and asked, "How you feeling man?" Gasping for air I responded, "I feel tired, I feel full of beer. Not inebriated by any means yet, but 5:19 is a good first mark. I've got some training to do." Though I was disappointed in the attempt, I learned a lot from it and knew where I could improve.

I managed to keep the beers down, and found the adrenaline in my system kept me pretty sharp at first. However, as it wore off and the alcohol flooded into my system, I went from sober to drunk in a matter of minutes. As my words began to slur together, I thanked everyone for coming and asked them to join me for burgers at a local restaurant.

The reception from the public to the video was outstanding. True to her word, my friend at TMZ pushed the video out via their media channels and my video soon had more than 87,000 views. To give a perspective, the most watched video of my 2012 win at the Olympic Trials had around eighty thousand views. The public had shown that they would rather watch me stumble around a track getting drunk than make an Olympic team.

Another plus was that my following on Twitter shot up another few thousand, and I was asked to talk about the race in various interviews. My agent even received the following email from the Oregon Sales Manager at Coors:

> *Be glad to hook Nick up with some cases of rocky mountain legend - Coors Banquet!*

The free beer and publicity made the event totally worthwhile—as did the response I got from my fans. I became known as the beer miler, and not a week went by when I wasn't asked by a college team to join them for their beer mile at the end of the season.

The take away I gained from the experience is that running needs to be fun, and it needs to be relatable. If I told someone I ran a mile in 5:19 they probably wouldn't care at all. Heck, if I told them I've run a mile in 3:56 I doubt they would care much. However, when I tell someone I drank four beers in 5:19 they are impressed. When I tell them I ran a mile while doing so they stare at me in disbelief, until I direct them to the YouTube video.

In a society that doesn't really appreciate the subtle nuances of distance running, we must do a better job at giving the average fan something they can relate to and enjoy. I have argued for years that the way we force feed our boring track meets to fans is not working. The loss of sponsors and lower ticket sales is proof of this. While I am not necessarily suggesting we add the beer mile to professional track and field meetings, there do need to be some changes. I have argued for shorter meets where alcohol and betting are allowed on site. These are not original ideas, but things European meet directors have been doing for decades—with much success.

The beer mile also allowed me to connect with fans that I wouldn't normally have connected with. As a sport, those responsible for the future of track and field need to be more concerned with connecting with the average fan and growing the sport tomorrow. Unfortunately, what I too often have witnessed from the USATF and IAAF are people who are more concerned with how they are going to pad their own pockets today, than how they can bring the product of professional track and field into tomorrow.

19

The beer mile, though quite painful, had been a fun way for me to say goodbye to the 2012 season. I took a few more weeks off after it and went on vacation to visit friends. Several dozen more beers and fish later I was starting to get over the pain of not medaling in London. It still stung whenever I thought about the fact that my time would have won an Olympic medal in every other Olympic Games, but I tried to remind myself that I was quite fortunate just to have been a part of that race, to have been a part of history.

One sunny fall morning in October I woke up and looked out my window at the Willamette River Valley. The air was crisp and the leaves were just starting to change color. I recalled a time when these things signaled the start of cross-country season, but those days were far behind me. Now when I smelled winter in the air it made me think of base training.

I went down to my basement where dozens of boxes of Nike gear had accumulated over the years and dug around until I found a new pair of my favorite trainers. Taking them out of the box I held one up to my nose and breathed deeply, smelling that sweet new shoe aroma. I took my time lacing them up and then jogged a few steps in place to see how they fit. The shoes felt amazing, but my body felt heavy and flat. I knew it would be a long road back to being race ready, but I had time to prepare.

I set out onto Pre's trail, the six mile bark chip loop that runs through Eugene, to log my first four miles of the 2013 season. As I clicked off those first slow, painful miles, I reminded myself that often there is a slight pull back in the times being run after an Olympic year. Perhaps people are tired, perhaps they are injured, or perhaps they are coming off of their drug cycle, I don't know. But whatever it was, the year following an Olympic Games can be full of surprises. I kept this thought in the back of my head the entire fall as I logged mile after mile.

As the weather turned from crisp to damn cold, I made the decision to once again fly south for the winter. A good friend, 2012 Olympic 1500 meter silver medalist, Leo Manzano, had told me about a city in central Mexico that he liked to train at called San Luis Potosi. This industrial city located at an elevation of six thousand feet has a topnotch training center called La Loma Centro Deportivo. Some of the world's best endurance athletes, including swimmer Michael Phelps, have called La Loma home at some point in their career. I was excited to see what this city had to offer, and to continue to work on my Spanish.

I booked a five-week stay at an apartment near La Loma with Leo and his training partner, Duncan Phillips. This brought me back to my favorite type of training, in the mountains, distraction free. For several weeks I pushed the training hard, and spent all of my non-running hours eating tacos and studying Spanish.

The trip to San Luis Potosi primed my system for the hard spring training that was to come. I returned to Eugene feeling fit and was able to crush my workouts. I set off for altitude again in March, this time to Flagstaff, Arizona for a month at seven thousand feet. Never before had I doubled down on my time at altitude and I was excited to see how my body benefited from it.

The hundreds of miles I had logged, and all the red blood cells I accumulated at altitude, had left my body strong and lean, but not particularly explosive. To race the 800 the right way an athlete needs to have a perfect combination of speed and strength. Although I was as strong as ever, I lacked a lot of the speed work and approached Coach Rowland with my concern.

I told him I was nervous that I wouldn't be ready to defend my national title at the USATF Championships in June. In his wise, heavily accented voice, he replied, "You may not win USA's this year, but you will make the team and will go on to win a medal at Worlds in August."

I was the five-time defending USATF Champion at 800 meters and the thought of not defending my title killed me. I thought back to how well Coach Rowland had prepared me for the London Games, and knew he was right. I decided not to question his plan and once again put my faith in him.

The USA Championships were held in Des Moines, Iowa that year and very few of us on the Oregon Track Club Elite were excited about racing there. In my experience, Des Moines in the summer is hot and humid, and the city struggles to fill Drake Stadium. The fans that do make it out are enthusiastic, however, and I wanted to impress them with my sixth straight win.

Once there, I found that my old rival, Duane Solomon, was intent on stopping me. We both advanced through the rounds easily and met on a hot, Sunday afternoon to see who would be the new champion. As always, Duane took the lead early on and set a very fast pace.

I found myself in the back of the pack after 200 meters. As the pace slowed I desperately wanted to move up, but was boxed in. I held back and tried to be patient. With only 300 meters to go I finally managed to break free and strode out to chase Duane down. I made up much ground going from eighth to second place in only a few strides. However, it was too little too late. Duane threw up his arms as he crossed the line in first, and I was only a stride or two behind him in second. Just behind me was hurdler turned half-miler, Brandon Johnson, who finished third to make his first world championship team.

I congratulated them both and then looked at the scoreboard to see the times. Duane had run a world leading 1:43.27 to beat me. My time of

1:43.70 was my second fastest time ever. Brandon had run a huge personal best, too, of 1:43.97. I was shocked that it had taken a sub 1:44 performance to make the USA Team. It was a testament to how far we had come as a country in this event in just a few short years.

We received our medals and then headed for the mixed zone to speak with reporters. I swallowed my pride and congratulated Duane. To minimize the emotional pain I felt I told the reporters what Coach Rowland had said about possibly losing USA's so as to be ready to win a medal at the world championships six weeks later. As I said it I realized I was placing a great deal of pressure on both Coach Rowland and me to perform, but knew that we both responded well to pressure.

On the other side of the mixed zone I found Coach Sam and Coach Rowland, and we discussed how the race unfolded and where I had made mistakes. Happy that I was on the team and headed to Moscow, we gathered up the rest of the Oregon Track Club Elite and went out for burgers and beers.

As the summer season continued it seemed that Coach Rowland's prediction was becoming more possible. From Des Moines I flew to Edmonton, Canada where I beat Duane for the win. I then beat him again at the London Diamond League meeting, the final stop before the world championships. As Coach Rowland, Coach Sam, and I boarded the plane from London to Moscow there was a new sense of excitement that we had never felt before going to a World Championship.

In previous years I had been ranked in the top ten going into Worlds, but never higher than fifth or sixth. This time I was in the top three. Duane still had the world leading time, but I had defeated him in our last two meetings. Mohammed Aman of Ethiopia, rounded out the top three and was (to some) the favorite, as he had not lost an outdoor race this year. I stepped onto the plane knowing if I failed to medal in Moscow, I would probably never win a world championship medal at all.

We touched down in Moscow later that afternoon and watched the sun set over a dense Russian forest as we rode into town. I was reminded of the time I visited here during my first season overseas, back in 2006. I smiled as I thought of those days when I had come to Moscow from Spain, after two weeks of living in a hostel and getting drunk every night. I had come a long way in seven short years.

I looked down at my body and recognized how much it had changed, too. Even though I did very well in collegiate sports, I had come out of college overweight and rather unathletic. The years of hard work by Coach Frank Gagliano, Coach Mark Rowland, and Coach Jimmy Radcliffe had transformed my body into an oval-running machine. I could feel each sinewy muscle of my legs and shook my head at the thought of the thousands of miles I had logged to make them that way. *Don't waste this opportunity,* I said over and over again.

We settled into our hotel and tried to get some rest. I was pleasantly surprised to find that USATF had given me a room to myself. Typically, only defending medalists get this luxury, but due to a mix up there had been an extra single occupancy room and someone made the call to give it to me. When they told me this I joked that perhaps they had pre-emptively given me the room because they were so confident that I would finally make the podium.

Though I do view USATF to be incompetent as an organization, I would be remiss if I didn't mention that there are some amazing and competent individuals who work there. Many of these hard working men and women have helped me immensely at various world championships, and for that I will always be grateful.

That first night I unloaded my suitcase, took a hot shower and, tired from the travel, settled into bed. I called my parents and my sister, who were back in the States packing their bags. They did *not* want to miss this race. The second night, however, I felt anxious and nervous and needed something, or rather, someone, to take my mind off the competition that would begin in a few short days.

My Swiss friend, Rachel, and I had stayed in touch after the London Games. We had reconnected a few weeks earlier at the Monaco Diamond

League meeting and she mentioned that she would be in Moscow for the world championships, working for the IAAF.

As I got ready for bed, I thought about how badly I wanted to see her. I wanted to talk to her about topics other than running and hear her beautiful accent. I sent her a text asking if she was in town yet. She responded that she had just arrived and was staying at a hotel that was located across the Moskva River from the hotel where I was. I sent her a few flirtatious messages, then asked if she wanted to come over. She accepted and met me in the lobby a few minutes later.

This meet was to be held in Luzhniki Stadium in Moscow's Olympic Park. It had been constructed for the 1980 Olympic Games, the Games that the United States boycotted. Although I had raced here before, it had been on one of the park's practice tracks rather than in the actual Olympic stadium. When I entered the marvelous arena for the first time it gave me chills.

I had raced on many tracks around the world, including several Olympic stadiums, but something about this one felt special. Perhaps it was the history that this stadium represented. I had personally met athletes who had made the 1980 US Olympic Team and were forced to sit at home and watch the Games play out on television as President Carter thumbed his nose at the Soviet Union. I was grateful to be here and grateful that Team USA had not boycotted these world championships, as many people suggested we should do.

I understood why many wanted a boycott, as Russian President Vladimir Putin had recently signed into law legislation that tread on the rights of its citizens, and made it illegal to spread what they called "gay propaganda." According to Putin, the rules were put in place to protect the children of Russia. The "anti-gay propaganda" laws, as international media now called them, made it illegal to publicly demonstrate or talk about being gay. Something as simple as waving a rainbow flag could get the flag holder put in prison. Needless to say, gay marriage was not up for discussion in Putin's Russia.

I had been a big supporter of equal rights for the lesbian gay bisexual transgender (LGBT) community for many years. This was not due to a close family member coming out as gay, or personally witnessing a friend being beaten for his or her sexual orientation. Rather, it was because I truly believe that sexual orientation lies on a spectrum, and that some humans are born with an attraction to the same sex. To discriminate against a group of people for the way they were born is just plain wrong.

My support publicly began when I heard that the Boy Scouts of America (BSA) were discriminating against openly gay troops and leaders. As an Eagle Scout from Boise's Troop 94, I was embarrassed and angered by the BSA's stance. I remembered my days as a youth working hard on my Citizenship in the Community merit badge and did not recall the practice of bigotry being part of the requirements. I posted a tweet to the Boy Scouts of America that let them know I would not support them until they did away with their discriminatory practices.

My tweet received a small amount of media attention, as athletes do not typically speak out with regard to political issues. I don't know whether that's because many athletes are afraid of offending fans or sponsors, but being politically active is not common among professional athletes. Although I have many political opinions, I had, for the most part, kept them to myself during the course of my career. Gay equality, however, was an issue I simply could not remain silent about.

A gay couple in California felt the same way and began a form of political protest called the NOH8 campaign. NOH8 is a creative way to spell "no hate." This movement was simple, yet powerful. It involved photographer Adam Bouska taking photos of celebrities with their mouths taped shut with duct tape. The tape silencing the individual represented the way the state of California, and the passing of State Proposition Eight, trod on the rights of gay couples to wed. Prop 8 was an initiative that passed in 2008 and banned same-sex marriage in the state of California.

A member of the NOH8 campaign learned of my support for equality and asked if I would come in and shoot a picture. It just so happened that I was scheduled to be in LA for a few weeks and was able to go to their Hollywood studio. The picture turned out quite well, and was posted on their website along with a quote I had given them: "It is an honor to be a part of the NOH8 Campaign. This civil rights issue will be the defining legal movement of our generation. To deny someone the rights afforded to others based on their gender or sexual orientation defies logic and is completely un-American."

My public support of gay rights in America had generated a fairly large fan base of gay men and women. As I prepared for my trip to Russia, some asked that I boycott the world championships in protest. Others asked me what, once I was actually in Russia, I would do to protest the anti-gay laws there. I was torn. I fiercely opposed the laws, but also knew I had a job to do.

After much deliberation I wrote a column for RunnersWorld.com where I denounced the Russian laws, but said that out of respect for the host nation I would stay quiet and focus on my reason for being there, which was to win a medal for my country. Many felt I took the easy way out and said that my silence was cowardly. I understood their position, but I also had a duty to my country to run to the best of my ability. I had worked for seven years to finally be a favorite for a medal, and placing well in Moscow had to be my number one priority.

As I entered the stadium for my first race I put political issues out of my mind and focused on getting to the finals. I won both my preliminary and semi-final races, which accomplished that goal. The eight men who would tow the line to race for the three available medals were the fastest men in the world. I was honored to be part of the field.

What was even more exciting was the fact that of all eight finalists, none had ever won a world or Olympic medal. The top three finishers would all be medaling for the very first time. Many said that it was going to be one of the most exciting finals of the entire championships, due to the fact that there was no clear favorite.

I kept this in mind as I prepared for the race. The sun had just started to set, but the evening was still warm as I ran laps around the warm up track. As usual, my legs felt better with each consecutive round. On this night, the night of the finals, I found myself feeling light and bouncy. I went through my warm up routine nervous, but confident. Coach Rowland and Coach Sam were both by my side, making sure my drills were done correctly, and offering words of encouragement and wisdom. When the call room announced it was time to head to the stadium I gave them both a hug goodbye.

The van that took us on the two-minute drive from the practice track to the stadium was small and smelled of sweat. I took my seat trying not to make eye contact with my competitors. Instead, remained focused on myself and what I needed to do to finally win a medal. The eight of us sat in silence as we crossed the park.

In the final call room I was able to put on my spikes and uniform and do some last-minute drills and stretches. With ten minutes to go before race time we were walked out onto the track. The stadium was nearly full, and the crowd of roughly seventy thousand people had started to get rowdy. This race had been highly anticipated and I could feel the energy in the air.

I ran a few strides and stripped off my warm-ups. My heart pounded in my chest and in my mind I repeated words that I had already said a thousand times that day: *don't waste this opportunity.*

We were called to the starting line and set free with a *bang* I had heard so many times before. This was my third World Championships final and I knew from experience how the first quarter of the race would unfold. There were several sprinters in the race, including Duane, and I knew they would all fight for the lead going into the second turn. As expected, they flew down the backstretch challenging each other for position while I brought up the rear, conserving energy.

Duane, adamant about leading, ran his first 200 meters in 23.53 to beat everyone to the curve. He had close to 10 meters on me, and I came through the first quarter of the race almost a full second behind him. I thought back to the 2008 Olympic Trials when Khadevis Robinson went out too hard and had saved little for his final sprint.

As we entered the home stretch for the first time the pace slowed and the pack began to bunch. I wanted to conserve my momentum, so I moved to the outside of lane two and began to move up. I was not accelerating, just maintaining my speed.

As we neared the end of the first lap I knew that with a tiny surge I could be up on Duane's shoulder. I dug down and quickened my stride for a few steps. I neared the lead, running even with Duane as we came through the first lap nearly tied.

The bell rang loudly in my left ear signaling the final lap and I glanced out of the corner of my eye to see that we had split 50.28 for our first lap. I knew that of all eight competitors I had run the most evenly paced first lap. Doing so had sapped very little of my strength and I glided along easily in the outside of lane one.

I heard Duane's labored breathing as we ran in sync down the backstretch, and felt fairly certain that I would be able to out kick him. I honestly hoped, however, that he would hang on for a medal. There was some jostling as we entered the final turn, but unlike Deagu, where I was bumped and shoved every step of the final 200 meters, now I was close enough to the front that I was able to run unimpeded.

We entered the home stretch and I thought of Coach Gags yelling "*flip the switch!*" at the 2008 Olympic Trials. I closed my eyes and dug deep, lifting my legs in a full sprint as Coach Radcliffe had taught me.

When I opened my eyes I saw that I was beginning to pull away from Duane and the rest of the field. I was rapidly burning through my kick, but was now a full stride ahead of the nearest competitor. The finish line was getting closer and closer and with only 50 meters to go I was almost certain I would be the next world champion. I struggled to maintain form as the lactic acid gripped my legs.

With everything I had, I urged myself to the finish line. As I did, I felt someone closing in on me. Out of the corner of my eye I saw a green jersey and knew it was Mohammed Aman of Ethiopia. For a moment we ran shoulder to shoulder and then, in the final 20 meters, he pulled away and I knew there was nothing I could do, he would win the race. I made a quick glance around me and lunged for the finish line.

I knew I had finished second. I threw up a fist, and grimaced at the same time. The feeling was so very bittersweet. On one hand I had finally won my medal, cementing my place in history as one of America's greatest half milers. On the other, I had come within inches of being world champion and might never have another chance to become one. As emotion flooded over me I heard my mother's voice in my head. "Win or lose, be the first person to shake everyone's hand."

I walked over to the new world champion and did just that. I then walked to the rest of the field and congratulated them. When I found Duane I gave him a hug and asked him how he finished. His response, sixth, hurt to hear. Though we were competitors and it damn near killed me every time he beat me, I had twice before finished sixth at a world championship and knew the frustration he was feeling.

I told him that he would learn from this race and go on to do incredible things. He, in turn, said he was glad one of us was going home with a medal. Through almost two decades of racing, I'm not sure I have met a classier competitor than Duane Solomon.

I patted him on the back, then jogged over to meet a representative of USATF who handed me an American flag. This was my sixth outdoor global championship meet, my fourth final, and now, instead of walking off the track with my head hung low, I was finally going to find out what it felt like to run a victory lap wrapped in the American flag.

I loved every moment of it, and stopped every few steps to pose for photographers. I looked into the stands and saw my family waving and blowing kisses. Tears streamed down the faces of my mom and sister. I desperately wanted to run up to hug them, but it was impossible, given the way the stadium was laid out. I waved and blew a kiss back, and continued around the track.

At the 200 meter mark I found Coach Rowland, Coach Sam, and Chris Layne who had all somehow managed to sneak their way down to the track. I was so grateful to have these men in my life. The "Symmonds Money Team," as Coach Sam called us, had finally earned our medal. I gave each of them a hug and told them I loved them. We posed for a few pictures and then I was asked to continue around the track.

When the victory lap was completed we three medalists were ushered into the mixed zone where we were mobbed by reporters. I spoke with media outlets from around the world discussing the way the race played out, and how it felt to finally have a medal.

One reporter from a local Russian paper asked me a very interesting question. He said he had read that I would remain silent about Russia's anti-gay propaganda laws as I worked toward winning a medal for my country, but asked that now that my job was completed, would I care to say something.

"As much as I can speak out about it," I said, "I believe that all humans deserve equality as however God made them. Whether you're gay, straight, black, white, we all deserve the same rights. If there is anything I can do to champion the cause and further it, I will, shy of getting arrested." I then dedicated my silver medal to my gay and lesbian friends, and thanked the Russian reporter for the interview.

I continued through the mixed zone, stopping to chat with reporters I had known since I first began my professional career. Everyone was thrilled for me, and excited for the tone that this race would set for the other American middle distance runners who were still to compete. I was taken to a press conference, and then to a room for drug testing. Just as with the Olympic Trials and USATF Championships, all medalists are tested for performance enhancing drugs. All I wanted to do was leave the stadium and find my family, but first I was required to provide 90 ml of urine. Thirty minutes and five bottles of water later I was a free man.

Still in my tights and singlet, I slung my backpack over my shoulders and ran outside. The meet had ended long ago and outside it was very quiet. I wanted to call my coaches and family, to let them know I was ready, then remembered that my phone did not work in Russia. Instead, I walked the half-mile to the practice track. Once there, I took a lap hoping to find Coach Sam or Coach Rowland. It was almost surreal how quiet it was on the track. The lights had been turned off and no one else was around. I looked up at the starry night sky and laughed. *So this is what happens after you win a medal?*

I had been through this process enough to know that I would eventually find my family and coaches and so, took the opportunity to walk a leisurely lap around the familiar oval. I knew my goal-oriented mind would brush this accomplishment aside soon, to make room for newer, loftier goals, but for just a moment I allowed myself to savor the feeling of having accomplished one of the hardest challenges I had ever set for myself.

When the lap was completed I caught one of the buses back to my hotel. As I boarded the bus I found Coach Rowland, Coach Sam and Chris Layne sitting together waiting for me. Together, we laughed and replayed every step of the race. They told me how they felt watching it and I told them how I felt racing it. So many times before we had shared this post race moment together, usually drowning our sorrows with burgers and beers. Tonight we would celebrate! With what else? Burgers and beers.

My family was waiting for us at the hotel when our bus pulled up. They ran up and hugged me; tears were still streaming down my mother's face. Inside we pulled up a table near the bar and sat down to appreciate the moment together. As I looked at my beloved family and my wonderful track family all together at one table, I felt truly fortunate.

The first round of drinks came and went. At one point a celebrating member of the USATF board headed to our table with a shot in hand. Without introduction the board member said, "I told everyone that I was going to take a shot for each medal that Team USA won here in Moscow. So this is for you Nick." With that, the fiery liquid was quickly downed. "And that, ladies and gentlemen," I said, "is the USATF for you!"

Our party lasted until well after midnight, when my parents called it a night. We said our goodbyes and went to get a few hours of rest. Sam and I went up to my hotel room where we again replayed the events of the evening. He tried to get a bit of shut-eye, but I knew there was no way I could sleep. Adrenaline was still pumping through my system. I sat down at my computer and began to answer the hundreds of emails, texts, and tweets that I had received. My loyal friends and fans knew how hard I had worked for this medal and were very generous with their kind words.

Around six A.M. I tore myself away from my computer to peek out the window. The sun was just starting to rise and I found myself famished, so I went downstairs and enjoyed the sweetest bacon and eggs I had ever tasted.

The next few days were a whirlwind of interviews, appearances, and meetings. Coach and I discussed taking a few days off to let my body recover and to deal with all the interview demands. Coach Sam stayed in Moscow with me so we could take in a few races and enjoy a bit of vacation. Most of the interviews I did were centered around the dedication I had made to my gay and lesbian friends. Apparently, I was the first athlete to openly denounce the new laws on Russian soil. With the 2014 winter Olympics set to take place in Sochi just a few months away, everyone was interested to see how the Russian government might respond.

My agent and publicist were inundated with interview requests and we managed them as best we could. The ultimate highlight was when I returned to the United States, to New York City, to tape the CNN program *AC360 with Anderson Cooper*. It was a true pleasure to meet such an accomplished reporter and, as expected, his questions were well thought out and thought provoking. Mr. Cooper was kind enough to give me a tour of the CNN studios and answer all of my questions about broadcasting and television.

I left New York to return to Oregon where I placed my precious silver medal in my safe. I lay back on my bed and looked out the window at the Willamette Valley. The summer of 2013 had been a summer full of adventures. In just a few short months I'd had more success and made more money than I ever thought I would in my entire running career. I thought about all the wild things I could do with the cash that was about to flow into my bank account as part of my medal victory: exotic travel, fancy clothes, and much more. I didn't need any of it. I had just spent the summer traveling through Europe, and had more free Nike gear than I knew what to do with. I was living my dream and all that was missing was a cold beer and my fishing rod. So, I loaded up my pickup truck and headed for the river.

20

Today, when I meet someone for the first time, the conversation in-
variably turns to what I do for a living. When I first turned pro I responded
with a grin and said, "I am a professional runner." That often led to quizzi-
cal looks and something to the effect of, "That's an actual job?" I soon
realized that "professional runner" left people to assume I was a broke
kid just out of college, living with my parents. They weren't too far off as,
unfortunately, many of us are!

As I got tired of explaining how running in circles could in fact earn
one a living I began to experiment with different responses. Sometimes I
said I was self-employed. While true, this is what drug dealers say as well.
Occasionally, I replied, "I'm on the US Olympic Team." Again, true, but
I always felt this came off as rather arrogant. More often than not I now
reply, "I'm in marketing," for this truly is what I do for a living.

Many people might say I make my living running, but I don't think
I have ever been paid to run. Rather, I make my living marketing products.
Professional athletes in track and field make the majority of their earnings
in three different ways: appearance fees, prize money, and endorsements.

The first two come from performing at meets. The money for our appearance fees and prize money comes from the meet sponsors whose names and/or logos are prominently featured on the bib numbers pinned to our jerseys. The last, and often most lucrative form of income is from sponsorships. Our primary sponsors are shoe and apparel manufactures that pay us to wear their products during training and competition.

Unlike our foreign counterparts, whose governments pay them large sums of money to train and compete, our federation here in the United States pays us little to nothing to represent our country. Thus, we are almost entirely dependent on corporate support to pay our bills. Knowing this, most athletes hire agents to find them sponsors.

In 2006, when I decided to turn pro and finally get paid to run, I chose Chris Layne of Total Sports Management to represent me as my agent. He negotiated my first deal with Nike that summer and renegotiated my contract with them after I made my first Olympic team in 2008. That second deal took me through the end of 2013. As the expiration of my contract with Nike approached, Chris once again set out to find the best contract for me.

Given that I had just won the silver medal at the 2013 World Championships and was currently ranked number two in the world, Chris felt that we had solid leverage to negotiate a very good deal. Nike, however, did not agree and suggested Chris shop my deal around to other companies. Essentially, Nike wanted to see what the market dictated I was worth.

Chris worked tirelessly with the other shoe companies to drum up interest and get a written offer. Although many companies expressed interest, only one invited me to take a trip to visit their corporate headquarters.

Brooks Running, a specialty running brand based in Seattle, Washington told both Chris and me that they were very interested in signing me, and asked that I make a trip up to visit with their team. In early November of 2013 I loaded up my truck and drove the five-hours from Eugene to Seattle.

Brooks is a small company in comparison to Nike and, while they had an impressive list of professional athletes, they had no track

Olympians on their roster at the time. The man responsible for negotiating their shoe contracts, Jesse Williams, greeted me upon my arrival in Seattle. Jesse, a handsome guy in his mid thirties, ran for Texas Tech in the late nineties. I had gotten to know him briefly during the summer of 2013 when the Nike Oregon Track Club Elite and the Brooks Beasts were based in the same part of London.

I spent several days in Seattle touring the Brooks headquarters, running with the Brooks team, and meeting with various departments from marketing to product development. I was amazed at how happy everyone was to see me. In my seven years with Nike I had never met with the apparel development or marketing teams to provide input. Here I was, not even under contract with Brooks, and they were asking for my advice. I liked being part of the process and could clearly see what a future with Brooks might look like.

As if reading my mind, Jesse pitched to me what that future could look like from the Brooks perspective. He concluded with the hope that Brooks Running and Nick Symmonds, LLC could form a partnership that would last well after I finished running professionally. I left Seattle very impressed with Brooks Running and hoped they would make a solid offer––and they did.

In the world of shoe contracts there can be huge variations from one season to the next on how much money is available for athlete endorsements. If there are several particularly talented athletes coming out of college, then companies may be forced to save what little money they have to try to get one or two of them. I will never know what prevented other companies from making an offer, but felt fortunate to have a solid offer from Brooks.

The whole process took a toll on me mentally, though, as did the cold weather in Eugene, so I booked a ticket to Los Angeles. Lauren had recently moved to Santa Monica and I had been spending more and more time there. I sub-let a small apartment just a few blocks from the beach and started logging in miles along the ocean.

As the end of the year approached my agent began to get calls from Nike asking where we were with my negotiations. Chris and I talked and we both agreed that the Brooks deal was the best we were going to get, so he emailed the offer to Nike.

Nike found themselves in a difficult situation with the terms of the contract. The Brooks offer did not have what are called, "reduction clauses." They offered me a guaranteed retainer for three years no matter how well or poorly I performed. Nike, on the other hand, was not interested in offering a contract without reduction clauses. What this meant was that if an athlete failed to perform to certain standards Nike had the right to reduce the athlete's salary by a certain percentage. The standards and percentages are outlined in the contract so both parties know what they are getting into.

Reduction clauses, however, make it almost impossible for an athlete to have any job security. One small injury, or an unlucky race, can easily cost an athlete a large percentage of his or her annual income. I had been fortunate during my seven years with Nike to be consistent and healthy, and had never been reduced. However, as I was about to enter my thirties, I felt it was time to finally have some security.

The reality was that I had, for the most part, enjoyed working with Nike. They had taken a chance on me when I was a no-name Division III graduate. I had cultivated relationships with many good people at their company and had been a part of the Nike Oregon Track Club from its inception. I didn't want to leave Coach Rowland and the Oregon Track Club Elite.

As promised, a deal from Nike arrived shortly. According to Chris, a rep from Nike prefaced the offer by saying, "We know Nick probably won't accept this, but this is our best offer."

The Nike offer, of course, included reduction clauses. To add insult to injury, Nike wanted a fully exclusive contract, which would prevent me from displaying any other corporate logos during competition (even on my skin), something that Brooks had not asked for.

Chris agreed with the Nike rep and guessed that I would not accept the offer, but told him that he would pass it along to me. When Chris told me what Nike's offer was I smiled. "Wow," I said, "they sure made it easy for me to choose Brooks!" Nike wanted so much more from me, yet they offered so much less in return. Add to that, when my agent spoke to them, he did not have the same positive feeling as he did when he spoke to Brooks. I knew it was time for me to leave the swoosh.

I told Chris that I would carefully craft a written response to Nike's offer and would email to them it first thing on Monday morning. My response was similar to the text that follows, but what you see below has been changed a bit, due to nondisclosure and other clauses in my new contract with Brooks Running.

To the Nike Sports Marketing Team,

I would like to begin by thanking you for your offer to extend our partnership through the 2016 Olympic Games. I value the Nike brand and my relationship with the Oregon Track Club Elite very much. I would like to compare the two offers I have been presented with, so that I can make sure I understand them completely. As it has been relayed to me by my agent, Chris Layne, the offers on the table are as follows:

Brooks: (X) per year average. No reduction clauses. Exclusivity on shoes and running apparel only. Displays of other corporate logos on my person during competition are acceptable.

Nike: (X) per year average. With reduction clauses. Exclusivity on shoes, running apparel, casual apparel, timing, and vision. Displays of other corporate logos on my person during competition are not acceptable.

Brooks is able to offer me a comparable training environment to the Oregon Track Club Elite, and is presenting me with a contract that allows me to court other sponsors and grow my business.

If I have this correct, then it is clear that the Brooks offer is better than the one presented by Nike. As I have very much enjoyed helping to build the OTCE brand from scratch, I would prefer to stay with Nike and continue our work together. However, it would be extremely disadvantageous for me to do so under the terms set forth in your offer. I would certainly entertain an offer that had more favorable terms.

Provided the offer you have put forth is, as you say, the best you can do, I must respectfully decline and will be signing a contract with Brooks on January 2, 2014. I wish you all continued success.

Sincerely,

Nick Symmonds, owner
Nick Symmonds, LLC

My email clearly outlined the pros and cons of each contract with the exception that OTCE is more accomplished than the Brooks Beasts. On the other hand, OTCE only recently began producing medals, after having been around for seven years.

The Beasts are a new and growing entity and, like the Oregon Track Club Elite, will take time to develop. As far as coaches go, Mark Rowland of OTCE is perhaps the best middle distance coach in the world today. Danny Mackey of Brooks Beasts is young, relatively speaking, and has yet to coach a world or Olympic medalist. However, in my conversations with Coach Mackey it is apparent that he has a philosophy and approach toward training that is very similar to Coach Rowland's. I believe that Coach Mackey will do great things in the world of track and field.

Furthermore, I feel that Nike has set a dangerous precedent by placing such a high value on the Oregon Track Club Elite. Over the course of my seven years on the team I saw many athletes come to OTCE, run well, and then be denied a contract or contract renewal. Nike created a phenomenal training environment in the OTCE. However, once an athlete had success in the group, Nike used that success against the athlete in the negotiation process because they knew the athlete would have a strong desire to stay. I'm not saying that is a bad negotiation tactic in the short term, but in the long run how does OTCE hope to continue to draw top talent if that talent knows they will be screwed when it comes time to renegotiate?

With only days left in my contract with Nike I knew I had to make a final choice: remain with the only shoe sponsor and professional team I had ever known, or try something completely new and sign with Brooks. The business side of me said I would make a terrible mistake if I signed with Nike. The personal side of me felt it would be better to retire than to have to work another day with Nike.

I wrote down all the pros and cons of each offer and placed them side-by-side. I knew a lot of people would tell me to stay with Nike as I would get to stay with Coach Rowland and OTCE. However, my gut told me that I should go with Brooks. They were the track less traveled, and choosing them would lead me to the new adventures and the possibilities I always looked for in life.

I made up my mind and called Jesse Williams at Brooks. "Jesse," I said, "Nike made an offer. That said, I would still like to sign with Brooks."

There was silence on the other end for a few seconds before Jesse replied, "That is fantastic news, Nick. We are going to accomplish some really incredible things together."

I wish I could say that I leapt for joy after making up my mind, but I did not, as the feeling was so very bittersweet. I thought about Coach Rowland and my teammates, about my house in Oregon and how much I had loved being a part of the Eugene-Springfield community. I also thought about how difficult the road ahead would be and how much pressure would be placed on me to perform.

All of these thoughts rushed through my head simultaneously. Fortunately, my parents had flown to Los Angeles for Christmas and I was able to talk through a lot of my worries with them. I could tell they were happy for me, and felt I had made the right decision. Their advice was sound and welcomed, but it did little to put all my fears at rest. During much of the Christmas vacation I stared at the ocean, wondered what lay in my future, and felt like my head was going to explode.

I was confused and lost. As I had done so many times before when I felt this way, I picked up the phone and called Coach Sam. As soon as I heard his voice, I began to cry. Through choked sobs I explained to him that I was afraid of everything changing, and how I didn't want to leave Coach Rowland. Sam and I talked for over an hour. Just as we had done during my transition from collegiate to professional running, and again during the transition from Coach Gagliano to Coach Rowland, we now, together, formed a plan that would take me through this transition.

The plan allowed me to have the support I needed to get through my first season with Brooks. Though Coach Mackey at Brooks would help me write my workouts, we didn't want to change much of what had been working so well with Coach Rowland. Sam suggested that I take many things into my own hands, and that I draw upon the wisdom of the years of running logs that I had saved. I also needed to take my massage and medical needs, items that had previously been taken care of by Coach Rowland, into my own hands. Finally, Sam and I agreed that for my short-term well being I needed to take this transition one step at a time.

Step one was signing my new contract and putting on a non-Nike pair of running shoes for the first time in seven years. Jesse was excited about the announcement and asked if I could fly to Seattle for a signing party. He booked me a ticket for New Year's Day. I continued to work through my own fears and began to focus on how I could best make use of the publicity that would come from the sponsor switch.

Earlier in the year I had done a photo shoot with celebrity photographer Stephen Wayda. This shoot, which was set up through my publicist, Hal Lifson, was unlike anything I had ever done before. Most shoots I had done before had been for sponsors or for magazines. These photos, however, were for no one in particular, but would be useful as I continued to build my brand. Stephen Wayda had built a reputation as one of the world's finest photographers through his work with *Playboy*, and proved to be as talented as everyone said he was.

I met with Stephen and his wife/assistant, Kara, on a private beach in Summerland, California, just south of Santa Barbara one sunny afternoon. The shoot began with me in jeans and a sweater posing next to some eucalyptus trees. However, by the end I was down to my birthday suit flexing as the surf washed in around my ankles. When I saw the results of the shoot I was astounded. Years of hard work on the track, combined with Stephen's incredible eye, had resulted in some beautiful, yet very tasteful, photos. Although I was nude, much was left to the imagination. I chose one of my favorites and posted it to Instagram with the caption:

FOR THE FIRST TIME IN SEVEN YEARS I AM WITHOUT AN APPAREL
SPONSOR. THUS, I AM FORCED TO WORK OUT IN THE NUDE UNTIL
A COMPANY COMES TO THE RESCUE.

As planned, the combination of the provocative image, along with
the news that I was no longer partnered with Nike caused quite a stir.
Among the running community there was much talk about why I had been
"dropped" by Nike and which company I would ultimately sign with. As
I boarded my plane to Seattle I smiled at a comment that read:

I BET HE HAS A CONTRACT SIGNED BY THE END OF THE DAY.

That follower's prediction was quite accurate, as I inked a deal with
Brooks Running later that night. I took a few photos in a neon yellow
Brooks jersey and recorded a thank you video to my loyal fans. I had only
gone sixteen hours without a contract, and was very grateful to once again
have a corporate partner. My story is somewhat unusual, though. Too
often the professional track and field athletes that we expect to win us
medals every four years are left penniless, wondering how to pay for their
basic needs, let alone expensive training.

21

After a few weeks of working with the amazing men and women at Brooks Running, I knew I had made the right choice. While I still harbored a strong sense of resentment towards Nike for, from my viewpoint, leaving me no choice but to find another corporate partner, I could tell right away that everything about Brooks matched my personality much better.

From day one Brooks asked me to provide input on product development, personal relations, and marketing. They allowed me to more freely express myself in my writing and in my interviews. I quickly formed a great working relationship with Jesse Williams. One day, as he drove me to the Seattle airport, he said, "Obviously we want you to run well Nick, but we believe we will get a return on our investment in you off the track as well." I felt like, finally, for the first time, someone appreciated all the hard work I had done.

I have continued to work hard on and off the track, both for myself and for my sponsors. Through running I have learned that hard work, and a little bit of cunning, can take someone anywhere they want to go. Often times I am asked what makes successful people successful. If I had to boil it down to one word it would be tenacity. No one has shown me this more clearly than Coach Sam Lapray.

Back in college, my Bearcat teammates and I recognized in Sam from day one the Midas effect, that incredible ability to turn everything he touched into gold. It took me a while to figure it out, though. Early on I could see that Coach Sam had amazing knowledge and a huge heart, but it wasn't until he and I were tested at the highest levels of running, business, and life that I fully came to realize what makes Sam a winner. It is his determination and tenacity to overcome anything that gets in the way of what he wants. Of all the gifts he has given me, this lesson is perhaps the most valuable.

I do not know for certain what the future holds for the sport of track and field, much less what it holds for me. I am a person who loves to have a plan, and as such, it terrifies me that I do not know exactly where my life will take me after I hang up my spikes. I do, however, feel a great sense of excitement for the next chapter of my life and can't wait for it to begin. I know that no matter what my future holds my loyal family and friends will be by my side to help me along the way.

I like to think that after I retire from competitive running, there will still be a place for me in the world of track and field. This sport has given me so much and I would very much like to give something back to it. It has taught me about the world and helped me see the really important things in life. Running has taken me on incredible adventures and set me up well financially. I believe the sport of track and field is one of the purest and most beautiful, and I very much want to see it grow and thrive for years to come.

Sometimes, however, I look at the professional side of track and field and feel that it is broken beyond repair. The often lazy and selfish people who control the sport frequently place their own interests above the interest of the sport. I imagine my role in the world of track and field after my retirement and wonder why I would want to deal with these people for several more decades. I constantly vacillate between wanting to continue the fight to improve professional track and field, and washing my hands of the sport entirely.

There are days when I imagine myself working for the USOC or the IOC to effect change at the highest level. I daydream about infiltrating their ranks and working tirelessly for the rights of the athletes. Then I remember that working tirelessly is not possible. The fight wears on you, and in my dream I am teleported to a tiny beach bungalow somewhere on a remote part of a Hawaiian island where all I do is surf and fish every day.

In reality, my life will probably consist of a little of both of those dreams. I will always be on the side of the athletes and every vote I cast or speech I make will have their best interests at heart, because I know first hand how hard the athletes work. This sport can live on without selfish bureaucratic imbeciles, but cannot live on without the athletes.

I often look at the more popular athletes, people such has Usain Bolt, Mo Farah, and Lolo Jones, and feel that the sport of track and field needs them more than they need the sport. I then look at my own career and my own unique set of skills. *Do I need the sport of track and field more than it needs me?* I don't know.

It is very possible that I, along with the vast majority of athletes in track and field, are replaceable. If I were to retire tomorrow I am certain that a young, hungry athlete fresh out of college would step up to take my place. He would go on to run fast times and make teams. Hopefully, he would also be able to earn a decent living.

Know, however, that I have the determination and tenacity to finish what I start. These are traits that track and field has taught me. I wonder, though, if these skills are being best put to use in the sport. All my experience has been as a professional athlete, but could the skills I learned on and off my oval office allow me to accomplish more, say, in the world of entrepreneurial business? There is only one way to find out.

I have learned that to be great at anything takes a great deal of sacrifice. For me, to be a great runner has meant giving up many of the things I want most in life. I have sacrificed time with friends, time with family, time at home, and personal relationships. I gave up some of the things that I loved most as a child, such as skiing, wakeboarding, summers at my cabin in Montana, and time at home in Boise. It has all been well worth the sacrifice, but I must admit as the end of my career draws near, I feel a stronger pull toward these things.

Perhaps the hardest part of the sacrifice has been personal relationships. As I'm sure you can tell, I have enjoyed being single and traveling the world. That was something I needed to get out of my system. I know that I would have made a terrible husband during this time in my life.

However, I recognize that one of the most important things a human can do with his or her life is to share it with another person. On the final day of my AP history class in high school, my favorite teacher, Mr. Skinner, left us with one final gem of wisdom. "The most important decision you ever make in your life," he said, "is who you choose as your partner. They will affect nearly every single moment of the rest of your time on this planet." That was heavy advice for my then eighteen-year-old brain, but it stuck with me.

Though I was not actively looking for a wife in my twenties, I enjoyed the process of getting to know women and finding out those qualities that were most important to me in a partner. These may sound like givens, but kindness, affection, quick wit, and a great sense of humor are must haves for me. They can also sometimes be the hardest things to find.

I like to imagine myself as something of a chameleon, someone who feels comfortable in any situation. I love to dress up in a suit and tie almost as much as I love being decked out in my old hunting clothes and hiking boots. I have a strong feeling that my life partner will have to share this sense of comfort in any situation.

I also am certain that the partner I am looking for, will, herself, be looking for a man who possesses certain characteristics. For most women, I am sure, "selfish" is not on that list of attributes. I have tried to give back during my career, and acknowledge that my lifestyle during my professional career has been a selfish one. I have asked so much from those around me, from my coaches, sponsors, and family and friends, often without being able to provide much in return, other than, perhaps, an inspirational performance.

When I look at the way my dad has selflessly loved my mother for decades, and think about how much he has given me, I know I want to emulate him. I want to love someone unselfishly and be there for every moment of my children's lives. But, I see those things and my job as a professional runner as mutually exclusive. So for now, I will continue to run in circles professionally, knowing that more great adventures await me.

That, above all, has been my favorite part of my career as a professional runner, the sense of adventure. It is the most addicting drug and one I will never be able to give up. Like a hopeless addict who switches to a nicotine patch, so will I have to find a way to feed my addiction.

To this end, I have set several goals for myself to help me transition to life off the track. I want to bike across the United States, backpack through South America, run a marathon, and finish a full Ironman. The loftiest goal I have set for myself athletically is to climb the tallest mountain on every continent. These peaks are known as the seven summits.

But, these goals all pale in comparison to the largest and perhaps most difficult goal I have set for myself in life: to fall in love, to faithfully share my life with someone, raise a family, and be a great father. These are my most important goals and I am confident that running has given me the skill set necessary to tackle them.

My mom likes to play a game where she asks if I have met my future wife yet. I usually respond with a shrug and a maybe. She then says, "I wonder what she is doing right now. Maybe she is hiking or out fishing or with her own family." At this point my dad usually interjects, "She is probably doing her high school algebra homework." This makes us all laugh.

Have I met her yet? I don't know, and I really have no idea what she is doing. What I do know is that there will come a time when my gut tells me that I would make a terrible decision to let someone go. This is the same instinct that has taken me down many strange paths, but also on many incredible adventures.

In the meantime, I will continue to go through life choosing the path less taken because it so often leads to wonderful and exciting possibilities. It allows me to live my life the way I want: for myself and for those I love most. I will leave you with the words of one of my favorite authors, Jack London. From the minute I read them they have helped shaped the way I live my life.

"I would rather be ashes than dust! I would rather that my spark should burn out in a brilliant blaze than it should be stifled by dry-rot. I would rather be a superb meteor, every atom of me in magnificent glow, than a sleepy and permanent planet. The function of man is to live, not to exist. I shall not waste my days trying to prolong them. I shall use my time."

THE END

Resources

Follow Nick on Twitter: @nicksymmonds

Follow Nick on Facebook: facebook.com/nick.symmonds

Follow Nick on Instagram: @nicksymmonds

Nick's Web Page: NickSymmonds.com

Nick's online *Runner's World* column:
runnersworld.com/nick-symmonds-oval-office

Nick's Favorite Running Websites:
RunnersWorld.com, FloTrack.com, LetsRun.com

Nick's Favorite Magazines:
Field & Stream, Outside Magazine, The Week

Charities and Causes Nick Supports:
Heifer International: Heifer.org
NOH8 Campaign: noh8campaign.com
PETA: PETA.org
Smile Train: SmileTrain.org
Humane Society of the United States: HumaneSociety.org

Nick's Corporate Partners:
Brooks Running: BrooksRunning.com
Melaleuca: Melaleuca.com
Hanson Dodge Creative: HansonDodge.com
Run Gum: GetRunGum.com
Soleus Running: SoleusRunning.com
Suja Juice: SujaJuice.com

Acknowledgements

It is pleasantly surprising to me how similar winning a race is to writing a book. Both take a great deal of dedication and perseverance, but more importantly, both require an incredible amount of help.

I would like to thank my publisher, Cool Titles, for helping me to share my story. I would also like to thank my editor Lisa Wysocky for helping to shape my grammatically poor writing into something readable.

Finally, I would like to thank my family for always supporting me in all that I have chosen to do. A special thank you goes to my mom, one of the finest English teachers in the world, who taught me how to express myself through my writing. This book is especially for her, the "dragon lady" of Bishop Kelly High School.

Cover photo by Becca Walls, Ladies & Gents Photography
Author photo and back cover photo by Stephen Wayda

About Nick Symmonds

Nick Symmonds is a professional athlete and a 2008 and 2012 Olympian for the United States of America. He was also a world silver medalist for 2013. He is the third fastest American ever at 800 meters, a two-time world championship finalist, five-time USA Outdoor Champion at 800 meters, seven-time NCAA Champion (Willamette University), and nine-time state champion (Idaho/Bishop Kelly High School, Boise). When Nick is not running he can be found climbing mountains and fishing in the Pacific Northwest.

About Coach Frank Gagliano

Frank Gagliano, "Coach Gags," is a former director of track and field at Rutgers University, former director of track and field at Georgetown University, founder of the Washington, DC based Reebok Enclave elite professional track and field team, coach of the Nike Farm Team in Palo Alto, California, and the first coach in the resurgence of the Oregon Track Club. At Georgetown alone, Coach Gagliano produced 140 All-America performers, seven individual national champions, and 23 Big East championship teams. Since coaching professionals exclusively, Coach Gags has trained countless numbers of athletes to USATF Nationals Finals, world championship teams, and world championship finals; as well as fourteen Olympians, and numerous Olympic finalists. Coach Gagliano has most recently brought his wealth of talent and knowledge back home to the New Jersey/New York area where he continues his tradition of excellence with his newest venture, the NJ/NY Track Club.

Book Club Questions

1. What initially motivated Nick to start running?

2. Nick's family was very supportive of his running early on (and still is). How did they support him and what did that mean to Nick?

3. In high school and early college Nick also ran other distances, such as cross-country and the 1500 meter. What made him zone in on the 800 meter?

4. Nick has had several injuries during his career. What motivates him to keep going during those times?

5. What do you think about the Beer Mile?

6. Who is Mortimer, and why is he important to Nick?

7. What one thing is most important to Nick as an athlete today?

8. For the 2012 season Nick auctioned off space on his left shoulder for a temporary tattoo so a sponsor could advertise there. Why?

9. Nick has a big personal commitment to help other athletes obtain sponsors. Why is that important to Nick?

10. What are Nick's biggest challenges, both personally and professionally?

11. Life on the road, traveling to different meets, can be challenging. What does Nick like and dislike about it?

12. What does Nick Symmonds represent in the sport of running today?

The John Wooden Pyramid of Success

John Wooden, owner of many unequaled and mostly unapproachable records, coached the legendary UCLA basketball teams to ten national championships between 1963 and 1975. His accomplishments on the court alone make him a fascinating person. But Coach Wooden is much more‹a philosopher and creator of the Pyramid of Success, which is a plain-spoken guide to achieving success that is packed with good, honest common sense. In this authorized biography, you will find the wisdom of this extraordinary man. Wooden allowed rare

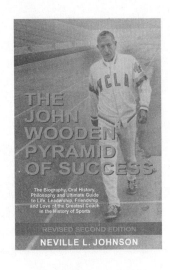

access to members of his family--brothers, children, and grandchildren who for the first time take you into his home life--as well as superstar athletes (Kareem Abdul-Jabbar, Bill Walton, Willie Naulls, Walt Hazzard, Gail Goodrich, Sidney Wicks plus many others) as well as nationally known broadcasters.

Woodenisms

John Wooden was arguably the greatest coach, the greatest leader, of all time. These Woodenisms, a collection of his wisdom and sayings, inspire, motivate, and prepare you for any challenge. Woodensims provide common sense, assist

you in being a leader and a team player, and also give you strength. Many of these Woodenisms have been distributed individually. They have also been used in print, and in presentations by Coach and other speakers. Now they are collected here, yours to cherish and enjoy as you strive for success.